Deleuze and Guattari's Philosophy of History

Continuum Studies in Continental Philosophy
Series Editor: James Fieser, University of Tennessee at Martin, USA

Continuum Studies in Continental Philosophy is a major monograph series from Continuum. The series features first-class scholarly research monographs across the field of Continental philosophy. Each work makes a major contribution to the field of philosophical research.

Adorno's Concept of Life, Alastair Morgan
Art and Institution, Rajiv Kaushik
Being and Number in Heidegger's Thought, Michael Roubach
Badiou, Marion and St Paul, Adam Miller
Deleuze and Guattari, Fadi Abou-Rihan
Deleuze and the Genesis of Representation, Joe Hughes
Deleuze and the Unconscious, Christian Kerslake
Deleuze, Guattari and the Production of the New, edited by Simon O'Sullivan and Stephen Zepke
Derrida, Simon Morgan Wortham
Derrida and Disinterest, Sean Gaston
Derrida: Profanations, Patrick O'Connor
Encountering Derrida, edited by Simon Morgan Wortham and Allison Weiner
The Domestication of Derrida, Lorenzo Fabbri
Foucault's Heidegger, Timothy Rayner
Gadamer and the Question of the Divine, Walter Lammi
Heidegger and a Metaphysics of Feeling, Sharin N. Elkholy
Heidegger and Aristotle, Michael Bowler
Heidegger and Logic, Greg Shirley
Heidegger and Philosophical Atheology, Peter S. Dillard
Heidegger Beyond Deconstruction, Michael Lewis
Heidegger, Politics and Climate Change, Ruth Irwin
Heidegger's Early Philosophy, James Luchte
Kant, Deleuze and Architectonics, Edward Willatt
Levinas and Camus, Tal Sessler
Merleau-Ponty's Phenomenology, Kirk M. Besmer
The Movement of Nihilism, edited by Luarence Paul Hemming, Kostas Amiridis and Bogdan Costea
Nietzsche's Ethical Theory, Craig Dove
Nietzsche, Nihilism and the Philosophy of the Future, edited by Jeffrey Metzger
Place, Commonality and Judgment, Andrew Benjamin
Sartre's Phenomenology, David Reisman
Nietzsche's Thus Spoke Zarathustra, edited by James Luchte
Time and Becoming in Nietzsche's Thought, Robin Small
The Philosophy of Exaggeration, Alexander Garcia Düttmann
Who's Afraid of Deleuze and Guattari? Gregg Lambert
Žižek and Heidegger, Thomas Brockelman

Deleuze and Guattari's Philosophy of History

JAY LAMPERT

continuum

Continuum International Publishing Group
The Tower Building　　　　　80 Maiden Lane
11 York Road　　　　　　　　Suite 704
London SE1 7NX　　　　　　 New York, NY 10038

www.continuumbooks.com

© Jay Lampert 2006

First published 2006
Paperback edition 2011

All rights reserved. No part of this publication may be reproduced or transmitted in any form or by any means, electronic or mechanical, including photocopying, recording, or any information storage or retrieval system, without prior permission in writing from the publishers.

Jay Lampert has asserted his right under the Copyright Designs and Patents Act 1988, to be identified as Author of this work.

British Library Cataloguing-in-Publication Data
A catalogue record for this book is available from the British Library.

ISBN: 978-0-8264-9953-0 (hardback)
　　　 978-1-4411-5295-4 (paperback)

Library of Congress Cataloging-in-Publication Data
A catalog record for this book is available from the Library of Congress.

Typeset by RefineCatch Limited, Bungay, Suffolk

Contents

Preface		vii
Acknowledgements		viii
1	Introduction: The "Joan of Arc effect" and the philosophy of history	1
2	Living in the contracted present – the first synthesis of time	12
3	The virtual co-existence of the past – the second synthesis of time	31
4	Navigating the dark precursors of the future – the third synthesis of time	54
5	Dates and destiny: the problem of historical chronology	71
6	Quasi-causes and becoming-causal	97
7	Why this now? The problem of actual historical events: the theory of beginnings	114
8	Why this now? Diagnosis of the now	143
9	Why this now? Co-existing levels of temporality	155
Bibliography		172
Index		177

Major texts dealt with in each chapter:

1 *L'Anti-Oedipe*
2 *Différence et répétition*, chapter 2 "La répétition pour elle-meme"
3 *Différence et répétition*, chapter 2 "La répétition pour elle-meme"
4 *Différence et répétition*, chapter 2 "La répétition pour elle-meme"
5 *Mille Plateaux*, 4: "20 novembre 1923 – Postulats de la linguistique"
6 *Logique du sens*
7 *L'Anti-Oedipe*, chapter 3 "sauvages, barbares, civilisés"
8 *Qu'est-ce que la philosophie?*, chapter 1.4 "Géophilosophie"
9 *Mille Plateaux*, 13: "7 000 av. J.-C. – Appareil de capture"

Preface

By now, there exist many excellent introductions to the philosophy of Deleuze and Guattari. But a great many readers around the world are past the point of needing an introduction. We are starting to see a good number of books that follow up on particular themes in Deleuze and Guattari in an extended way, drawing out implications systematically, analysing the arguments in the texts in detail, and forcing Deleuze and Guattari's concepts to confront tightly related series of philosophical problems. This book is written for readers who are familiar with Deleuze and Guattari's texts, and who are sympathetic to their concepts, but who are interested in challenging the arguments in the text to see how far they can be taken.

Many of the concepts and arguments from Deleuze and Guattari that I discuss are summarized by commentators, but have not yet been subjected to the detailed and demanding scrutiny that the great philosophers of the past, from Aristotle to Husserl, have been subjected to. There is a lot of free speculation of my own in this book concerning issues in the philosophy of history. But I have tried to tie it to close textual analysis. For example, I have attempted to make some headway in analysing Deleuze's arguments for the "pure past" in *Différence et répétition*. Likewise, I have attempted detailed conceptual analysis of Deleuze and Guattari's thesis that "becomings do not come from history but fall back into it" (*Qu'est-ce que la philosophie?* 92), along with their treatment of Nietzsche's saying that "All the names of history, it's me" (*L'Anti-Oedipe* 28), as well as many other principles. Deleuze and Guattarian thought stands or falls on whether claims like these can be analysed and demonstrated. My view is that their theses on history are, in a still useful sense of the term, true. I would like to prove that, and then to prove some other things.

Many of the interpretations in this book of Deleuze and Guattari's arguments are bound to be controversial. I look forward to reading alternative interpretations and arguments that other writers might be incited to offer in their place.

It goes without saying that the point of analysing a philosopher of history is ultimately not to know what the philosopher thinks, but to investigate what history is.

Acknowledgements

I would like to thank Professors Costas Boundas, Keith Ansell Pearson, and David Goicoechea for inviting me to present early versions of chapters 5, 6, and 7–9 at their excellent conferences. I would also like to acknowledge the many formative conversations I have had about Deleuze and Guattari with the excellent Deleuzians, Olivier Serafinowicz and Mani Haghighi. I would also like to acknowledge the contributions of Deleuze-oriented philosophers who were in the past doctoral students of mine: Karen Houle, Jim Vernon, Antonio Calcagno, and others. I thank a number of people for their support, discussion, and scholarship: Catherine Malabou, Len Lawlor, Alice Craven, Gisle Johannessen, and many others. I thank the University of Guelph for its generous research leave support. And of course, I thank Jennifer Bates, and Hector.

1 Introduction: The "Joan of Arc Effect" and the Philosophy of History

Deleuze and Guattari's philosophy of becoming seems at times opposed to the very idea of historical succession. But suppose that we want to do without the concept of history, or to rebuild a concept of history without succession. Some quasi-historical phenomena would still need to be explained: events, memories, retroactive interpretations, dates and causes, precursors and themes, series and sequences and destinies and continuities and breakdowns, not to mention the actual occurrences that have shaped the geo-social world. How might we conceptualize these phenomena free from the constraints of succession? If events are not related in terms of progression, then they will have to be related in terms of co-existence or simultaneity. If the relation among events is not causal, then it must be one of mutual distribution or circulation. If the subjects of events are not successively individuated, then all the names of history must be able to erupt at any moment on the body without organs.

Since it is not obvious on the surface that Deleuze and Guattari even have one, we should note what it usually takes to constitute a philosophy of history. Normally, it covers five topics: (1) A philosophy of history must distinguish between events that are historical, and two sorts of non-historical events: natural occurrences, and everyday social occurrences. (2) It must determine how much empirical or other evidence is required to justify claims about history; it must also have a theory concerning how to diagnose the meaning of historical events. (3) It must articulate a principle for ordering events. This includes both a general theory of chronology as well as a principle for organizing themes and their recurrences in history. (4) It must have a theory of historical causality (whether in terms of the great man, or classes and masses, or providence, or material conditions). In some way or other, it must explain, for each event, why it happens when it does. (5) Finally, it should sketch the main stages of actual human history. Put in these terms, it will become obvious that Deleuze and Guattari do have a philosophy of history.[1]

Two things that Deleuze is best known for, both in his solo works and with Guattari, are: (a) the neo-Bergsonian theory that time is not divisible into past, present, and future, but involves a circulation of events in a co-existing "cone" of the pure past; and (b) the concept of virtual events on a plane of consistency that is prior to the rigid, state-regulated historiographies of successive states of affairs. Given the ontology and the politics of Deleuze and Guattari, it is bound to seem controversial when I say that they are proposing a philosophy of history. Nevertheless, they are clearly interested in both major and minor events of what we normally call world history, and their writings are filled with analyses of such phenomena as dates and chronologies, causes and quasi-causes, and events and event-assemblages. So a systematic and creative development of Deleuze and Guattari's philosophy encourages us to create concepts for a philosophy of co-existential time as philosophy of history.

In this introductory chapter, I analyse one important variant on the theory of co-existential history, namely Deleuze and Guattari's conception of the "names of history". In this, and the ensuing chapters, I pose the following question: What degree of distance between events can still be accounted for, once events are characterized as co-existing?

Deleuze and Guattari introduce the theory of the "names of history" in *AO*, but the logic of time required to make it work is found in the three temporal syntheses in Deleuze's *DR*: the present Chronos of habit, the past Aion of pure memory, and the future of the eternal return. Since the past sustains not only innumerable names of history, but also a plurality of histories of history, we will find multiple distinctions between successive and simultaneous series.

What is a historical person or event? How does a phenomenon become historical for someone who looks back on it from the present? The theory of the names of history is introduced in *AO* to explain how such a person as Nietzsche existed as *homo historia*. Nietzsche is no self, but rather "the Nietzschean-subject who passes through a series of states, and who identifies the names of history with these states: 'all the names of history, it's me' " (*AO* 28). The names of history are not figures who were once present and became past, but exist as a subject's passage back through historical personae. A historical subject identifies not with a person but with a name. This is a three-termed relation. "It is not a matter of identifying with persons, but rather identifying the names of history with zones of intensity on the body without organs, and each time, the subject cries, 'It's me, so it's me!' " (*AO* 28). To identify with a figure from the past is not to identify with an identity, but with a zone. For that matter, the historical personage could not have been entirely self-identical in the first place, since she in turn will have circulated through the names of history on the periphery of her own zones of intensity. In any case, one's own body is hardly one's own, since the zones on that body are liable to become somebody else; the body without a self is the body on which all subjects circulate. The name of history is activated when *I* name it, and when I name it *as me*, but it does not so much replace me as fold in with me, and make me "*homo historia*". "No one has ever made history as much as the schizo has . . . He consumes all of universal history at once" (*AO* 28).

Even traditional concepts of history try to do something like this. For they do not try to present the past as something directly available to the present, either in terms of our immediate knowledge of the past or in terms of the direct causal impact of the past on us. Rather, history treats the past as a mode of intensifying certain patterns of present activity. History is about what becomes of the present when the past catches up with it.

History is "morphogenesis"; "everything commingles in these becomings" (*AO* 101). The schizo is the paradigm case of one who "made history, who hallucinated and experienced the delirium of universal history" (*AO* 101). "(I feel that) I am becoming god, I am becoming woman, I was Joan of Arc and I am Heliogabalus, and the Great Mongol, a Chinese, a redskin, a Templar, I have been my father and I have been my son" (101). Once a person is open to having their functions defined by past figures (and every person, and plenty of non-persons, are open to this), it could be any sort of past character or collective that does the determining. Nations, cultures, and gods circulate on a *homo historia*'s body in the same way that Joan of Arc does. Familial, social, and political groups, some concrete and some abstract, cut across the names of history, commingling with "the Commune, the Dreyfus Affair, religion and atheism, the Spanish war, the rise of fascism, Stalinism, the War in Vietnam, May 68 . . .", and so on (116). There are too many lists of names of history in the text to cite them all here. Often the lists overlap (Joan of Arc is co-listed again with the Great Mongol and Luther, 121). Any one of these, or any combination, could suddenly begin to define a present-day person's opinions, desires, or actions, given the right moment of susceptibility. In brief, history is not the past, but the circulation of events.

As important as this is, the names of history is not one of the more thoroughly explicated of Deleuze and Guattari's concepts.[2] We can begin to interpret it with two remarks.

First, a name of history is a running effect; just as we speak of the Kelvin effect or the Doppler effect in physics, Deleuze and Guattari posit a "Joan of Arc effect or a Heliogabalus effect – and so on for all the names of history" (*AO* 103). An "effect" in this sense is a virtual pattern, an abstract sequence of possibilities, which becomes actual whenever certain conditions and driving forces fall into place. Joan of Arc performed some acts, and now those acts can take place on our bodies, following more or less the same kinds of series, offering more or less the same potentials for decisive changes of direction, creating contexts and milieus for new acts of Joan of Arc, assembling surrounding people into Joan of Arc's new allies and enemies, and so on. Joan of Arc is a diagram, an abstract machine, a vibration of potentialities; Joan of Arc happened once to a person some centuries ago, and can happen again on anyone who has a body. On the one hand, the Joan of Arc effect runs on *us*; it has status as a retrospective effect (164) and not as a pre-determining cause.

On the other hand, it does not depend on our personal knowledge or imagination, but vibrates through us as an after-effect of its *own* virtual reality. When we become Joan of Arc, the issue is not whether we do so in an objectively accurate way or not, but how long the effect can maintain its specificity before it commingles into another effect.

The second point is that names of history do not lose their singularity in the course of their migrations across the bodies of others (*AO* 101). In Deleuze and Guattari's "machinic" account of movement, specificity is everything: the extensive and intensive magnitudes of each character shift, the degree of collectivity, the precision of expression, the layers of articulation, the speed of interpenetration, the dating of concepts, and so on. If the borderlines between different historical running effects are in a sense undecidable, they are not in any way indeterminate (to use an important Derridian distinction – any given ambiguity is a particular and determinate one). This is one reason why individuation, i.e. the overcoded identification with a transcendent historical model, is very different from singularization, i.e. the flexible mapping of transecting lines. It is also a reason why the names of history are always minority figures (125). In contrast to Deleuzian minoritarian history, centrist or Statist history stabilizes subjectivities and limits the revolutionary eruptions of the names of history. A few pages before the end of *AO*, some revolutionaries are listed (lists are symptomatic of a flexible spirit): "a Castro, an Arab, a Black Panther, a Chinese on the horizon? A May '68 . . ." (454). Centrist history, in contrast, represses the running effects that constitute co-existential history; to say the same thing, it represses revolution (454).

The fact that names of history must be singular in order to commingle raises the problem that I want to focus on, namely how history can preserve an element of succession within a general structure of co-existence or simultaneity. We can raise this problem in two ways: first, in terms of the logic of simultaneity itself; and second, in terms of the remnants of succession across the simultaneous names of history.

In phenomenology, simultaneity is treated as a function of succession. For Husserl (1966),[3] our perceptions of an object occur successively. Two objects of consciousness (the car speeding by, and the gum I am chewing) are present simultaneously when two series of successions converge. Each flow of perceptions related to a given object retains its predecessors and anticipates its successors. We can measure how far we have come in experiencing each object, and then we can put the two chains of succession on the same time-line. Simultaneity identifies a degree of fulfilment of one object, with a different degree of fulfilment of another, and a different degree of fulfilment of yet another, and so on, until we have constituted the simultaneity of all objects of consciousness at once. In short, for two objects to exist "at the same time" means that even though each object has its own rhythm of coming into presence, the two chains of succession inhabit the same time-line. Of course, the problem is whether the successive experiences of different objects really fall on a common (subjective or objective) time-line. But whatever the technical difficulties in the theory of converging time-lines, Husserl says, there is "no simultaneity without succession".

In contrast, the Deleuzian names of history entail simultaneity without succession, and as a corollary, simultaneity of difference and not of identity. But what does simultaneity mean, if not a moment that two or more ongoing events share? What would simultaneity mean if events did not each have their place in the order of succession? Deleuze and Guattari certainly do not have in mind a *totum simul*, a frozen bloc universe, but what is the nature of succession in a world where the past never stops having running effects?

In addition to the formal problem of what simultaneity without succession could refer to, it seems that the names of history themselves retain some internal elements of succession. The theory of the names of history begins with Bergson's observation that memory does not always retrieve events stepwise in reverse order, but rather can jump to any point in the past. Any body with a memory houses all virtual pasts at once. Yet each of those pasts, like the Joan of Arc effect, has its own *internal* successions of events (first her divine visitations, then the battles, then the flames, and so on) without which it would not be the Joan of Arc effect. A present-day person must run through some version of *that* series in order to be running the Joan of Arc effect at all.

Even if succession is merely an artifact created when we map the stages of what is primordially a set of co-existing possibilities, that succession still needs to be accounted for. At the very least, we cannot actualize all the virtually co-existing historical possibilities at once; at any given moment we have to select among alternatives. And of course, even virtually co-existing events are dated relative to one another. When, for example, the Joan of Arc effect is running on our bodies, it gives all our battles a low-tech character. For in an irreducible sense, the virtual reality of Joan of Arc comes *before* the virtual reality of atomic weapons, in spite of the fact that it might be a very modern politician with an atomic arsenal at his disposal who is undergoing the Joan of Arc effect by waving his arm as if to brandish a sword. The effects, as events, may co-exist, but their contents are nevertheless dated. Succession remains an issue not only because the body expresses one effect after another in time, but also because each effect is an effect that dates from a particular moment in history. Hence, to identify a zone of the body with the singularity of a determinate effect, that effect has to be kept at a distance from other effects, and even has to be diagrammed for its historical relations relative to other effects, even while it may be running at the same time as more ancient or more modern effects in a commingling and unpredictable series of mutations.

To be sure, Joan of Arc is already a multiple event, which includes unaccomplished possibilities that Joan died before achieving, puzzles and mysteries that Joan failed to solve and that generations to this day keep trying to solve, consequences for her contemporaries that Joan never heard about, influences from previous events that Joan never realized, unanticipated beginnings of future ways of life, unconscious desires that Joan would have been horrified by – all of which may still resonate when the Joan of Arc effect runs today. Immediately after Joan of Arc's death, in fact, several impostors sprung up around France, collecting funds for imaginary battles. Some attracted followers for years afterwards.[4] And by our century, the Joan of Arc effect has already been reshaped by innumerable interpretations of Joan of Arc, which have added to the ways that the events may now resonate in us. The Joan of Arc effect instigates a set of problems for a body to solve (theologico-political problems, military-gender problems, juridical-conspiratorial problems, and so on) rather than a particular set of acts to perform. For that matter, Joan of Arc did not have a Joan of Arc blueprint from birth, so she herself had to *become* Joan of Arc by running the Joan of Arc effect on her own body, becoming a simulacrum of a form that had no original before her.

In short, the Joan of Arc effect is multiple, uncompletable, virtual, and performative. All of these levels of the event are initiated as running effects on somebody's body. Someone may start running the Joan of Arc effect on just one of its dimensions (assuming it will function as a feminist, or a mystical, or a patriotic exemplar), only to find several other dimensions of fifteenth-century socio-religious attitudes welling up as well. Such consequences may arise because the simulator has read books about the period, but others may enter his bodily responses just because gender–Church relations, for example, have been resonating since that time without his knowing any history about it. Some elements of the Joan of Arc series will intersect with other fifteenth-century motifs, but other elements might suddenly diverge into other martyr figures from other times or other religions, and still others might mutate into entirely different series: the sword in an evangelical politician's hand might become a smart bomb, one's appeal to the divine word might strengthen one's adversary's faith, the *guerrillière* might become cyborg. The period-related elements, the succession-related elements, and the co-existing elements drawn from anywhere whatsoever, can quasi-cause each other at any point. The simultaneity of the effect first constitutes the possibility of diagramming a successive series of events to make use of; then, it disorders that series. It passes into the effect by habit (as present), it contemporizes the series in memory (as past), and it returns to it in difference (as future).

Now, there would be no ontological paradox if we could say that in history, events themselves occur successively, and that it is only in memory that those events are retained simultaneously. But Deleuze has independent arguments against historical succession in general.

Before we make this argument, we should note that the term "history" is used in two ways in Deleuze and Guattari's writings.[5] In some cases, as in the phrase, "the names of history", the term "history" appeals to the schizoanalytic phenomena of libidinal production (*AO* 117), the overflow of codes and alliances (*AO* 155: "the end of history has no other sense"), contingencies, ruptures, collectivities, retrospections, bifurcations, and lines of flight (*AO* 140: "universal history is one of contingencies"), differences without origin (*DR*), neo-archaism and ex-futurism (*AO* 309), rhythms and refrains (*MP*); in short, "history" is sometimes a "historical rhizome",[6] an equivalent term to "becoming". Deleuze says that these usages are possible thanks to the way Foucault has reinvented the term "history" (*F* 51).

But because of the use of the term "history" in Hegel on the one hand and certain empiricists on the other, Deleuze and Guattari frequently say that "history is always written from the sedentary point of view". In this sense, becoming should be described by nomadology, "the opposite of a history" (*MP* 34). In these passages, history is treated as the opposite of becoming, which "replaces history" (*MP* 200). "All history does is to translate a co-existence of becomings into succession" (*MP* 537). Those who think according to that concept of history take what is itself a flow of becomings, and overcode it according to a conjunctive synthesis in the form "So that's what this meant" (*AO* 79–80). "History has made itself one with the triumph of states" (*MP* 490) and the filiation of the father. Among its many ontological errors, Deleuze and Guattari argue, history takes events as "supposedly fixed terms" (*MP* 291); it assumes that events have their primary causal impact on just those events which they resemble (in the terms of *DR*); it treats events as if they were entirely determined by prior causes unaffected either by chance or by subsequent events, and it reads events teleologically (*MP* 537). In all of these senses, history is the reactive force (in the terms of *NP*) that paranoiacally keeps itself from engaging with the living past.

In the final analysis, it is because Deleuze can speak of history *either* as the (good) schizo's deterritorialization of events, *or* as the (bad) paranoiac's segmentation of events, that he can say, paradoxically, that "history [in the schizo nomadic sense] is made only by those who oppose history [in the paranoiac centrist sense]" (*MP* 363).

These definitions suggest the general reason why co-existence is a feature of events themselves, and not merely a feature of the way we remember events. An event brings together supple flows and rigid segments, without having a "power centre" to regulate the flows (*MP* 275–7). Because every event is multiple, a cause is not a unique proximate condition, but a communication across various series of events. A historical event has not so much a cause as a "quasi-cause", a series of "non-causal correspondences forming a system of echoes, of reprises and resonances, a system of signs, in short, an expressive quasi-causality" (*LS* 199, Series 24: "On the Communication between Events"). And since each event becomes a different event once such communication occurs, it "communicates with itself through its own distance, resonating across all its disjunctions" (*LS* 207). That is the reason why history cannot be explained as a succession of individuated phenomena along a single causal line.

Here we see again the relation that this book will problematize. How is it that the simultaneous co-existence within an event, which makes it co-existent with any other event that it intersects with, forms a system of distances? How is there temporal distance within simultaneity?

To make matters more complicated, there is not just one logic of simultaneity and one logic of succession; there are three of each, because there are three syntheses of time (in the second chapter of *DR*). There is the contracted habitual time of the present, the embedded memory time of the past, and erotic groundless time of the future's eternal return. I will analyse at length these three categories of time in chapters 2–4. At this point, I just want to hint at the complexity of a theory of simultaneity. While in one sense there are three distinct logics of time corresponding to the forms of present, past, and future – the logic of succession, the logic of co-existence, and the logic of dark precursors, respectively – the logic of succession has its own way of conceiving of present, past, and future, and the logics of co-existence and of precursors each have their own ways of conceiving all three. As a result, there exist nine forms of present, past, and future, hence nine forms each for succession and simultaneity, and nine movements of the name of history.

To schematize this very complex theory of time in a nutshell, and to apply it to the philosophy of history: the synthesis of the present shows how successions are contracted into mutually relevant systems; the synthesis of the past shows how all events co-exist simultaneously in a kind of storehouse where mutual influences are carried out; and the synthesis of the future is a practical synthesis where we choose how to make use of successions and simultaneities, and to constitute a series free for chance and free for flight. Events are singularities, but they carry pre-histories and post-histories along with them. Genuine novelty paradoxically requires that all events already co-exist in the form of an unbound system. That is why the future is the eternal return, in that every event qua future throws the dice of the past and affirms whatever line of continuation communicates its excess. As soon as one series of co-existences passes over into another, a new series already exists. The point of passage is a "dark precursor".

We will see in chapter 4 how this final synthesis explains the simultaneity of simultaneity and succession. The general problem of history concerns how a past event can be both simultaneous with the present and also distant from it. This will be explained by the way that each event must be at once a past, a present and a future in independent senses. As a present, each event is one in a succession. As a past, it is virtually contemporaneous with every event, but in a way that makes it a cause of all of them. As a future, it is a bifurcation point that forces movement. In all three phases, time is a type of simultaneity; but in the present, the passing event is also successive in the form of chronology; in the past, the virtual event is also successive in the form of causality; in the future, the groundless event is also successive in the form of event-bifurcations. (These three topics – chronology, causality, and actual events – constitute the topics for chapters 5, 6, and 7–9 of this book.) This remains to be demonstrated, but the results of this book will look something like the following.

The succession of befores and afters is a triple by-product of there being three simultaneous simultaneities. What takes the place of the classical concept of history is nothing other than these multiple forms of co-existence with their multiple subordinate forms of serial distribution. Once it is proved that an event's present status and its past status are independent yet simultaneous, it will follow that the succession-effects of the names of history run simultaneously, and that the past is a real place on the body.

FOUR TRADITIONAL TOPICS IN THE PHILOSOPHY OF HISTORY

Something happened a long time ago. What does that mean? It means that it is happening now, but in a peculiar sense of now.

We set out to explain how Joan of Arc could literally be on our bodies right now, without it ceasing to matter what Joan of Arc's dates are. We can say four things about how succession segments events backwards from simultaneity, by touching on four traditional issues in the philosophy of history. In the course of this book, we will develop issues in the philosophy of history that emerge in the terms of Deleuze and Guattarian philosophy, but for the moment, we will say a few words in their terms about issues that develop in traditional philosophies of history.

First is the issue of the freedom to reinterpret history. Following Nietzsche, there are two forces of succession: a reactive succession whereby we submit to a predecessor, and an active succession whereby we add a power to a predecessor (in the terms of *NP*). These both look like responses (the first objective, the second subjective) to the same kind of succession. But in fact, reactive and active retrospection constitute two entirely different kinds of series: the first constitutes history as nihilism, the second constitutes names of history as zones of intensity. The theory of succession as causal determinacy is a theory we simply reject, on account of its erroneous assumption that events have power centres sufficient to determine one result rather than another. But the theory of succession as the passage of power across mutually communicating events, implies the inheritance of the freedom to interpret.

Second is the question whether history proceeds continuously. Too much or too little interruption, and there is no history. Too much segmentation of history into names of history generates the great man of history theory, and as a result, succession and co-existence both degenerate into solipsistic historiographies based on despotic interpreters. Too little segmentation generates the theory of deterministic mass movements, and as a result, succession and co-existence both degenerate into repetition of the same. If there is to be a history in which *all* events matter and yet *each* event matters on its own, then there must be a dialectic of continuity and discontinuity, fluidity and segmentation. Each event must be a threshold in which co-existence is laid out in dynamic succession, and succession is contracted in interactive co-existence.

Third is the question whether an event, like the origin of capitalism, 'could have'[7] occurred in another time or place than it did. I devote the last three chapters to this very complex problem. In spite of their theory that events are incorporeal transformations whose source is virtual, and independent of particular states of affairs, Deleuze and Guattari do not want to say *tout court* that any event whatever can occur at any time in history. This is a difficult point in their philosophy of history, but the key to their reasoning is that an emergent event requires "a whole *generalized conjunction* that overspills and reverses the preceding apparatuses" (*MP* 564–5). It may sound odd to hear Deleuze and Guattari analyse history in terms of whole conjunctions instead of partial disjunctions, and in terms of a systematization of predecessors instead of free becomings. But in fact, it would be a mistake to identify free becoming with isolated phenomena or disengaged possibilities. The freedom to take a chance with a new event requires the resolve of staking everything on a whole system of chances. To speak of the origin of a phenomenon like capitalism is to posit that the whole determinate periodic history of nations and other assemblages can be simultaneously interpreted as its pre-history and its post-history. Events are singularities, but they are also abstract machines that produce pasts and futures along with them. The disengaged question of what "could have" happened is an idealist's search for possibilities; in contrast, the affirmation of the co-existence of all that happens, as a particular array of relations, is a schizo's rigorous temporal mapping of virtualities.

The fourth question is whether events of the past are accessible directly or only through intermediaries. This is to ask whether the Joan of Arc effect will run differently on our bodies than it will have run on bodies in the fifteenth century, on account of the intermediary events between then and now that in some ways dilute its effect and in other ways advance our technologies for expressing it. Of course, our ways of becoming Joan of Arc are different from Joan's, but after all, "becoming and multiplicity are the same thing" (*MP* 305), and the effect of history is a return of the different and not a return of the same. This makes the fact of successive intermediaries an indispensable feature of co-existential time. But on the other hand, as soon as we are related to the past, any event of any given period might be the one that our bodies reanimate. In this sense, becoming-historical is never simply a matter of continuity or progress (*MP* 289). To have a history, as opposed to just having a single predecessor that in turn has a predecessor, means to be able to search out any moment of the past and use it without regard to intermediaries. Becoming-historical means getting from A to B by means of an anti-memory that deterritorializes what happened in between. When the names of history are identified with zones of intensity on the body without organs, the body becomes a pure past, and makes decisions on a libidinal future, and so the virtual body becomes the place that takes up the place of the concept of history.

NOTES

1 A philosophy of history should also apply Kant's four schematisms of time: time-series, time-fullness, time-order, and time-scope. For Deleuze and Guattari, these are covered by theories of pure past, events, dates, and quasi-causes, respectively.
2 The names of history are close to Deleuze and Guattari's notions of abstract machines in *MP* (e.g. the "Lenin abstract machine"), and conceptual personae in *QP* (e.g. the philosophical motifs of Descartes' piece of wax, or Proust's madeleine). Jacques Rancière (1992) makes interesting companion reading, but is not directly related.
3 Edmund Husserl (1966), s. 38 pp. 76–9; also *Beilage V and VII*, pp. 109–11 and 115–16.
4 Pernoud and Clin (1986, pp. 337–44). That historians still debate whether an attempt was made to poison Joan with bad herring during the trial (on "The Day of the Herrings", pp. 320–30), and that such a question cannot but seem of world-historical significance to anyone who studies it in detail, testifies to the power of assemblages in constituting events. One level of incorporeal enunciation in the "names of history" is the fact that the name "Jeanne d'Arc" was not used for the historical figure during her lifetime (pp. 313–16).
5 There is a helpful article collecting passages showing the two uses of the term "history" in Deleuze by Guillaume Sibertin-Blanc (2003). Sibertin-Blanc attempts to synthesize the two uses by means of categories that are ontological and extra-historical, for example, by reading Deleuze on Spinoza concerning powers of action. He does not focus on resolving the two senses at the level of history itself.

To my knowledge, there are no books that try to do the sort of thing I am doing. Manuel De Landa's excellent *A Thousand Years of Nonlinear History* (1997) takes Deleuze and Guattari's discussions of history in a more materialist direction. Michael Hardt and Antonio Negri's *Empire* (2000) has become a classic application of Deleuze and Guattari to political history, but is not focused on the temporal ontology of history. Éric Alliez's masterful two volumes (so far) of *Les Temps capitaux* (1991, 1999) lay out the historical background of Deleuze's philosophy of time in relation to politics, but not with a focus on philosophy of history. The approaches to Deleuze's politics in the writings of Paul Patton, Rosi Braidotti, Philippe Mengue, Todd May, and Eugene Holland are all important, but different from what this book is doing with the history of political events.

There are some excellent analyses of the relevant arguments of Deleuze's texts, particularly those of Juliette Simont, Francois Zourabichvili, and Veronique Bergen, not to mention other excellent books and articles about Deleuze by Constantin Boundas, Charles Stivale, Dan Smith, Manola Antonioli, Keith Ansell Pearson, Bruce Baugh, Jean-Clet Martin, Peter Hallward, the contributors to the journal *Chimeres*, and many others. Like all books written on Deleuze today, mine implies a response to the controversial but important interpretations and critiques of Deleuze by Alain Badiou.
6 Éric Alliez and Félix Guattari in *AH* (1986, p. 181) distinguishes the "historical rhizomatic" from capitalism's claim to be the "destiny" of human history.
7 I use double quotation marks when quoting the text. But when I cite a phrase that someone might say, but which is not actually a quotation, I use single quotation marks. This punctuation will be used extensively in chapters 7–9, when I discuss various potential versions of the question, 'Why did such and such an event occur at the time it did?'

2 Living in the Contracted Present – The First Synthesis of Time

Deleuze and Guattari's philosophy of history relies on Deleuze's analysis in *DR* of the three syntheses of time. This chapter explicates the first of these: the synthesis of the present. Deleuze's second synthesis is the best known: the "pure past", the virtual co-existence of all time. Many treatments of Deleuze describe in appealing ways his account of time, but little work has yet been done to analyse his arguments for it. As a result, Deleuze's first synthesis of time, the time of organic succession, is not as well known.[1] When discussed at all, succession is generally treated as the false or superficial notion of time that co-existence is meant to replace. But Deleuze's philosophy does not devalue the categories of life and desire that characterize the temporality of succession. All three syntheses are clearly meant to co-exist as independent series of temporality. Furthermore, Deleuze's description of succession is not merely a standard account of time setting the stage for his original contributions concerning co-existence; it is full of provocative and original arguments in its own right. Most important, the details of Deleuze's account of succession in the first synthesis of time are precisely the premises that entail the necessity of the second synthesis.

The second chapter of *DR* is one of the most important and rigorous in Deleuze's corpus. It contains many explicit arguments, in addition to many other passages that I construe as arguments. Despite the length of my treatment of Deleuze's three syntheses of time, a great deal more could be said about how to construe and develop the arguments in the text. I hope and expect that over the years, philosophers will be poring over the details of Deleuze's arguments, and that a variety of different analyses of the text, at least as detailed as my own, will appear in print.

The first problem of interpretation concerns methodology. From the beginning of the chapter, Deleuze talks about the present as a contraction of instants, using a Humean model. Yet his method is not explicitly either phenomenological or positivist, transcendentalist or associationist. Nor is there a presumption that the account of time will fit into an ontological system (as in Hegel). What methodology prompts Deleuze to begin a theory of difference with the topic of time, and what methodology is he using to choose a starting point for thinking about time, and to draw consequences from there on?

The stated project of *DR* is to consider whether a form of difference precedes unity, totality, and identity. Time synthesizes an event simply by virtue of holding together different moments. The theory of time is thus an experiment in thinking difference without identity. This does not entirely explain why time should be chosen as the paradigm difference-synthesizer (e.g. as opposed to space, number, or writing), and perhaps Deleuze would not want to say that time is a more fundamental assemblage than, for example, sense, sensation, or desire. Nevertheless, Deleuze supports Bergson's idea that living matter produces memory, and in this sense, any differential interaction is temporal.

Assuming, then, that time is a legitimate first topic, how do we start describing it? We might begin with the concrete experience of time, and indeed Deleuze cites the "lived present" early in the chapter. But "experience" could mean anything from Humean impressions to Husserlian lifeworlds, and indeed, the fact that Deleuze combines these two vocabularies without comment suggests a difficulty. Throughout his corpus, Deleuze interprets subject as "superject", reducing subjects to local conjunctions of images produced by objects. On that basis, so-called "experience" is no more a starting point than any other formed matter in flux. In this context, it is not accidental that Deleuze starts with Hume. For Hume, "experience" need not be founded on subjectivity; it is first of all a conjunction that allows data to "count as one" (to use Badiou's phrase). A Humean model of sense-experience might be neutral enough to serve as a starting point for a theory of time, allowing us to appeal to facts of experience without a phenomenological reduction. But as we will see, the neutral starting point will make some later stages of the argument hard to evaluate.

A final methodological issue concerns the rigour of Deleuze's argumentation. Deleuze clearly says that the second synthesis follows "necessarily" from the first (108); in other passages, it is less clear whether he intends his analyses to be read as deductive arguments concerning the unfolding structures of time and repetition. I plan to analyse chapter 2 of *DR* as one long and rigorous argument. This approach raises issues concerning systematicity and logic, sense and implication, consistency and rhizomaticity. But the final test of whether Deleuze's texts should be read as rigorous arguments is whether we can generate Deleuzian conclusions from Deleuzian premises, whether that procedure throws light on the Deleuzian plane, and whether it allows us to do things with Deleuzian concepts that we otherwise could not do.

THE SYNTHESIS OF THE PRESENT

(i) Cases and instants

Deleuze begins by asking how repetition is possible (96). Suppose we consider the occurrence of some "element", and then consider it as an occurrence again. If we consider the two occasions independently, there is no schema for retaining the location of the first once there is a second. Such a repetition "changes nothing", as Hume says. It has no meaning with respect to the content of what is seen, even if the "mind that contemplates" them could remember having seen the first after the second occurs. In fact, there can be no genuine memory if the recurring elements are taken as individual elements. This is why, on Deleuze's construal, Hume begins his account of repetition not with "elements" (e.g. where A occurs, then A occurs again), but with "cases" (e.g. where an A–B conjunction occurs, then an A occurs, anticipating a reoccurrence of B).[2] Once we begin with a case, a double content, we can explain how a second occurrence recalls a first, namely by incorporating it. The repetition changes something, and the second appearance lets the first's possibilities be grasped. The repetition is the moment when the event's parts get distinguished (the second part of the first case being anticipated by the first part of the second case), and in which those parts recall one another (whether the part-to-part relation is one of identity, causality, or independence). The mind "extracts" (*soutire*) a difference from the repetition.

In two ways, this is a surprising interpretation of Hume. First, Deleuze's interpretation makes atomistic positivism the enemy of Hume's empiricist associationism. Deleuze takes Hume to be a relational thinker who starts with association, imaginative combination, and sympathetic bonds, and who realizes that if the mind had only discrete elements to work with, it could do nothing of what we know it does. Second, Deleuze takes Hume to be no more subjectivist than objectivist. For the mind can only operate once the objective content is relational. Repetition is the foundation for subjectivity, not the converse. So far, this is traditional metaphysics, from neo-Platonism (the first number is not One but the indefinite dyad), to Hegel (being begins with becoming), to Husserl (objective intentionality depends on protentions and retentions).

If a single case makes a difference, i.e. if it appears *as* a singular something, it is because it appears twice. Its first appearance, as an isolated element, never takes place as such. The first time it appears is when it appears for a second time, namely when its antecedent looks similar yet different from its consequent. The faculty of associating elements is what Hume calls "imagination" (at least on Deleuze's interpretation – we are not testing his reading of Hume's texts here). Association is a faculty of "retention", but not a receptacle for holding images. It "contracts" two moments into one temporal unit, yet retains them qua different. In this sense, it "founds" the two impressions that it contracts into one.[3] In sum, if an impression is to be grasped, it has to include a difference, and each of the differentiated moments must be able to call into play the others. Calling the double into play is repetition. For this reason, Deleuze says, repetition is not primarily memory, reflection, or conscious understanding, but a "synthesis of time" (97).

This is an important stage of Deleuze's arguments for the priority of passive over active synthesis, time over memory, co-existence over succession, becoming over history, and synthesis over instants. "A succession of instants does not make time, it unmakes it just as much" (97). A succession is not sufficient to constitute memory. It is at best material for synthesis.[4] On this point, Deleuze employs Kantian transcendental deduction (and attributes it to Hume): we know there is a "lived present", a grasped content (97); succession alone will not explain it; therefore there is a faculty of repetition in imagination that synthesizes that content. Though Deleuze introduces "lived present" and "instants" as though they were natural and obvious, they recall many well-travelled problems. Why does Deleuze use the vocabulary of "instants" at all, instead of starting with, for example, (Bergsonian) durations, or even (Hegelian) vanishings?

Perhaps Deleuze's argument should be read as a *reductio* against instants, not as a theory of how instants are assembled. But the "instant" does after all have some genuine status, even if not an originary status. Although we cannot have constructed the lived present out of instants, the present case nonetheless includes temporally different parts; it "retains" past instants, and "anticipates" future instants. Past and future instants have status as backward and forward referents of the present. Instants are non-originary and non-eschatological constructions that the present retroactively and proactively targets *as* elements in order to interpret itself.[5] Past and future do not refer to instants *outside* the present, but they do refer to "dimensions of the present itself *insofar as* it contracts the instants" (97).

We have to ask the text three questions: (a) Why does time begin as a present instead of as past or future? (b) How are past and future immanent in ("contracted" in) the present? (c) Why do past and future appear first as instants?

(a) Time is the present just because the first experience is a case, a repetition, a contraction of a plurality into a singular phenomenon, hence something that appears all in one together before us, affirmed as what there is, as presence. In spite of Deleuze's differences with Hegel and Heidegger, his argument, like theirs, hinges on an inference from contraction to presence, from co-presentation to Now-ness. A purely independent element would not be located on a time-line. In contrast, while a synthesis of moments is spread out over time, it is at the same time, a synthesis *for us*, here and now. A past composed of successive elements would be no past at all unless it were taken as such in a present; the past is nothing more than the present's way of arraying present content itself (*mutatis mutandis* for the future).[6] In short, original experience is a synthesis, and even though synthetic time is extended, it necessarily appears contracted into the present all at once.

(b) Every synthesis, therefore everything that could be something, is a present and only a present. But precisely because it is a synthesis, there is a schema *in the present* for the co-presence of the multiplicity that *made up the present*. Synthesis displays the present precisely as a past-present-future array. It does not matter whether the parts are objective moments ordered necessarily, or subjective moments ordered accidentally; either way, the present appears as *already*-having-been-multiple, hence as having a past dimension. Similarly, it appears as an ongoing contraction of *whatever* will be coming up, hence its future dimension. (This passage also describes present life as an apprenticeship building on the past for the sake of the future (101).)

(c) The third point follows. Again, the present is multiple; the presentation of the multiple as multiple is the presentation of synthesis as divisibility; and divisibility leads back to instants.

Deleuze (drawing from Hume) describes the movement within the present from past to future as a movement from particular to general. This has three consequences. First, it introduces the concept of "envelopment" (97). In a present synthesis, a moment converts a particular instant into a general field of unfoldings.[7] This does not mean that particulars are givens and universals are constructed. Particulars are just as much products of the synthesis whereby a temporal field is contracted into a present moment; the instants that have already passed result from counting backward. We might think of time as the folding and unfolding of a topological field. When folded over on to itself, the field is present one small square at a time, with its other parts moved around back – present but backgrounded. When unfolded out again, the presents get reorganized, and new foregroundings take place. Instants are always being reformulated on the shifting topology; as the smallest possible points of view, they are in a sense real. In sum, the smallest points, and their order of presentation, are dependent on the folds and unfoldings of the general field that envelops them.

(ii) Passive synthesis

The second implication of the move from particular to general follows. The general field is the sphere of synthesis, hence synthesis does not depend on agent subjectivity; therefore, the present is "passive synthesis" (97).

This notion of passive synthesis is difficult. Even in Husserl, from whom the term "passive synthesis" is drawn, there is a problem of interpretation. At times, Husserl means syntheses that the experiencing subject simply accepts as given, without conscious deliberation or action, sometimes without noticing that they have taken place. The stream of experiences we have upon waking up, or the backgrounds that we experience without attending to, are examples of passive synthesis. They are synthetic, since they involve spatial configurations, interpretations in relation to memories and conceptual schemes, and so on. But they are not, on the surface, products of active interpretation. Yet if we press beneath the surface, even these sorts of experiences involve subjective procedures. Spatialization involves an orientation of the body, memory involves recall, conceptual schemes require information processing. Phenomenology has to conclude that so-called passive synthesis is really a case of low-level active synthesis, which constitutes objects capable of showing themselves to us while we are relaxing. Passivity is a stance of habituation that we actively take up, or fall into. Though it is not clear that this is what Husserl meant, this interpretation is consistent with phenomenology. But such a reading is not consistent with Deleuzian principles, which require a more radical passivity. For Deleuze, again following a Humean spirit, the active subject is not a prior condition of object-configuration, but is one configuration among many that come into being as syntheses fold into one another.

Happily, Deleuze's paradoxical conclusion is that a passive being can *do* more things than an active being. This is parallel to Deleuze's argument in *DR* chapter 1 that the univocity of being allows more differentiation than multivocity. If being were multivocal, then each individual thing would be determined by the particular essence appropriate to it. But since being is univocal, each thing is free to pick up determinations from any other in a smooth space of characteristics and forms. Likewise, passive synthesis frees the mind from whatever structures of action would have limited its capacity for novelty. This sketch makes some version of the mind's passivity plausible and palatable, but we need to explain why the temporal movement from past to future within the present, read as a movement from particular to general, is passive.

It is primarily because synthesis is immanent that it is passive. To put it bluntly, immanence implies that as soon as there is something then there is everything. As soon as there is anything, there has been a contraction that has folded a multiplicity into a singular presence. This 'already' confers on synthesis the status of having taken place before any subject comes to look at it; it renders synthesis passive. It is synthesis in the sense of being thought together, and in (Heidegger's) sense of coming-into-presence, but it is passive in the sense of being an internal relation rather than a succession of points awaiting action. Of course, it requires energy to realize these internal relations, and the passive–active relation will be problematic in concrete experience.

The third implication of the transition from particular to general is that passivity implies a time arrow, an asymmetry or non-reversibility of temporal movement. Stengers and Prigogine (to whom Deleuze refers) emphasize this problem in modern physics. An object can change state in either of two directions, rising or falling, heating or cooling, increasing or decreasing according to any given property. Formulas defining time in terms of change of state are thus indifferent to the direction of time, so classical physics cannot account for the time arrow that ordinary experience exhibits. Stengers and Prigogine appeal to thermodynamic entropy to argue that certain kinds of change are irreversible (i.e. a system can only lose energy, not gain it), and hence to argue that physical time does have an irreversible arrow after all.

Deleuze's argument for a time arrow is not based on physics, but nor does it depend on the old tunes that pass for introspective description. If there is a time arrow, the logic of contraction-production must demonstrate it. Contraction produces internal references from each one of its parts to the others. The movement from one particular to another is reversible, but the movement from a particular to a general whole introduces a difference in kind. Without requiring active intervention, the particular has the status of something already present, whereas the general has the status of opening into infinite extensions. The move from particular to general within a singular contraction follows an irreversible arrow from past to future within the present.[8]

Now, if passive synthesis throws so-called instants into a contracted generality, can we still speak of a "succession" of moments, or can we speak only of a single moment in flux? Deleuze says that repetition "implies" three proceedings (*instances*) of time (98): the "in-itself" of time that cannot be thought; the "for-itself" of passive synthesis; and the "for-us" of active synthesis or reflective representation. Up to now, we have been presenting the second as the origin of temporality. But the first suggests a flux in the living present prior to passive synthesis. Deleuze's discussion of time in LS Series 1 and 2 begins with a similar distinction between the measureless flux of becoming and measured instants in succession. One of the most difficult problems in interpreting Deleuze's account of time concerns the status of flux. Is there a flux that is indeterminate in relation to what actually happens in time? Is the contracted whole (one sense of history) indifferent to the distance between events as they occur in succession (the other sense of history)? The more emphasis put on the unthinkable flux, the less contact there will be between simultaneity and succession, and the more indeterminate time in general will appear. Conversely, the more that flux is embedded *in* the interplay between distance and simultaneity, the more articulated time will appear. I am arguing in general for the latter, both as a reading of Deleuze and as a working theory of time. In any case, the in-itself, pre-thought, measureless time cannot become present without a contraction of two or more determinate moments. The present may well be a flux "in itself", but it appears "for us" only after its passive synthesis is broken down into instants or else built up into successions.

The moments that succeed one another "for us" only emerge from the flux once we attend to them. There is a temptation to treat such secondary reflections as mere illusions. But that is not Deleuze's move. In *NP*, reflection produces *real* reactive forces; in *ES*, it produces *real* cultural artifices. For better or worse, the production of succession produces actual individual moments. This is important for two reasons. First, since we showed that instants cannot by themselves produce synthesis, they need to be explained as offshoots of synthesis. Similarly in *AO*, flows and interruptions are primary, but their secondary reifications into part-objects exist in their own manner. As in *AO*, a synthesis can be analysed both in its schizo version and its fascist version, its synthetic version and a degenerate individuating version. But why must degeneration take place, and why must it take the form of instants? In *AO*, the reasoning is that a *desire* to pursue a flow invests itself in each of its moments, setting the stage for object-choices, phobic responses, and other modes of getting stuck in an instant cut off from its milieu. In *DR*, perception does a similar job, sweeping across a field until it lands on something to grasp. Anything along the flow can be what perception fixes upon as the already-there. In order to be perceived passively, there has to be not-yet-exhausted material that can potentially be attended to actively.

The present's immediately contracted singularity must therefore be able to show itself secondarily as successive representations of part-moments held together in present memory. But succession, the degenerative function of the present, now takes over as Deleuze's primary definition of present time. It is not unusual for a phenomenon to be dominated by its degenerative aspect. But we have to keep in mind that the logic of the present is no longer univocal. "The present" can refer to the logic of contracted passive synthesis, or to the logic of successive memory-representations.

(iii) Organism and intention

The justification for Deleuze's use of the term "memory" to describe representational succession depends on the connection of passivity with habit. Deleuze gives an organic account of habit.

The appeal to organic life to explain temporality is unexpected here. First, we wonder why Deleuze would have started with a perception model of temporal repetition only to bring in an organic model later on. It can seem on the one hand that Deleuze is trying to deduce the organism from features of passive perception, or on the other hand that features of the organism are brought in *ex machina* to solve problems that arose for the perception of time. My attitude has been that, when reasonable, we should read the text as a deduction, and it seems to me that Deleuze's argument does derive organicism from the passive synthesis at the origin of perception.

Yet in chapter 1, Deleuze argues that the greatness of Leibniz and Hegel is that both recognized the limits of organic explanations in metaphysics. The concept of organism suggests a genetic limit to differential transformations, whereas perception has the advantage of being open to any content from anywhere. But in chapter 2, Deleuze equates the organism with "contemplation" (99–100), equating a kind of organic materialism with a kind of perceptual idealism. The point is that organic perception is neither exactly subjective nor exactly corporeal. A perception is simply an "intentional" *content*, the presence of some object. (With Husserl, perception is "consciousness of" something, but for Deleuze, it is more "of" than "consciousness"). Content is the object-form lived as the present. Content for an organism is life in the presence of objects, or life-with-objects, or life shaped by objects, or life that adapts to, and engages with, objects.

To derive memory from contraction, we need to connect the concepts of organism, habit, and intentionality. The organism, defined less by physiology than by forces of engagement, contains pre-conscious aspects of habit. We are used to thinking of habit as an activity we learn as a result of our own endeavours rather than a synthesis that takes place for us in the objects themselves. As an example, Deleuze says that in organisms, the integration of certain nutrients in our cells is passive synthesis (100). Cellular heredity is a synthesis of the past; it is body memory existing in the present organism. Similarly, organic "need" is a passive synthesis of objects with a futural function. Deleuze's examples in the same passage of "apprenticeship" and "instinct" are more adaptational than physiological, but they suggest the same passive syntheses of the past and future referents of life. It is difficult to draw a firm line between passive and active syntheses, and Deleuze says that a full account of synthesis (which he does not promise to give) would describe manifold variations and "levels" in the interactions of passive and active synthetic forms of life (100).[9]

Deleuze's justification of organicism is far from complete, but it is enough to draw the three conclusions we need in order to derive memory from organic perception: first, that habit means drawing something off; second, that drawing something off is a kind of contemplation; third, that contemplation is a sign-function and hence a kind of intentionality that entails memory.

First, habit means "drawing something off", or "extracting something" (*soutirer*) (101–2). Deleuze used the term "extraction" in the first paragraph of the chapter (96) to make the point that the mind comes into existence when a difference is "extracted" from repetition and made into an object for contemplation. The difference extracted is in one sense the mind itself (the mind becomes subjective when some content is foregrounded); and is in another sense repetition itself (a flux becomes objective when some content is backgrounded).[10]

Deleuze aims to show that two different extractive functions follow from contraction: a sign function, and a self-reference function. Together, they constitute the proto-intentionality we need in order to draw memory out of habit. Each part of the argument appeals to an organic phenomenon, but the underlying principle is that it is the heterogeneous content of contraction that extracts external sign-references and internal self-references.

The organic phenomenon that Deleuze uses to introduce the sign function is the difference between an animal sensing the presence of water, and an animal suffering dehydration (100). In the first case, the animal makes use of a sign; in the latter, it does not. Deleuze does not define "sign" here, but we might say that the contraction of a duration into a present makes it possible for one content to refer outside itself to another. Signs are not primarily representations of objects, but rather the cross-references of heterogeneous elements that have been contracted into a single case without erasing their difference. The contraction is, in one sense, just the two contents together, but in another sense, it extracts a meta-character from the ensemble, a relationality functioning in a minimal sense as a sign. A sign is still passive because it is nothing more than contraction, yet it is incipiently active in expressing the external other.

The organic phenomenon that Deleuze uses to exhibit the self-reference function in contraction is that animals gain pleasure not just from one body part at a time, but from generalized excitations and relaxations of the body as a whole (*autosatisfaction*) (101–2). An animal has a feeling of life, a second meta-character added to that of the sign: perception through *self*-reference added to external reference. The organism is both the synthesis of objective contents and the self-referencing system of contents. Deleuze cites the Plotinian thesis that there are "contemplative souls" in our muscles and our nerves (101). The process that contracts contents enough to make the body work, also turns them into a self-referential whole. The parts of such a whole have an interactive momentum; they are mutually defining; they become inseparable from the whole *as* parts of a whole; from then on they signal the existence of the whole; they refer to a whole which in turn refers back to them. It is a property of immanence[11] to be on the one hand a multiplicity of consistent, self-referencing contemplations,[12] and on the other, a single bloc of sense even across incompatible parts.

The combination of the externalizing function of signs and the internalizing function of auto-reference provides organic synthesis with an object-pole and a subject-pole: sensory-motor intentionality. How does this make habit into memory, passivity into activity, present into past?

We are about to see what effect organic habit has on the synthesis of present time. But we first have to be clear about the three levels[13] of repetition and generality (103). (1) Repetition at the level of immediate contraction produces generality in the sense of elements belonging together. (2) Repetition at the level of contemplation produces generality in the sense of reference to a whole. (3) Repetition at the level of a continuous ego produces generality in the sense of totalizing representation. The last is inherently "third", the medium in which the flux of repetition is reduced to representations. Overall, the mutual reference among contents of perception is the beginning of self-contemplation. The three levels of repetition move towards a broadening of generality, and an increase in subjectivity (representing itself as being more subjective than it is), or more precisely, an increase in self-reference. The repetition of elements in flux ends with a meta-function of self-conservation in which instants are at the same moment divided, serialized, and made present. The threefold distinction posits division as the mediation between undifferentiated temporal flux and the differentiated flow of the present. To express this last point, Deleuze says that "difference exists between two repetitions" (104).

We can describe the three levels of repetition either (a) as a sequence (*en longeur*) where the first results in the third by the mediation of the second, or (b) as a common foundation of different experiences (*en profondeur*), where the three unfold as functions of the same repetition. On the second description, it is the synthetic act (repetition) that makes division (difference) possible.[14]

We can now draw temporal consequences from the theory of habit as quasi-intentional, quasi-organic contractive self-contemplation. These consequences lay out the attributes of present time, and also prepare the way for a temporality of pure past (with a new past-present-future distinction). We started with a kind of time that contracts past and future within the present. But we now have an unstable situation. "Only the present exists", yet there are extra-present aspects of the present, namely the past and future as sign functions and auto-reference functions. These generate what Deleuze calls "intra-temporality" (98), a difference in time from time itself. There is now a sense in which the "present passes", and this will entail a second synthesis of time outside present time.

The original argument (98) for the presence of past and future in the present (intratemporality) was drawn from perceptual contraction. That argument established for present time the attribute of being quantitatively one-many. I construe three more arguments for intratemporality in pp. 105–8. The second draws from need, and attributes rhythm to present time. The third draws from signs, and attributes the past perfect form to time. The fourth combines needs and signs into questions, and attributes a field-structure to present time.

In preparation, Deleuze gives an odd argument (105) for why there is any multiplicity in the present at all. One would think that this had already been established, since each time is a contraction of several times. The variation that Deleuze gives here appeals to "physical possibility". Why can we not, he asks, "conceive" of the present independent of time passing, i.e. as a "perpetual present"? Strictly speaking, we cannot conceive of time as if there were no passing whatsoever, since time is contraction. But why can we not imagine that each of the "succession of instants" contains a contemplation of the same infinity, in such a way that the present content would be "co-extensive" with all time?[15] If all the contracted instants covered the same duration, no difference of intratemporality could be extracted. Deleuze's response is that while we can indeed "conceive" this kind of present, it is not a "physical possibility". It is not clear what force the appeal to physicality has, but based on what Deleuze says next, it seems the reason time cannot all be reduced to one coextensive present is that different physical beings at different times have their own temporal needs.

(iv) Need and fatigue

The argument for intratemporality based on need: the content of each moment of time functions as a point of view, contemplating the content of other moments.[16] Each content measures the "duration" of time passing, and the measurement "varies" depending on its perspective on neighbouring points of view. Each species, each individual organism, indeed each part of each organism, has its own measurement of time. Therefore, time passes at many speeds at once. The only thing that followed from simple contraction was that there is a quantitative flow of moments sharing a homogeneous measure of time. But with the premise that organisms contemplate from points of view, we introduce variable quantifications of duration. Deleuze highlights the counter-intuitive fact that since contractions occur at different rates, two "successive" instants can both be "contemporaneous" with a third. For time is not a single series of cases, but an indefinite number of superimposed time-lines, each measured by the sign-functions immanent in some time-content. This defines time by movement; it defines the form of time by the content of time. We might say with Leibniz that each monad expresses the history of the world according to the rhythm of its own time-line, so that one and the same event is found in different places on different time-lines. If a given content B is immediately contracted with A on one time-line (from one point of view), but on a different time-line is contracted with A after an intermediary contraction with C, we can say consistently both that B occurs two moments after A, and that it occurs one moment after A. Or, since the first time-line held steady between A and B while the second was in movement, A and C are successive with respect to the second time-line but contemporaneous with respect to the first. Different time-lines define variable durations, so different time-moments are superimposed upon one another.[17] This problem is at the root of Bergson's argument (against Einstein) that relativity permits a unity of time, albeit a multi-dimensional unity. The same problem is at the root of Husserl's analysis of "simultaneity". Contemporaneity, for Husserl, occurs when intentional streams, each flowing at its own speed and requiring its own order of perceptions, nevertheless necessarily fix from time to time on points shared by each other's time-lines. It may be difficult to discern which points are shared by two time-lines, or to define "at the same time" without regress. But the conclusion from this first stage of the argument from need is that an organism temporalizes itself by apprehending "diverse" durations of the present at the same time.

From variable duration, Deleuze infers the interplay of need and fatigue (105). The fatigue in question occurs when an organism tries to contemplate something but is unable to contract it into its own duration-line, as if there is no room left in its time-line, or as if it has exhausted its ability to go further. An organism is fatigued not when it has done so much that it has no energy for more, since contraction is by definition momentum, but rather when its contractions have slowed to a near halt. Fatigue is not like getting tired of not fulfilling one's needs; it is like failing to generate needs. We know from Deleuze's work that need is not lack; as long as one keeps one's desires passive, maximally needy, then they will be fulfilled by just about anything. Contraction is always successful in propagating momentum. Needs are always satisfied, and fatigue is the internal and external limit of that need. Externally, fatigue occurs when satisfaction is complete, so that any remainder is outside the organism's sphere of concern. This fatigue is the state of having nothing left to do. Internally, fatigue is contraction that never gets started, a need satisfied with having nothing. This fatigue is the state of having no idea what to do. Need and fatigue come into focus when the momentum of satisfaction (when contraction accelerates, it is need) alternates with loss of momentum (when it decelerates, it is fatigue). Need is the futural dimension of the present; fatigue is the present's satisfaction with the past (though need is sometimes driven by the past, and fatigue can be futural drift).

The "present extends between two surges of need" (105). It is not just that after one need is satisfied, another always begins. A single need surges up twice: once at the beginning, and again when satisfaction fulfils it. The present endures by filling itself up until it absorbs its two limit-points. The extended present is the time in which the past has a future that satisfies its past.

The intratemporality of past and future in the present is therefore "inscribed" in the present's needs and its variable speeds (106). Need is the "for-self of repetition, the for-self of a certain duration" (106). Intratemporality is the structure of the present as such, of differential time-lines extracted from the limits of points of view. "Starting from our contemplations, all of our rhythms, our reserves, our reaction times, the thousand interlacings, the presents and the fatigues that compose us, are defined. The rule is that one cannot go faster than one's own present, or rather, one's presents" (106). Past and future are the present's way of being at, between, and beyond, its own limits. They are the present's rhythmic extensions of presence into other presents. They add length to present moments and depth to the time-lines measuring the present.

(v) Signs

The third argument for intratemporality is based on signs. Here, past and future are treated as ontological levels of the present, rather than as time (or time-lines) added on to the present. The argument from need added variable quantity to homogeneously quantified perceptual time. The argument from signs adds qualitative intratemporality.

As we have seen, contemplation is present in every instant's point of view as a signifier; as signified, it subsists as the past or future dimension (of the present). This lets Deleuze say that temporal signs "refer to" past or future, but "belong to the present" (106). This is not quite to say that signs are *in* the present. The sign is a relation, and is not in one instant more than in another. The sign is a sign *of* the present; it refers to past and future *through* the present, and indeed refers to them *as* features of the present. The sign is therefore not just a reference *from* the present *to* the past or future, but also a sign directed *to* a feature of the present itself, albeit not its feature of immediate presence. Furthermore, the sign is not something that exists in the present, but is the very essence of being present as such. Deleuze appeals to the Stoic description of a scar as a sign not of a past wound but rather of "the *present* fact of *having had* a wound". I will focus on the attribute of present time introduced by "having had". Deleuze raises issues quickly, but I linger on four points.

First, using Stoic vocabulary, Deleuze says that "natural signs" refer to the presence of past and future in the present, whereas "artificial signs" refer to fictional pasts and futures, extensions out of the present. From the standpoint of the present, the latter raises a paradox. The present's own artificial signs refer to a past and future at once real for it (as the limit-case of its reference beyond the present) and unreal for it (since it cannot contract that other time into its own).

Second, natural signs posit past and future fully as other dimensions of the present, not just as extensions of the present. Earlier, we conceived past and future as the multiplicity of moments in one big present. But now we are not thinking of variable quantity but of an ontological difference between signifying present and signified past and future. Points of view are variable not just in duration, but in the way they posit virtualities (by the ways they interpret content).

Third, to explicate " 'the present fact of having had a wound' ", we need a distinction between "something that happened" and "something having happened". What does this grammatical form refer to? Deleuze's phrase in French (in quotations in the text because it paraphrases the Stoics), refers to the " '*fait present d'avoir eu une blessure*' " (106). Here we have (a) the participle (what the present refers back to as its own history); and (b) the infinitive of the auxiliary verb, "to have", not exactly possessing, but we might say quasi-possessing the past. Referring into a past (or future) from a present requires, first, letting the past take on a status that is not simply that of a later present, and second, positing an intermediary that is not just present and not just past, but past in the quasi-possession of the present.

The puzzle of "having had" shows that the conception of the past as a dimension of the present has not given us enough resources to describe the past that the present itself has begun to signify. The clue that the past is not just a dimension of the present is that the past has created these paradoxes in the present. The present contracts, and in so doing signifies a doubled time, an auxiliary past; but while incorporating that past into its contraction, it has no solution to the question of what kind of past it contracted itself from. In short, the present generates paradoxes due to its simultaneous need to signify the past and its inability to enunciate the co-existence of past and present within the present. It will be up to the past qua past to define co-existence as a generative principle, but to do so, it will have to enunciate the co-existence of past and present within the past.

The present is intratemporal because it doubles as a present-present and a present-past. The present passes not by moving from present to past; it uses the past within it as a kind of energy reserve to dip into in order to motivate continued contractions.

Fourth, Deleuze offers the difficult formula: "the sign is the contemplation of the wound, it contracts all the instants that separate me from it into a living present" (106). Each instant, as it passes, separates itself from me in the present; but what the instant signifies pulls the instant back to me. Distance, followed by cancelling the distance: this is how the present reads itself as history. Further, in the sign, the present reads itself as *me* reading *my* history. The "me" in the text is no doubt precarious. We have already seen that it is only on the artificial, self-representational level of synthesis that the ego takes form. But it is precisely at this level that the paradox of the present shows itself again and again, namely when the past is (inevitably) represented. For it is at one and the same level that instants are represented individually, that the past is represented as independent of the present, and that the history of the present is represented as mine.[18]

Deleuze's last argument for intratemporality in the present arises because both need and sign consist of "gaps" (*béances*), and a gap in sign-functions is expressed as a "question" (106). The issue for intratemporality concerns the nature of a "problematic field" (107). Contemplation endures through time by small discontinuities, since any question challenges some element in the habitual anticipation-fulfilment chain. And it endures by large discontinuities, since it asks the fatiguing question, "What difference does it make?" Questions bring to fruition the generality of the present, by extending the gap problem throughout the domain of signs. Traversing time by gaps is not just a negative mode of unhinging expectations, but also a positive mode of stringing together all the little "finite affirmations" carried out by all the little leaps of judgement by all the syntheses of contemplative souls contracting one thing with another. In sum, the questioning soul gives present time the structure of a "field". The present does not just include past and future contents; it problematizes them all at once, and this, finally, is what makes the present intratemporal. We can still say that the difference between past and future is a difference of rhythms and interpretations, but we will now define a rhythm as a sign covering two beats under one question. In short, the past is not just what has happened so far, but also the discontinuity of affirmation on a general field.

To summarize, the past is a dimension of the present in four senses: (a) the past is the other instant contracted into the present (in the tick-tock of present perception); (b) it is the variability of time-lines (in the rhythms of present organic habits); (c) it is the virtual having-been of "my" history (in the signs of present contemplation); and (d) it is the field of discontinuities (in the gaps of present questions).

(vi) Consequences

Let us consider what Deleuze's theory of the present does, relative to other philosophical accounts of the present.

First, in Deleuze's account, the vanishing present does not play its traditional role. In ancient theories of time, the key issue is whether the present exists and the past and future do not (since there is no time at which past and future are actual; past and future consist only of memories and anticipations in the present), or else past and future exist but the present does not (since as soon as we point to the present, it has ceased to be; the present is specious). In one sense, both sides of the controversy can be found in Deleuze. The non-existence of past and future can be found in his argument that past and future are dimensions *of* the present. But Deleuze's subordination of past and future to a processual present does not deny those dimensions as such. In a similar way, the non-existence of the present can be found in Deleuze's critique of individuated instants. But here too, his subordination of the present instant to extended duration does not deny that time can count as present. Deleuze's concept of the present thus incorporates what the Ancients *opposed* to the present. For the essence of the present is to contract the *other* moments. So when Deleuze says that from the standpoint of the present, only the present exists, the "present" here already includes features we normally attribute to past and future, and vice versa. This is typical dialectical argumentation.

My reference to dialectic is not gratuitous, since Hegel is the philosopher of the vanishing present (*Phänomenologie des Geists* s. 95–6, 106–7). Like Deleuze, Hegel does not deny that the Now actually appears. Rather, his argument works by showing that the Now is already *another* Now, that the Now is always a plurality, a universal, a having-been, a subjectivity and not just a facticity. Hegel introduces multiplicities of temporal quantification into the present, and multiplicities of qualitative subjectivities into temporal quantification. His move is not to deny something about the present but to add so much into the present that it no longer looks like what we thought the present was going to be. In this way, Hegel's logic of negation is not a logic of absence, of lack, or even primarily of antithesis – it is a logic of genetic multiplication, negation via hyper-affirmation. To clarify why Deleuze does not take seriously the view that the present does not exist, it is of value to note Hegel's reason for not taking it seriously: namely, that what makes a Now be another is not that it vanishes, or simply is not there, but that *more* Now extends it into something else.

Second, in Deleuze's account, the immediacy of the present does not play its traditional role. Here the relevant contrast is between Deleuze and Derrida. Derrida critiques the equation of present time with present objects, using the problem of deferral. An object cannot be experienced all at once, an expression cannot be explicated exhaustively, a context of interpretation cannot be determined without ambiguity, and speakers/perceivers and listeners/tribunals cannot be decisively marked off as autonomous consciousnesses, or as independent language-users, or as curable unconsciousnesses, or as continuous biographical histories. The presence of objects is deferred for perceiving subjects whose self-presence is likewise deferred. Consequently, the present cannot be located on a time-line, and one cannot tell which point in a complex protention-retention chain a content fits into. For Derrida, these facts undermine presence. Now, in various ways, Deleuze follows similar routes in affirming the multiplicity of object-forms, the foreignness of language, the splitting of the ego, and the non-locatability of temporal moments. But for Deleuze, none of this undermines presence. The reason for this difference hangs on what expectation one had for the term "present". If one expected the term "present" to refer to an individual moment in time, then one should stop using that term in the face of temporal complexes. But if one expected it to refer to a field that from the first instance includes serial, contractual, multi-dimensional, perhaps inherently unmeasurable, non-individuable, swarming blocs of movement, then one can continue speaking of that whole mass as "present". This difference between Derrida and Deleuze is terminological, but not without consequence. For Derrida, undermining presence introduces absence; for Deleuze, multiplying presence incorporates difference but not absence. For Derrida, the fact that the same event occurs on different points along different time-line measurements, means, more or less, that there is no Now-point. For Deleuze, the same fact means, more or less, that all such points are Now-points. Indeed, for Deleuze they are all the same Now-point – though not from the standpoint of the present, for which all the points are contracted in multi-layered succession, but from the standpoint of the past, for which all the points are affirmed in simultaneous co-existence.

At this point in Deleuze's text (108), there is a blank line, a brief summary of the "paradox of the present", then the statement: "We must not draw back from the necessary consequence: there must be an other time in which the first synthesis of time carries itself out. The latter refers necessarily to a second synthesis" (108).

NOTES

1. The best commentators on this text, in my view, are Zourabichvili (1994), Simont (1997), and Ansell Pearson (1998).
2. The relation between elements and cases is complex. Deleuze (98–9) contrasts Hume's beginning with A–B cases (on a model of cause–effect: tick-tock) with Bergson's beginning with A–A successions (on a model of clock time: tick-tick). Cases have their contractions within, whereas elements have their contractions between them. In one sense, the case seems "closed", since its repetition is accomplished without going outside. But in another sense, the case is internally dynamic, "open" to proportional variations. In contrast, the element seems self-enclosed and indifferent to successors; in another sense, it is open, since when the clock ticks 4, it is open to being various kinds of 4: 4 a.m. or 4 p.m., 4:00 or 4:30. Deleuze concludes that case and element "refer" to one another. A case presupposes the elements that are contracted within it, and the elements "surpass themselves" in a case-complex. While Deleuze wants to give Hume and Bergson equal play, his argument makes Hume's "case" foundational. Passive synthesis tends to experience tick-tick as tick-tock.
3. "Contraction" sometimes designates one phase of a process whose other phase is dilation (as in Bergson), but here it designates the "fusion" of both phases (101).
4. In *DR*, Deleuze, discussing Hume, identifies succession with simple coming-after, and repetition with synthesis. In *ES* (62–4), discussing the same point in Hume, Deleuze identifies "repetition" with simple "coming-after", i.e. with mechanical, quantitative sequence; he identifies the synthesis of "contraction" (also "genesis" and "progression") with "habit". However, the essence of the two texts is the same.
5. For various levels of retroactivity as backward reference, see Lampert (1995a).
6. In *LS* Series 2, Deleuze gives a parallel argument that the time of bodies (as opposed to incorporeal events) is the present. A mind remembers a past or anticipates a future; but a body is nothing other than its actual states at any given time, so it exists only in its own present. The situation becomes more complicated once Deleuze ascribes incorporeal attributes to bodies.
7. *LS* (22–3) makes a similar equation of past and future with particular and universal. Yesterday is a particular; tomorrow is open to interpretation.
8. The move from particular to general is the past's "living rule of the future" (97), a phrase from Hume that Deleuze also discusses in *ES* (103–4).
9. This is the focus of Simont's (1997, p. 307) account of the first synthesis. The ticking of a clock constitutes a habit of material vibrations that are neither subjective nor objective, active or passive.
10. In *AO* (50), the synthesis of "conjunction" is said to "extract" a "subject" from what is previously a flow of connections and disjunctions. Once there is conjunction, its locus will begin to have reflective and then projective functions. Desiring machines exist in the full sense at the same time as subjectivity is extracted from a flow.
11. In *CS* (99), Guattari defines a "plane of immanence" by means of "auto-references".
12. Daniel Dennett's multiple processing model of mind and organism in *Consciousness Explained* in the 1980s is reminiscent of Deleuze's in the 1960s, not to mention Merleau-Ponty's *The Structure of Behaviour* in the 1940s.
13. The distinction is confused by the fact that it is laid out in two different ways on 103 (and reprises the threefold distinction on 98; see my p. 14). Each version uses slightly different vocabulary, and puts the three levels in a different order. All the versions indicate the same relation between indeterminate and determinate flows by the mediation of successive differences. If anyone would like to work through the details, email me (jlampert@uoguelph.ca).

14 In other ways, division (difference) makes synthesis (repetition) possible, as when social division generates repeating systems of confrontation.
15 Keith Ansell Pearson (1998) gives two construals of the argument that the present is not co-extensive with time. (1) "The fact that the present is constituted through need and synthesized temporally through acts of repetition means that there can be no present which could be co-extensive with time" (101). Ansell Pearson takes this to be the same as the argument from need, while I construe them separately. On my construal, need implies duration, but Deleuze is concerned that duration might be one single complex present co-extensive with all time. (2) "The time of the present is fundamentally paradoxical since in order to be 'present' it must not be self-present, that is, it must pass, and it is the passing of time that prevents the present from ever being co-extensive with time" (pp. 101–2). The second clause looks ahead to Deleuze's argument for the pure past. The first clause, concerning self-presentation, is what I call the argument from signs or self-reference.
16 Ansell Pearson (*ibid.*, p. 101) construes this argument differently: "Repetition and need are inextricably linked since it is only through the repetition of an instant that need can express itself as the for-itself of a certain duration." On my construal, need is not brought into the argument as a given in order to deduce duration; rather, duration demonstrates that enduring beings have needs. It is difficult to be certain which construal is best.
17 Zourabichvili (1994, p. 72) construes the whole first synthesis of time this way. Need demands density of interpretation, and fatigue allows slackening of interpretation. Temporality is a milieu that both allows, and covers over, lacunae in the actual instants of experience.
18 In the last paragraph on the synthesis of the present (107–8), Deleuze distinguishes the self (*moi*) as subject from the self as "a thousand habits". (a) The self of the thousand habits is a contracting contemplation. (b) It is neither simple nor plural, but a "system", exemplified by Beckett's "larval subjects". (c) It is not active, but a "machine" that extracts itself from its contents, and hence extracts its "right" to find itself. (d) It does not "have" modifications, but is "the modification of something else". (e) On the other hand, "one is only what one *has*" (107). "One" is the neutral milieu that "has" a self.

3 The Virtual Co-existence of the Past – The Second Synthesis of Time

The transition to the second synthesis of time, the pure past, is one of the most important moves in the philosophy of Deleuze. Anyone who knows anything about Deleuze knows his theory that the past in its entirety co-exists with the present. The entire theory is developed within eight pages of *DR* (108–15). As exciting, and as useful, as this idea is, it is essential that we be able to demonstrate it. In this chapter, I am going to analyse the details of Deleuze's arguments for the pure past, to require the most rigorous demonstrations possible, and to mine every aspect of these pages that I can find that might be used to construct a decisive proof. I will also pull together parallel arguments in other texts of Deleuze.

Some of these arguments compare temporal phenomena and conclude that there are different temporal structures; others argue that the present cannot explain time (because it is either contradictory or contains presuppositions) and conclude that the past is its ground.

ARGUMENT 1: THE ARGUMENT FROM CONTAINMENT

The present contains the past as an immanent dimension, and this at first seemed enough to explain the phenomenon of the past. But as the dimension of the past in the present was explicated in terms of rhythms, signs, and virtual fields, something about the past was being posited within the present that the present could not contain. None of these analyses proved that there is a past not structured by the present, or demonstrated what such a past could be. But the point at which the present ceases to be self-explanatory is the point that introduces the logic of the past as such.

Let us preview what the passage promises to demonstrate: "We must not draw back from the necessary consequence: there must be an other time in which the first synthesis of time carries itself out. The latter refers necessarily to a second synthesis" (108). First, Deleuze announces an "*other* time", as opposed to a further characterization of the present. The promise is that we are about to be shown a phenomenon that cannot be explained by the multiple time-lines that branch out from the present.

Second, he announces an "other *time*". An atemporal synthesis cannot resolve the paradox of the present, but a temporal synthesis can.

Third, the necessary addition to the synthesis of the present is to be a *synthesis*, as opposed to a thetic unity, a simple time-form, or an abstract time-constant. But it is not yet clear what "time-synthesis" can mean if it is not about time passing, i.e. if it is not a synthesis of the present.

Fourth, and most important, the second synthesis is said to be that "*in* which" the first must be carried out. This is the key to the argument for the pure past: the present requires some kind of container – a context, or medium, or ground – in order to pass, and in order to be the present incorporation of all time-passage. What does "in" refer to in the case of time? Simont (308) takes the question, "*in* what does the present pass?" to mean, "*with* what does the present contract?" On her construal, the present must be "susceptible" of passing, of ending, hence of being past (309). The present is "in" the past in the sense that it depends on the past superseding it. This construal is plausible, but Deleuze seems to affirm a more literal sense of the past as container of the present.

Fifth, the past is that in which the present "carries itself out". The first synthesis will not simply be reduced to a phase of the second; the second will provide a milieu in which the first continues to operate independently.

Deleuze articulates two questions unanswerable from the standpoint of the present (108). The first is "*why* the present passes". The second is "what prevents the present from being co-extensive with time". The second is not obvious. Is Deleuze asking whether some lacuna within the extended present prevents it from filling the scope of time from end to end? Is he asking why eternity does not consist of a single present instant? Or is he just asking why we need to posit anything other than a series of presents? The first two seem like straw men. For that matter, why should time have "co-extensivity" as a property in the first place? Even if the present should turn out to be fragmentary (in fact, contraction is the contrary of fragmentation), why is that a problem? The idea that another kind of time has to be posited in order to fill up the time-scope, suggests that time *should* be a filled continuity, co-extensive with itself. But why should it?

Further, the first question, namely *why* the present passes, is not obvious either. Obviously, Deleuze is not looking for a final cause, but what sort of first or proximate cause, explanation, origin, transcendental and/or material condition, or energy source are we looking for? Are we being told now that contraction does not even explain why two times subsist in one present, even though that was demonstrated in the preceding pages of text? The text here is written (like Hegel's) as though we need to hear from Time itself that contraction is necessary, and not just from the subjective standpoint of the perceiver. But this is not a proof. The passage referring to the past as a container of the present is suggestive, but the metaphor of containment is not entirely helpful, and the arguments remain to be given.

ARGUMENT 2: THE ARGUMENT FROM THE PARADOX OF THE PRESENT: THE PARADOX OF TIME PASSAGE

The paradox of the present is the premise from which the existence of an independent synthesis of the past is said to follow necessarily: a "pure past" distinct from the present's version of the past. The core of the paradox is that the synthesis of the present, in order to be originary, must already be intratemporal; in order for the present to ground past and future, it must already have contracted past and future. It is the paradox of the "present that passes" (108).

There are many variants. The present "constitutes" time, yet it passes in the time "constituted". It is simple yet plural, the whole yet the parts, infinitely determinable yet finitely determined. It is the abstract, changeless form of passing, yet also the concrete, changing instants that pass. The present passes away, yet "never leaves the present". It is the only kind of time there is, but it incorporates kinds of time other than itself. We might have said that this is the paradox of time as such, not just of present time. We will see, though, that these paradoxes only hold for present time, time that passes; past time, time that is not passing, has its own paradoxes.

The essence of Deleuze's arguments for a pure past is that nothing about the present explains how it "passes". The commonsense view is that a present moment is all there is at that moment, and that time passes when a second moment comes along and takes its place, causing it to move into the past. But if the present is all there is in the present, how could the second moment enter (as if from somewhere else) into the present, in order to displace it? If we assume that time does pass, and that it passes in the present, it follows that some structure of time other than the present must explain that passing. Something must explain how a moment of time can ever be a past moment. Deleuze calls this the pure past. His theory, to lay it out in advance of proving it, is that a temporal moment does exist in the present, and that that moment is, at a certain point, past, but that it is not the fact that it was once present that explains how it becomes past. A given temporal moment is a present, and that same moment is also a past. Its presentness and its pastness are equally essential to it, exhibiting two distinct features of time. To put it simply, an event's presentness consists in the way it comes into presence bit by bit, expanding and contracting; the same event's pastness consists in the way it persists as a whole in a kind of storehouse of memory and potential reactivation. One and the same event, while it happens, is a passing succession, and at the very same time, but in a different temporal sense, it is a retrievable unit that will be available at, and in that sense contemporaneous with, i.e. the past for, any and all later times. The presentness and the pastness of the event co-exist as two distinct structures of the event while it happens, at exactly the same time.

Not all of this follows from the fact that the present contains a paradox, but what does follow is that something other than the present has to be introduced in order to explain how the present works.

What is at stake is what it means for time to "pass".[1] At least since McTaggart's *The Nature of Existence* (1927),[2] many philosophers have denied that time "passes". Often, those who deny time passage appeal to post-Einsteinian space-time; they reject the observer-independence of the present, and plot temporal differences on Minkowski diagrams in order to show how before–after sequences (as seen from different points of reference) can be calculated together. Usually, they take their main opponent to be Bergsonian lived duration. Deleuze allows that time does pass according to the standpoint of the present; but he argues that in the past, which alone explains the present, time does not pass. Deleuze takes this compromise denial of the ultimacy of time passage to be Bergsonian.

Deleuze's appeal to the paradox of time in order to sidestep time passage works like this. The synthetic present does not strictly speaking pass; it expands (and contracts) outwards from one moment towards a temporal periphery. Since the present contains its own expansion, other moments within that expanse successively present themselves as the central Now-points. Because of the expanse, time seems to pass. The present never leaves the present, but is already elsewhere, indeed everywhere in time, constituting all of time. Distinct times in succession are produced consequent to the undivided temporal totality where all the instants co-exist. Succession presupposes co-existence.

This exposition of the present expanse sounds like it already explains the passage of time. But Deleuze construes the paradox as an argument that time passage requires a different structure of time altogether. Expansion shows the "effect" of the passing present, i.e. it describes the apparent passing of time, but it does not explain "why" time passes. This is a puzzling moment in the text. Why do present expansions not fully explain how time just is the passage from one Now to the next? For that matter, why should Deleuze not come right out and conclude that the present does not actually pass when it expands, thus obviating the need for a second synthesis?

Indeed, many philosophers since the nineteenth century replace substances and forms with processes. Hegel and others propose that things are the processes themselves; that when the force runs out of the process, the thing is gone. Why should time not be thus exhausted by contractions and expansions; why should it require some other temporal substance to hold it together, some container or medium? If time is exhausted by contractions, then, for example, once a memory is too distant to be contracted into the present, it disappears, since no container holds it; why is that consequence incorrect?

But perhaps the claim that time passage takes place *in* time does not really entail a container, but only means that times pass in relation to the *whole* of time.

ARGUMENT 3: TWO ARGUMENTS FROM THE WHOLE (*C1* AND *C2*)

The argument from qualitative change in the whole (*C1* 18–22): (In all the arguments for the pure past in the *Cinéma* volumes, Deleuze cites Bergson). Moving in space from A to B requires succession, but "when I have reached B and have had something to eat, what has changed is not only my state, but the state of the whole which encompassed B, A, and all that was between them" (*C1* 18). The change of the whole is qualitative, and so at the end, the whole, and not any present moment, gives meaning to the passage from beginning to end. Qualitative change makes the process "open" (20), since it means the thing can become something new. Time, when seen as a whole, is not just the succession of movements, but an indivisible duration that takes all the past and the present as a unit. Deleuze does not always valorize wholes, but here he does, to the extent that a qualitative change occurs over a bloc of time (also *C2* 108).

The argument from acentricity (*C1* 85–91): from a perceiver's perspective, objects appear successively in the flowing present. But Bergson's theory of perception says that images are created in, and exist in, the objects perceived. An object vibrates and sends sound waves into the air, which eventually enter an ear. Once an image is captured by a perceiver, it exists in a subjective perspective. But images themselves exist all around us at once. And because images themselves are not centred in a subject, but are rather "acentred", they do not exist in any particular succession. They co-exist at various stages of transmission through the media of light and air. In this "acentred universe where everything reacts on everything else" (*C1* 90), events from various moments of time co-exist on a temporal plane. Deleuze's arguments in the *C* volumes naturally depend on examples from particular films, so we need a more direct demonstration of the pure past from Bergsonian premises.

ARGUMENT 4: THE ARGUMENT FROM TWO TYPES OF MEMORY (*B*)

Deleuze frequently articulates his theory of the "pure past" with reference to Bergson's theory of "pure memory" in *Matière et mémoire*.

Bergson's premise distinguishes (a) the kind of memory in which one looks back to the past by retracing one by one the steps that led up to the present, remembering experiences in reverse successive order, from (b) the "pure" memory in which an experience from any point in the past can pop up into present experience. Both types of memory clearly exist. Deleuze draws three consequences of the second to infer the pure past (*B* 48–53). The first consequence is that the memory of any point whatever is unconcerned with how distant the memory is from the present. Therefore, it belongs more to the past than to the present. The second consequence is one of Bergson's main theses in *Matière et mémoire*. The first kind of memory image is an extension from the present, expressed in the present; it exists in the mind and body of the rememberer. But given that the second kind of memory image is not tied to the present, and is not at the present moment experienced, what is its ontological status? Bergson says the past memory does not exist anywhere in the present, not even in the brain, since the brain exists in the present. Once it gets retrieved in the present, it is no longer strictly speaking a "pure memory", but a present experience image that refers to a past event. Bergson concludes that pure memories exist virtually, but not actually. The status of a memory is that *if* it should get expressed in a present, then it will reveal the past, but until it does, it exists in a virtual status of its own.

The third consequence is that moving from a present to a past image requires a "leap" (*B* 51–5). Once we leap into the past, we enter a zone where the whole past is equally available: the "past in general". We do not bring images of the past into the present, but relocate our minds in the past, where the virtual images are.

In short, the past is detached from the present, its reality is virtual, and the whole past co-exists as a totality. These theses coincide largely with the four Bergsonian paradoxes of time that Deleuze lays out in *DR*. But there are difficulties in translating the arguments based on "pure *memory*" in *B* with those aiming at the "pure *past*" in *DR*. For this reason, I am not going to work out the details of the comparison here.[3]

ARGUMENT 5: THE ARGUMENT FROM FUNDAMENT

DR 109 constructs a not entirely helpful metaphor. The synthesis of the present, or Habit, Deleuze says, is the "foundation" (*fondation*) of time; the synthesis of the past, or Memory, is the "fundament" (*fondement*) of time. The present is the "ground" of time and the past is its "sky". More helpful is the idea that the present "occupies" or "possesses" time, whereas the past "appropriates" time. The present orders successive occurrences each in their place; the present is territory on the map of time. In contrast, we might say that the one who draws the map of time has a distant perspective, surveying commensurable events from a wider perspective, placing them on, and appropriating them for, a common time-line.

In this picture, it is the second-order, or reflective, determinability of events in time that "*makes* the present pass". The mapping of events as an array of pasts transforms the present immediacy of lived time. Deleuze calls the reflective synthesis of time "Memory", in contrast to the Habit of taking each event as it comes. The appeal is not really to a sky-level overview, but to the "alliance" of two co-existing temporalities (109): time qua measure and time qua measured. This is not an argument, but it previews the important idea that the map of time does not pass through time.

ARGUMENT 6: THE ARGUMENT FROM THE SURFACE AND DEPTH OF BODIES (*LS* SERIES 23, "OF THE AION")

This argument has three stages.

(a) The argument from the measureless (depth)

In *LS*, Chronos and Aion more or less play the roles of the syntheses of present and past in *DR*. Chronos is the regulated, "immanent measure" for the changing states of bodies over time. Deleuze asks, "Is there not a fundamental disturbance of the present, that is, a ground which overthrows and subverts all measure, a becoming-mad of the depths that slips away from the present?" (*LS* 193). Deleuze calls this the "measureless", the "bad Chronos", which "has already given way to another reading of time". It is not entirely clear what Deleuze is appealing to in saying that the orderly movements of bodies have something measureless in their depths that undermines succession. It seems the idea is something like the following. Temporal succession depends on the way that bodies are always in the process of being blended. But if bodies are in flux, no body can explain the successive states of it or any other body. Succession yields an infinite regress of appeals to objects, a system of causes that cannot form a unity. Orderly succession ultimately lies in disorder.

Deleuze calls this a "shift of orientation" away from succession. The shift takes place at the level of succession, but grounds an independent logic of Aion, namely that set out below in the second stage of the argument.

(b) The argument from the incorporeal ground of language (surface)

Changes can be expressed according to types, independent of whether a body changes in one direction or another. At any instant at which a body could get bigger, it could also get smaller. Deleuze calls these types, which exist as possibilities and are expressed in language, but which never occur in any present, "incorporeal or surface effects" (194). The reason the present is a field of confusion is that there is a temporal "instant" just before possibilities diverge. "[The instant] is the pure moment of abstraction whose role is, primarily, to divide and subdivide every present in both directions at once, into past-future, upon the line of the Aion" (195). This is not an instant that extends into past and future by causal modification, but is an instant of sense ("sense is the same thing as event" (195)) that contains whole sets of alternatives. Part of an event consists of possibilities that exist in a past that never became present.

(c) The argument from the actualization and counter-actualization of the whole in the part (to prevent confusion of depth and surface)

> How could there be a measurable actualization, unless a third present prevented it at every instant from falling into subversion and being confused with it? ... What is excessive in the event must be accomplished, even though it may not be realized or actualized without ruin. Between the two presents of Chronos – that of the subversion due to the bottom and that of the actualization in forms – there is a third, there must be a third, pertaining to the Aion. In fact, the instant as the paradoxical element or the quasi-cause that runs through the entire straight line must itself be represented. (196)

It is not enough for Aion to be a separate species of time; Aion must explain how events can become actual in spite of virtually containing counterfactuals, and how events can remain in flux in spite of becoming actual. While *LS* refers to Aion as "*the pure empty form of time*" (165) just as *DR* does, *LS* builds the pure past into the *confusion* in the way the present passes, not just into the mere fact that the present passes. *LS* thus requires a stronger premise concerning the present than *DR* does. But if the premise in the argument in *LS* is true, it promises to provide a stronger explanation of how the past becomes concrete. The past will not remain a merely formal map of memory, but a force field of quasi-causes. This may explain why *DR* has to introduce a third kind of time (the future) in addition to present and past, while *LS* builds the third (as quasi-cause) into the second (the past). We will consider time as cause in chapter 6. For now, the point is that the non-actualized past must somehow be represented in the event without being present.

ARGUMENT 7: THE ARGUMENT FROM REPRESENTABILITY

This argument of *DR* is that a given moment can be a present only if it is contained in a temporal flow, i.e. only if it is representative of, situated in, and a generalization of, a temporal whole. The argument from representability contains an embedded argument from generalizability.

The presumption that a present moment presupposes another present implies that some mode of time is already past. On the surface, it would seem that relative to the present moment, it is the other present that is the past. But the heart of Deleuze's thesis is that the present that has been, the "former present", is not the primary sense of the past. The former present is a present, which the past is presently the past *of.* A child is born in the present, for example, and later, when an adult, she will speak of her birth, a former present, in past tense. But Deleuze's point is that it is not qua former *present* that the moment is past. The past grounds the very possibility that something could become former. The past is not any present moment – not even a former present – rather, as Deleuze likes to say, the past exists "between" two presents.

The past is "the element in which we aim at (*vise,* glimpse) the former present" (109). This is an epistemological thesis about cognizing the past qua past: the past is the *form* by which a former present remains visible. If a present were simply present, then once it ceased being present, it would not be cognizable at all. For a present content to be retained, it must be retained not as former present but as simply former. That is, a present cannot be retained at a later present simply as a former present, since a present cannot contain anything that is not presently present; therefore, if there is such a thing as a former present (and surely there is), it must not be part of the present, but must co-exist along with the present in a different temporal form, i.e. in the past.

But now, how do we reconcile this argument with the central feature of the synthesis of the present? There, we showed that the contracted past *is* contained *within* the extended present. One way to take the text would be to read it as an Antinomy, as if the left column were a reductio argument proving that unless the past is contained in the present then there is no past, and the right column a reductio proving that unless the past is distanced from the present then there is no past. Yet Deleuze seems not to reject both, as antinomies deserve to be, but to affirm both. Another reading would be to distinguish two phenomena of pastness: there *is* one kind of past that simply is retained as the former part *of* the present, and another kind that is *between* two presents, mediating the former present so that it appears *as* an independent past. The second kind of past would be found in the representation of an event that is no longer ongoing. But does this prove that the past is not contained in the present? If the argument were that there can be *no* past within the present, it would be plausible to posit the independence of the past. But since one kind of past does exist within the present, why can the other kind of past not exist within the present as well? Even if the past must be represented, why can the present not represent it in its cognitive content?

For that matter, why is there no past unless it is represented? Deleuze in other texts opposes representationalism, but here the text insists:

> The former present is to be found "represented" in the current one . . . But now, the former present is not represented in the current one without the current one being itself represented in this representation. It belongs essentially to representation to represent not only some thing, but also its

own representivity. The former and the current presents are thus not like two successive instants on the time-line, but the current one necessarily entails (*comporte*) an additional dimension by which it re-presents the former one and in which it is also represented. (109)

The obvious reason that not all former presents can be dragged along as the tail of the current present is that some former presents are so distant, in quantity and quality, that they cannot be retained merely as faded presence. Some presents no doubt have what I will call soft representational status, remaining in the temporal field of vision, as when an image of a moving train lingers in the blur of shifting perspectives. But the fact that one present has a successor would not guarantee the continuity of time, unless *every* present were retained in the successor. That requires that memory retain more than either perception or habit can.

The past makes events representable qua events, by extracting them from their particular present contexts. Yet the past is not representable in itself, since the past is never what is presented in the present. The key is what the past accomplishes while we live in the present. While living in the present, if we see what is happening *as* a flow, we are seeing it *as* the present; if we pick out and represent an event-content in such a way that it becomes a topos of thought, then it has the same status as an event in the distant past. The event has become a free-standing occurrence rather than part of a flow. The past occurs whenever something is in this way extracted from the flow and highlighted. An event is past as soon as it can be an item on a list, and this guarantees that every event, not just some, gets retained.

From the standpoint of the past, the present is simply the most recent representable, thus past, event. In fact, we often experience the present as if it were already past, already a topic to contemplate rather than a process to wait out. The presentness of the event is its causality in relation to its environment; its pastness is its thinkability, its sense. Presents too distant to be felt can only be retained by hard representations, i.e. when they are represented in present thought as alternate possible worlds in time.

The argument for the existence of a past independent of the present hangs on the three representations mentioned in the passage quoted above: the past is represented in the present; therefore the present is represented in the present; therefore there is a generalized medium of representation over and above the passing present. It is difficult to see why the second and third follow, until we analyse generalization.

ARGUMENT 8: THE ARGUMENT FROM GENERALIZABILITY

When we think of the past as retained in the present (within the synthesis of the present), past moments are particulars and the present is the generalization that contains them; in contrast, when we think of the present as the most recent edge of time (within the synthesis of the past), most of which has become past, then each present, including the now, is a particular, and the past is the general term covering all the presents. This difference in what counts as general by itself is enough to prove that present and past embody independent logical structures. We call "habit" the retention of a succession of particular pasts in the form of the present; we call "memory" the representational reproduction of a succession of particular former presents in the form of the past.

In *PS* (and *LS*), Deleuze associates the generalized past with incorporeality and eternity, since it expands beyond any set of empirically present particulars. This is the target of Badiou's (1997) claim that Deleuze is a philosopher of the atemporal.[4] But this is of course only one side of what Deleuze says. Deleuze does refer to the generality of time as the "extra-temporal", but he equally calls it, "time in a state of birth"; he calls it "eternity", but also says that it "envelops the multiple in the One and affirms the One in the multiple" (*PS* 57–60). For Deleuze, the past is atemporal only in the sense that it generalizes from, and thus "complicates", the present.

This strengthens the argument from representability. In the synthesis of the present, each past represents the form of the present, and the form of the present is general. So each present not only presents its own content, it also presents a generality; therefore it contains a multiplicity of re-presentations. From this it follows that the present presents what is not present, i.e. the generality of the past, the "additional dimension" within which all the past moments are represented. The very generality of the present, which holds together past particulars, demonstrates that each present is a particular held together by the generality of the past. We can now reconsider representability.

ARGUMENT 7 (REPRISE)

Insofar as the past's generality subsumes all moments including the present, it conserves present moments as former presents. This does not prove that every moment must include a representation of another, and so does not prove that there must be anything general about time. But *if* there is a general time into which the present fits (a premise that is plausible even though not yet proved), then the past is a kind of storehouse that includes all times.

This is a good moment to comment on the metaphor of the past as a "storehouse" of temporal moments. The flaw in the metaphor is that it suggests inert memory packages, whereas we know both from Bergson and from neuropsychology that memories persist interactively, circulating in and through each other while we are not thinking of them. Memories are not just retrieved but reactivated and folded into new variations. Nevertheless, the storage metaphor is not all bad. Just as social temporality is radicalized when the state puts commodities into a central storehouse (see chapter 9), so also, time-consciousness is transformed when memory stockpiles events.

In *C2* (62–73), a similar argument, based on the nature of description, suggests that the past represents time as a whole. One can respond to an event by habit, following it up the same way each time it occurs; alternatively, one can respond to an event by describing it over and over, choosing new elements in the event to attend to. To describe an event is to go *back* to it, to disengage its drive in the present towards a future. Deleuze cites the flashback form of cinematography. Describing events over and over shows that events undergo forking paths. In contrast to habit, description highlights the virtual in the event, and makes as much use of false as of correct memory. It is thus "pure memory" (*C2* 77), implicating the whole series of actual and possible events.

Generality, representability, describability, listability, and storability are not just sundry characteristics of the past. An event is past precisely because it is repeatable in these ways. The present qua present vanishes; but the present is re-presentable, hence it already obeys the rule of the past. It is not just that memories are lost if they are not stored; it is that the reproduceability of an event is something other than its duration, and the name for reproduceability is "the past". It would be going too far to say that present duration is not part of time, but in a sense, time is conserved not by duration but by re-presentation.

Deleuze suggests that the mechanisms whereby a former present is represented in a current present are the Humean categories of association, contiguity, and resemblance. This is odd. In Hume, association is a rule of habit; but Deleuze equated habit with the first synthesis of time, not the second. Later in the chapter, Deleuze switches to different categories of the past, namely desire-assemblages. But the fact that he describes the second synthesis by re-using categories borrowed from the first is important for what I call Deleuze's multiple-level theory of time. This is what makes reading the text so complicated: basic structures are re-used at a secondary level even when they are not the grounding structures at that level. Even in passages where Deleuze writes of the second synthesis without reference to the first (or in other contexts when he discusses events that overtake states of affairs, or abstract machines that overtake strata, or revolutionaries who overtake figures of state), those slow-moving anachronisms remain part of the picture. For it is not that the quasi-simultaneous past dissolves present endurance into nothing; it re-configures, as it re-uses, those mechanisms of ordered retention that contract the present into short durations. The nature of time is that a plurality of temporal structures co-exist.

ARGUMENT 9: THE ARGUMENT FROM PROLIFERATING DIMENSIONS

The former and current present are "not like two successive instants" (*DR* 109). For as we have seen, (a) the contiguity of two successive moments is not sufficient to ensure that the first will be recollected in the second; and (b) representation, which adds another dimension to mere contiguity, is necessary for recollection. The current present, in other words, "carries along necessarily an additional dimension" (109). The temporal meta-level (namely, reflection) required to account for time passage makes time an assemblage of former and current sense rather than primary retention. Time thus has more to do with the necessity that a secondary meaning be represented in every present than with the contingency that a given present has a successor. A current present relates to another present externally, whereas the past is internally present in the present. Paradoxically, it is the past, and not the present, that expresses presence in the present.

Similarly, the future, qua represented in the present, has the same logical character as the past: "the current present is not treated like the future object of a memory but like that which is reflected at the same time that it forms the memory of the former present" (109–10). What gives the present a future is not that some subsequent present might come along, but that the present is already representable in all future moments, beginning with its own.

This is a typical Deleuzian point. It is not that I first experience what is happening and then either anticipate what will happen next or retrieve what happened earlier. Rather, I first experience this moment as a memory, as a content in my repertoire, and then I observe it vanishing. I experience it first as past and subsequently as present. When I say, for instance, "Look, I'm dancing", or "That man is stealing a wallet", the expressions appear in present tense, but the experiences respectively designate a repertoire, and witness to what just happened, before I wonder what is coming next or what has led up to it. The past is the immediate presence of the experience and the present occurs as an afterthought when the experience is just about to become former. The synthesis of the past has two aspects (110): on the one hand, reproduction, recall, and memory, and on the other hand reflection, recognition, and understanding; the first establishes the experience qua past and the second then represents it in the present.

Argument 9 makes use of this observation to demonstrate that the past exhibits a "constant augmentation in dimensions, in their infinite proliferation" (110). Whereas "the passive synthesis of habit constituted time as the *contraction* of instants under the condition of the present, the active synthesis of memory constitutes it as the *interlocking* (*emboîtement*) of the presents themselves" (110). Presumably, this means that each present moment reproduces all others. The reason this differs from contraction in the living present lies with the infinite proliferation of dimensions, an infinity that is not containable in the present no matter how great the present's capacity to contract other moments. The present can contain one additional dimension (namely the chain of actual remembrances), but only pastness can contain an infinite number of dimensions. When Deleuze says there are three syntheses of time (present, past, and future), this is misleading, since the second contains an infinite number of temporal structures. But how is proliferation generated, and what "dimensions" is Deleuze referring to?

Since Deleuze gives no explanation of this apparently crucial point, I will speculate. Each present synthesis contracts all of time according to the way it is retained in the present experience. The present moment is its element, and the totality of retained time is its added-on dimension. The present does have rhythms of memory-retention, but the time-line that culminates in the present passes through each former present just once. In contrast, each past superimposes its memory sequence on to other pasts, all of which are simultaneously represented in a present. Past and present syntheses both constitute totalities of experience, but when we attend to the past qua past, we recognize that other totalizations of the same experiences are possible at the same time. To use a vaguely Proustian example, when we experience the past in a piece of food, we experience simultaneously a personal history of family life, a bodily history of taste, a contested history of culinary politics, and so on. When we experience something as belonging to the past, we experience it as part of a set of *histories of past elements*: histories of clinics, of revolutions, of cinema, and so on. The past emerges not as one dimension; it is precisely as many dimensions that it counts as the past.[5]

In short, we experience a scene not as the present, but as an element in a scheme that has already been structuring the past, and that thereby structures the scene as past. It is because the present is given sense by layers of structuring that the past is not made up of former presents but is a "pure past" made up of patterns that existed in their own right before a present is synthesized into them. This is transcendental synthesis "proper to memory itself" (110).

ARGUMENT 10: THE ARGUMENT AGAINST DISPLACEMENT – THE FIRST PARADOX OF THE PAST

The long paragraph at 110–12 lays out Deleuze's famous "four paradoxes" of the past. The short argument he gives for the first is also a general argument for the synthesis of the past. This is perhaps the most appealing of all his arguments:

> It is hopeless to attempt to reconstitute the past on the basis of one of the presents that wedge it in, either the present that it was, or the one in relation to which it is now passed. In effect, we cannot believe either that

The Second Synthesis of Time 45

the past is constituted after having been present, or because a new present appears. *If the past had to wait for a new present in order to be constituted as past, the former present would never pass, and the new one would never arrive.* (110–11, my italics)

The argument proposes a thought-experiment. Imagine a present content. There it is, the full and exclusive content of what is there in the present. The present is nothing but present, and nothing else is present except what is present. Now, the reader is asked: why would what is present ever pass? (a) Take the hypothesis that the present would somehow exhaust itself and just depart on its own. But why would it? If something is present, *why* does it stop being present? *Why* does time pass? As Parmenides says, if something is, it should remain what is. Since what is is, nothing in it makes it pass out of being. Only something other than the present can do that. (b) Now take the hypothesis that the present is forced to pass when another present comes along and takes its place. *How* is another present supposed to come along? If the original does not pass on first, where will the new present arrive? Is the new present supposed to push the old one out of the way? Why does a new present not add on to what is present without displacing the old? And where does the new present come from: is there a store of new presents arranged serially that click into the present position one after another, dislodging their predecessors? Neither hypothesis is plausible. A present is not going to get out of the way, and if it does not, the next will not arrive.[6]

Of course, other theories of change might avoid the absurdities of a temporal instant that refuses to get out of the way. Nature is not going to stop dead. But the point is that we cannot start a theory of time with the present and expect to explain the past. Pastness must be a temporal property of the event that does not result after something has happened to the present (just as the future cannot just be presents that have not happened yet). Its pastness must be as much a part of the actual event as its presentness is. The event must have its character of being past independently of, at the same time as, its character of being present. This is what Deleuze calls the first paradox of time.

Deleuze gives a good variant in *C2*:

What is actual is always a present. But then, precisely, the present changes or passes. We can always say that it becomes past when it no longer is, when a new present replaces it. But this is meaningless. It is clearly necessary for it to pass for the new present to arrive, and *it is clearly necessary for it to pass at the same time as it is present*, at the moment that it is the present. (105–6, my italics)

The only time when a present can become past is while it exists. It cannot become past after it no longer exists; for when something does not exist, it obviously cannot do anything. It must become past at the very same time that it exists, while it is still present. To be sure, an event can *be* in the past when it is not present, but it cannot *become* past, it cannot *be passing* into the past, except while it exists.[7]

In sum, the argument for the first paradox of the past begins by demonstrating that the present cannot pass into the past on its own steam, and then demonstrates that becoming-past must be part of an event independent of its being-present. The conclusion is that the present and past of an event co-exist at the same time:

> This is the first paradox: that of the contemporaneity of the past with the present that it *has been*. It gives us the reason for the passing of the present. It is because the past is contemporaneous with itself as present, that every present passes, and passes in favour of a new present. (111)

Now, it is not clear why the contemporaneity of past and present gives the *reason* why the present passes. The theory that an event is past at the same time as it is present seems rather to dissolve the problem of why an event in the present passes into the past. The present does not pass into the past, says the theory – it is already past while it is present. We know what it *means* for the present to co-exist with the past, namely that an event simultaneously has the properties of present temporality (it ticks on by, it calls upon sensory-motor syntheses, it interests and fatigues, and so on) as well as the properties of past temporality (it is re-presentable and re-usable, graspable as a whole, and so on). It is clear why from the perspective of the present, the event passes, and why from the perspective of the past, it is already there. But how does the past's perspective *explain* how, or indeed even concede that, the present passes? Perhaps the intent of Deleuze's argument is precisely to cure the reader of the temptation to think of the present passing. But that is not the way the text is written.

For my part, I would like to see a direct argument that the contemporaneity of past and present explains why the present passes. Perhaps the fact that events have a temporality of the past, laid out so as to be seen as a whole, entails that the present must pass through all of an event's phases successively without stopping. Perhaps the fact that events are meaningful as whole repertoires entails that agents have a temporal momentum that keeps them passing in a sensory-motor way through their present surroundings. Along these lines, a few sentences into the second paradox, Deleuze says, "the past does not make one of the presents pass without making another one come to pass (*advenir*) . . ." (111). The fact that events *qua* past make sense as whole histories entails that the present must continuously replace what it is attending to with its meaning-conferring successor. These sorts of arguments seem persuasive to me, but Deleuze's text does not pursue them.

ARGUMENT 11: THE ARGUMENT FOR TOTAL CO-EXISTENCE – THE SECOND PARADOX OF THE PAST

The second paradox of time seems to follow directly from the first, but there is a difficulty in articulating the exact nature of Deleuze's argument: "A second paradox follows (*en sort*): the paradox of co-existence. If each past is contemporaneous with the past that it has been, the *whole* past is contemporaneous with the new present in relation to which it is now past" (111). The claim is that if Past A is contemporaneous with Present A, and Past B is contemporaneous with Present B, then Past A will be contemporaneous with Present B, and Past A will be contemporaneous with Past B. The two antecedents express the first paradox of the past; the two consequents express the second. But why do these consequents follow? Why can each present not have precisely one past that is contemporaneous with it (the first paradox), without Past A being contemporaneous with Present B (the first consequent in the second paradox)? Even given that the past is an independent time-scheme, can it not consist of a series of moments that are not all contemporaneous (the second consequent)? The idea behind the second paradox is that if one past is contemporaneous with one present, then that past will be contemporaneous with everything past and present. Why?

I construe the first consequent, that all pasts are contemporaneous with each present, in the following way. The premise that the past of an event does not follow in sequence from its present (since it is contemporaneous with it) means that no past follows in sequence from any present. The order of sequential succession is not relevant to whether two events should be interpreted in relation to one another. Any event can count as a recurrence of, a representation of, or a memory of,[8] any past theme or event. All pasts therefore co-exist with any present.

But now, even if we accept the first consequent, does it follow that all past moments are contemporaneous with each other? Why is the thesis that every moment in the past is invoked by every present incompatible with the past having a serial structure? I construe Deleuze's argument on the basis of his remark that while the past makes the present pass, the past "does not itself pass" (111). If the past is the "pure form of time", a temporal map unaffected by movement, then both of the consequents above will follow. All pasts on the map will co-exist without temporal difference, no matter what temporal differences there are across coordinates of the present. But if that is the argument, then Deleuze's notion of the pure past seems closer to eternal form than to multi-contemporaneity. Certainly, there is a temptation to see Platonism when Deleuze says in this passage that the pure past is like an *a priori* form underlying temporal change, and that "we necessarily speak of a past which never *was* present" (111). But clearly Deleuze categorizes the past as a type of time; it cannot merely bypass movement, it must *endure* as a whole alongside the passing present.

This is in evidence when Deleuze says of the past that "its manner of being contemporaneous with itself as present is to posit itself already-there (*se poser déjà-là*)" (111). Obviously, Deleuze does not mean that the past is in the present déjà vu, or that it makes the present feel preordained. It is more that the event, in the mode of the pure past, makes one think, "Now this is really something", or, "There's a story in this", or, "Where have you been all my life?" The idea that each Now is a keeper also explains how the Past A that is contemporaneous with Present A remains contemporaneous when Present B arrives. Even in common sense, when someone does something – reads a book or snubs a friend – and is definable without delay as the one who has learned something or the one who has lost someone, the pasts that arise with the present remain permanently part of the same life (smart and alone). But common sense is difficult to demonstrate ontologically.

ARGUMENT 12: THE ARGUMENT FOR PRE-EXISTENCE – THE THIRD PARADOX OF TIME

Deleuze introduces the third paradox again as a deduction: "the paradox of pre-existence thus completes (*complète donc*) the two others" (111). Its claim is that "the pure element of the past in general pre-exists the present that passes" (111). Deleuze's terminology sounds like pre-determination, but of course, he does not mean that the Ideal event pre-exists its actualization, and he does not literally mean that events chronologically *have* taken place before they *do* taken place. He emphasizes two things about the past:

(a) The past "is not itself represented" (112). That the past pre-exists the present means that the pastness of an event is given not as a second presence, but alongside presence. Pastness is not visible the way the presentness of the event is. Pastness is the logical capacity of the event to undergo inexhaustible transformations; it is the virtuality of the event.
(b) "The present designates the most contracted degree of an entire past" (112). That the past pre-exists the present means that the present can be "seen as a particular" (112) only when it is recognized to be the culmination of the whole past up until now. The present becomes present only once it is experienced as the particular moment that sums up, in a contracted way, the entire past at once. An event only enters the present scene as a result of the whole past, up to and including that event itself, ending up, finally, having already come to that point, emerging into actuality.

Do these two claims of the third paradox follow from the second paradox?

Does the premise that the whole past is contemporaneous entail that the past is silently contracting into the next present? Why should the past, all sitting there at once, contract at all? To see why, we have to remember that there are after all different presents, and it is these passing presents that have non-passing versions as their pasts. So even insofar as events, qua past, do not pass, they are still relatively distinct from one another. My breakfast is still different from my lunch, even if they are all in my stomach together now; my childhood is still different from my adolescence even if the latter has retroactively reinterpreted the former. I will deal with this problem in the next chapter, namely how events can be ordered once pure time renders them contemporaneous. My point here is that Deleuze's paradoxes of the past only follow if, when he says that all pasts are contemporaneous, he allows that events retain a differentiated status. This is certainly what Bergson has in mind when he describes the "cone" of memory, in which different eras of a person's past float about in virtual images, organizing themselves into new combinations. Bergson too, at the end of chapter 3 of *Matière et mémoire*, refers to the problem of "localization", of how to individuate contemporanized events, of explaining how and why they get intensified one after the other in memory. This problem leads to the fourth paradox.

ARGUMENT 13: THE ARGUMENT FOR LEVELS – THE FOURTH PARADOX OF TIME

Deleuze introduces the fourth paradox not as an inference, but as a property of the third paradox: "The present is the most contracted degree of the past that co-exists with it, only if the past first co-exists with itself in an infinity of diverse degrees of relaxation and contraction, in an infinity of levels" (112).

Deleuze offers various phenomena to make this plausible. One is drawn from ordinary experience: "We have the impression" that the different successive events in our lives "play out 'the same life' at different levels" (113). Another is drawn from the inevitability of constructing narratives: successive events play out "the same history" (*la même histoire*, the same story) (113). A third is not so much evidence as an appealing array of categories for describing contemporaneous events at different levels of the past: "non-localizable liaisons, actions at a distance, systems of replay, resonance and echoes, objective chances", and so on (113), which Deleuze collectively calls "destiny". Destiny does not mean one is unable to control one's life; it means there is a way of living that makes use of all of one's virtual possibilities. Deleuze suggests (without proof) the intriguing possibility that each person has the "freedom to choose the level" (113) of the past on which they will contract next. Finally, once all pasts are available in full at every present, it follows that each person can contract on (in later texts, "territorialize on") elements in the pasts of other people, and even on non-human lives.

Deleuze makes a similar point in $C2$:[9]

> From this point of view [of recollection], the present exists only as an infinitely contracted past which is constituted at the extreme point of the already-there. The present would not pass without this condition. The present would not pass if it were not the most contracted degree of the past. ($C2$ 130)

We know that the present contracts anticipations of past and future into the present. Here, it is the past that is said to contract. The past as a whole, all that has happened, becomes intense in the present moment. However the past comes together, that is what the present contains. One might say that time is defined as the increase of what has happened, so the present is the cutting edge of the past.[10] The present cannot pass until it is put into a sequence of events already there. If the present somehow passed but did not fit into the past that was already there, if it did not get released from its contracted state into a relaxed state of belonging with other possibilities, it would not make it into the past, but remain an anomaly of the present. In other words, the present can only pass if it passes *into* a series.

Now, everyone knows this idea of Deleuze that we live out the same life at different levels. Has this conclusion been demonstrated? The synthesis of the past began with an argument for the co-existence of a past status alongside the present status for the same events. Co-existence was then universalized for all pasts. The co-existent whole was then said to preserve "levels", which in turn contract into new presents. "Relations of succession and simultaneity" (113) characterize not just the past but relations between present and past. As we were promised, the past includes a dimension of the present, as each of the three syntheses of past, present, and future internally includes the others. But features of the present are now recast according to the logic of the past. The fact that contemporaneous events are interpreted on different levels constitutes the dimension of the present within the past. Similarly, the past's capacity to contract into something *next*, a capacity that may never be actualized, constitutes the future dimension within the past.

This emphasizes that events in the past have their own virtual movement, even if nothing is actually passing empirically. Like ideas that get worked out while we sleep, pasts undergo constant combination. All possible combinations are logically generated, and even if they all exist at the same time, each makes some other combination possible, hence "*the ever-increasing co-existence of levels of the past within passive synthesis*" (113). The metaphor of the past as a storehouse is no longer adequate (except for the tale of the department store whose mannequins come alive at night). Paradoxically, events in the present change, but do nothing but be themselves; events in the past do not change, but never stop producing.

TRANSITION TO THE THIRD SYNTHESIS

We have described how the past includes serial differences and combinatory processes, but the theory only works if we can explain *how* the past relaxes and contracts. Deleuze poses a version of this problem in the last paragraph on the synthesis of the past. It sounds more like a problem of application than ontology, but the challenge of application begins the argument for a third synthesis of time, the synthesis of the future. The synthesis of the future as a third independent structure of time, with past and present re-cast as its internal dimensions, is once again presented as a necessary inference from properties of the past. On my construal of Deleuze's argument, what the past requires is a search engine. The future will be defined in terms of the practices of navigating the co-existing levels of the past. If phenomenology is the science of the present, and ontology the science of the past, pragmatics will be the science of the future. The present is motor; the past is field; the future is drive.

Deleuze's last paragraph on the past says that "The question for us is to know whether we can penetrate the passive synthesis of memory. To live, in some way, the being in itself of the past . . . How to save it *for ourselves*" (114–15). Assuming that the pure past has now been proved, how do we live in the past? What makes one memory stand out rather than another, given that all memories are contemporaneous with all presents? What will we remember next? How is it even possible to remember one thing at a time? How do we penetrate the solid block of the past and manoeuvre through it? In habit, similar presents awaken similar pasts, but in memory, all pasts are interpenetrating, so something has to happen if the block is to be opened up. Something has to be forgotten. The "echo" between past (independent of the former present) and present (within which some past is chosen) is

> a persistent question, which is developed in representation like a problem field, with the rigorous imperative to search (*chercher*), to respond, to resolve. But the response always comes from elsewhere: all reminiscence is erotic, whether it concerns a city or a woman. It is always Eros, the noumenon, who makes us penetrate into this pure past in itself, into this virginal repetition, Mnemosyne. Where does it get this power, why is the exploration (*exploration*) of the pure past erotic? Why does Eros hold both the secret of questions and answers, and also the secret of something insistent throughout our whole existence? Unless we are not yet making use of the last word, and there is a third synthesis of time . . . (115)

The past, to be past, and not just a reified version of the present, must be searchable, explorable, problematizable, penetrable, and livable. I will emphasize the arguments from searchability and livability to demonstrate the existence of an independent synthesis of the future. In short, to be past, the past must have a future. To put it simply, what allows us to penetrate the past and choose one moment in it rather than another is not that one is objectively more salient; it is desire. Neither habits nor memories make a past come alive the way that the theatre of desire can. But why is desire the structure of future time, and not simply a preference held in the present concerning the future?

NOTES

1. *ES* 103–4 has an early version of the argument that for the present to pass, the past must "push" it.
2. McTaggart's (1927, chapter XXXIII) B-series (time defined as objective before-after, in contrast to the A-series (time defined as subjective past-present-future) has something in common with Deleuze's pure past. McTaggart's C-series (chapters XLV–L), which analytic philosophers neglect on account of its Hegelianism, describes a kind of time that is at once dynamic and static, and might be still more suitable for comparison with Deleuze.
3. The best exposition of Bergson's cone of memory that I know is that of Leonard Lawlor (2003, pp. 43–59).
4. As an interpretation of Deleuze's corpus, Badiou's 1997 work is one-sided, as most commentators say. But it should be remembered that it was published in the Hachette series "Coup double", whose authors are expected to exhibit their own original philosophies while commenting on some great philosopher.
5. In *PS*, the problem of the passing present is not how one instant has a successor, but how a whole line of experience slides into the background as another line within the present takes over. Deleuze's example is that since learning takes place on several lines at once, with progress in one implying relapse in others, there exist many dimensions of time (*PS*, 36). Zourabichvili largely draws from *PS* to interpret Deleuze's pure past. He makes the good point that before we can ask about the quantitative succession of presents, we have to ask about the "lateral" set of temporal "milieus" (1994, pp. 73–4). What the "passing" present passes across are the heterogeneous characteristics of an event. With this in mind, Zourabichvili says that for Deleuze, "time is the intensity of the body" (p. 80). This explains why a singular event is smeared over many moments, i.e. why its time-function may not be its time-location (pp. 117–18).
6. These puzzles, along with the four paradoxes, are rehearsed in *B* (53–7).
7. This assumes that becoming-past is a process. But given that the idea of time "passing" has been criticized, is the argument beside the point? It seems to me that even if we decide that time "passage" is a bad metaphor, and give a deflationary description of time in terms of markers on a time-line or tenses in sentences, Deleuze's argument for the contemporaneity of present and past works just as well. For example, tense qualifiers that distinguish between "A postman walks by" and "A postman walked by" become possible at the same time, qualifying the neutral content "a postman walking by". Or to use Deleuze's cinematic examples, a scene by itself does not express whether it is being played in the present or in a flashback; going strictly by content, we cannot tell the difference between past, present, and future (109).
8. Alain François (1998, p. 78) takes the argument for the co-existence of the whole past in each present to be based on the fact that every present experience includes memories of the whole past.
9. While Deleuze often uses the terms "co-existence" and "simultaneity" interchangeably, here he distinguishes them (*C2* 132–3). "Co-existence" refers to the way several pasts are

available at the same time (in memory); "simultaneity" refers to the way several present points coincide (in flashbacks). When a past splits off from the present, there is a "crystal" of time; when the past stretches out from the present in concentric circles, there are "sheets" of time; when several presents are simultaneous, these are "peaks" of the present (*C2* 130–3).

10 For an important version of this theory of time, see John Mbiti (1995).

4 Navigating the Dark Precursors of the Future – the Third Synthesis of Time

Deleuze's analysis of the synthesis of the future occupies over 50 pages of text (*DR* 115–68), far more than the other two syntheses together. There is a development in these pages, but not the same kind of tight step-by-step argument. These pages include lengthy excursions to other authors. They introduces many new ideas that are highly suggestive, and have become deservedly famous, but which are not exhaustively developed in the text. I will not attempt a close analysis of the entire third section of chapter 2 of *DR*. I will begin with the arguments for the third synthesis that appear early in the section. Then I will say how I read the general flow of the argument in this section. Then I will focus on Deleuze's four main comparisons of the three syntheses. To a large extent, these comparisons constitute his argument for the third synthesis. Finally, I will say a few words about how Deleuze's famous notions of the "dark precursor" and the "object = X" contribute to the theory of the future. In the final analysis, my view is that Deleuze's theory of the future in this chapter is correct in its approach, but that it does not adequately solve the problem it is introduced to solve. Showing how temporal co-existence can be penetrated requires more emphasis on actual historical events than *DR* calls into play.

Pure co-existence (the past) raised the problem of how series of events can be traced, how events can be remembered, how searches can be engineered, in short, how there can be moving historicality (the future) within temporal co-existence. In the last part of chapter 2 of *DR*, Eros makes time thinkable.

Deleuze's theory of desire as production rather than lack is important, but I am not going to analyse the theory as a whole. In this particular chapter of *DR*, desire is defined as the power to search through the store of events. "Desire . . . appears not as a power of negation or as the element of an opposition, but as a force of searching (*force de recherche*), questioning and problematizing" (140–1). Searching through the living past requires that one invent pathways that force different events to communicate (or that allow one to be forced to encounter them). Desire has to search through disguises and masks of all kinds (138–45); it has to see various experiences in terms of the same "problem", even if "displaced" (142). In the search for lost time

The Third Synthesis of Time

(Proustian time aims at the future rather than the past), the relevant past "is there where one finds it only on condition that it is searched for where it is not" (135). For the pasts that the future searches for are not former presents, which do exist where they are, but are no longer of use; the pasts are the virtual events that have insisted without necessarily having been represented in empirical fact, and that hence belong to innovation.

The issue of the future concerns how a general past can be re-instantiated in a new, singular present[1]. In *B* (60), Deleuze cites Bergson saying that it is one thing to "translate" our experience from a present orientation into the past, but another to "rotate" on to a useful angle on the past. All these variants concern how the event can be both distant from, and simultaneous with, itself.

The questions that define a concern for the future are thus: Why does this particular event resonate with that? What should I bring out of the past next? How can I divide the past into parts of unequal value? How can I serialize moments that exist simultaneously? How can I make only certain moments of the past return to the present when they all co-exist? What problem does my life so far pose? Where does the very question of what to do next come from? If the database of the past does not say what to think next, or what to remember in what order, then there has to be a third synthesis of time. The present's answer to these questions is that the most recent past is the most salient; the past's answer is that anything can come up; what is the future's answer?

The future makes objects determin*able*. In Deleuze's interpretation of Kant, this is what time in general contributes to events (the subject contributes determining structures and the object contributes the undetermined given (116–18)). This makes the third synthesis of time an "empty form" (119), removing any ground for putting events in one order rather than another. The rug is taken out from under the search procedure, but the whole system is thereby made searchable by any parameter one chooses.

In different terms, the future makes events adaptable. It puts events, which had become available yet abstract in the past, back into play precisely in time. In that sense, the synthesis of the future *is* time. Just as the present *is* all of time in the sense of events in passage, and the past *is* all of time in the sense of events on record, so the future *is* all of time in the sense of events in play.

We have thus already seen two preliminary arguments for the existence of a third synthesis of time equiprimordial with, and independent of, the first two. The first is that the second synthesis needs something for its own functioning that only the third synthesis can provide. The second is that the third synthesis can account for all of time on its own terms – futurity describes not just events that have not happened yet, but all events insofar as they are ordered by search, problematization, and choice. In addition, two explicit arguments appear early in the text.

ARGUMENT 1: FROM GROUNDLESSNESS TO ETERNAL RETURN

Deleuze (using Klossowski on Nietzsche) identifies the problematization of the past and the affirmation of the future with the "eternal return". Each return wills a different production of the same past. "In its esoteric truth, the eternal return concerns, and can only concern, the third time of the series. It is only there that it can be determined. This is why it is literally said to be a belief of the future, a belief in the future" (122). The whole temporal structure of the past is superseded by the new temporal structure of the future (it not just that old events are replaced by new events): "The ground has been superseded by a without-ground, a universal de-grounding that turns upon itself and makes it so that the only thing that comes back is the future to come (*ne fait revenir que l'à-venir*)" (123). To make the argument short: groundlessness constitutes the future. If it were not de-grounded, disentangled from its contexts, disinvested from the pleasures it provided, rendered free for new interpretations, the omni-contemporaneous past would be a frozen instant. Habit in the present at least projects like into like, but memory of the well-grounded past would forever repeat the same image in the same frame of mind. Fortunately, the very omni-contemporaneity that superimposes the past over the present loosens the bonds between any given past and its successive explications. Since the past contains the *totality* of possible events, there is no time beyond it to serve as the ground of events; by definition, totalities, and only totalities, are ungrounded. The past is a totality; totalities are ungrounded; ungrounded events exist *only* as future possibilities.

This argument for futuricity uses the negative character of ungroundedness. The other argument uses its positive indeterminacy.

ARGUMENT 2: FROM CIRCULATION TO ACTION AT A DISTANCE

Deleuze sets the third synthesis the task of explaining a common experience:

> If we consider the two presents, the two scenes or the two events (infantile and adult), in their reality separated in time, how can the former present act at a distance upon the current one, and be a model for it, when the former must receive all its effectiveness retrospectively from the latter? (138)

For example, childhood events normally do not operate on us continuously, but only once we are psychically ready, after an adult event triggers them, i.e. at a distance. If events were all contemporaneous *tout court*, then childhood events ought to operate on all presents; but they do not. Therefore, there must be a temporal synthesis that keeps events circulating in a neutral mode, so that they always can be, but need not be, activated. The future thus depends on something like chance. Further, events must be neutral so that they can take on the form that the future gives them. A temporal object, in Deleuze's adaptation of Kant, = X. Repetition is constituted

> between the two co-existing series formed by the presents, in function of the virtual object (object = X). It is because it constantly circulates, always displaced in relation to itself, that it determines transformations of terms and modifications of imaginary relations within the two real series in which it appears, thereby between the two presents. (138)

In other words, even if one moment in question is in the past, and the other is in the present, the relation between them is in the future, determined neither by one nor the other, but by the possible meanings and causes they create together. Each event makes the other = X; each neutralizes and then redefines the other, by putting it into a time-slip. Our childhood affects the present; the future explains how.

It is clear why the past, as universal contemporaneity, cannot explain action at a distance. But why can the present not interpret the past, without introducing a third logic of the future? Deleuze suggests that the present's way of actualizing the past tends to mythologize it, and the future is assigned the task of preventing that from happening (145). His demonstration of the synthesis of the future primarily consists of drawing subtle distinctions like these between the three syntheses.

Deleuze proposes four major schematizations, comparisons, and genealogies of the three syntheses (116–68).

(i) THE THREE SYNTHESES OF TIME AS THREE REPRODUCTIONS OF REPETITION (121–4)

Luther repeats Paul, the Revolution of 1789 repeats the Roman Republic, 1848 farcically repeats 1789, and so on. History does not consist in similarities between events, but in the actual reproduction of historical events in new forms. "Repetition is the historical condition under which something new is effectively produced" (121). The question is which ontological levels of the prior event are reproduced in the later event. The answer depends on which of the three syntheses of time is employed:

> It is in the first place for themselves that the [French] Revolutionaries are determined to lead their lives as "resuscitated Romans" . . . thus under the condition that they identify themselves necessarily with a figure of the historical past. *Repetition is a condition of action before being a concept of reflection.* We produce something new only on condition that we repeat

– once in the mode that constitutes the past, and once more in the present of metamorphosis. And what is produced, the absolutely new itself, is in turn nothing other than repetition, the third repetition, this time by excess, the repetition of the future as eternal return. (121–2)

To summarize: (a) in the mode of the present, Paul "metamorphoses" into Luther; (b) in the mode of the past, Paul is the "condition" for Luther; (c) in the mode of the future, the "excess" generated by repeating Paul spills over as Luther.

What is interesting and difficult is that all three forms of historical reproduction (present, past, and future forms) are in this description things we expect from the present, namely expansions of one event into another. The present is first expressed in a version proper to the present itself, then in versions appropriate for the syntheses of past and future. Yet because the versions culminate in the future, all three are recast into things that we expect from the future, namely self-exceeding affirmations of novelty. In short, Paul expands into Luther in the past, present, and future modes of Paul's present; and simultaneously, but following a different logic, Luther exceeds Paul in the past, present, and future modes of Luther's future.

Deleuze provides this futurist version of the same three reproductions two pages later, in relation to Nietzsche's book *Zarathustra*:

> The before occupies the largest part of [Nietzsche's] book, on the mode of the defect or of the past: this action is too big for me ... Then comes the moment of the caesura or of the metamorphosis, "The Sign", when Zarathustra becomes *capable*. The third moment is absent: that of the revelation and affirmation of the eternal return. (124)

If we line up past, present and future with before, caesura (an interesting way to refer to the specious present), and after, then we can say that (a) the past is distressingly too big to use; (b) the present is just our size (when we become capable of metamorphosing from past to present); and (c) the future is again too big, but affirmed as rightly so. In other words, the past does not determine how to relive it; the present is comfortable to remain basically the same, however much it changes; the future affirms the new world opened up by every new possibility that arises. Ultimately, *DR* gives no direct method for searching the past for the sake of the future – it only affirms that it is to be done. The future is not a direction for successfully continuing the past, but a range of successors affirmed no matter how the dice fall. For an event to exist in the future just means that it is affirmed. It is odd to use affirmation as the definition of a temporal category. But temporality does not refer to a moment when an event happens as much as it refers to levels on which an event co-exists.

The three modes above cast past, present, and future all into the future.

The past is only too big, and the present only the zone of capability, in relation to what is to be done: "We see that in this last synthesis of time, the present and past are in turn no more than dimensions of the future: the past as condition, and the present as agent" (125). The reference to agency introduces the second three-part schematic of the chapter.

(ii) THE THREE AGENCIES OF REPETITION (125–6)

"The present, past, and future are revealed as Repetition in all three syntheses, but in very different modes. The present is the repeater, the past is the repetition itself, but the future is that which is repeated" (125). The last clause makes the future sound a lot like the past, but the point is that the future is a difference extracted from repeating the past. The third synthesis "ensures that, for itself, repetition is difference in itself" (126).

What is new in this second schematization is the role of the (self-effacing) agent of repetition. (a) The present is the repeater: on the one hand, repetition in the present repeats habitually or passively; on the other hand, the repeater undergoes "a metamorphosis of the agent" with each repeated experience (126). (b) The past is repetition itself: events simply *are* their repetition-function. (c) The future is that which is repeated: "the work is independent in relation to its author or agent" (125). In relation to difference, (a) the present extracts differences, (b) the past includes differences, and (c) the future is "difference in itself" (125–6).

As always, what complicates this schematization are the twists of intradimensionality in the layering of the three syntheses. The first twist is that the issue of who is behind repetition is a question that one only asks in relation to the future. The present passes without thinking, the past is just there, but the future has to make a choice, and thus has to choose who is to choose. So it is the future that first attributes the present to an agent, but it is also the future that refutes that agency when it turns the future-qua-present into a future-qua-future. "In the future, the present is no longer anything but an actor, an author, an agent destined to be effaced" (125). The temporality of futurity, in short, both creates agency for the sake of choice, and annuls it so that what is authored can stand on its own.

This last point raises the second twist in the multi-layered intradimensionality of the three syntheses. As the schema says, an event qua past is an event qua repetition. So dividing the three syntheses of time in terms of three repetitions is something that the past would do; yet by dividing the three repetitions in terms of agency, the future is taking the past's category of repetition and dividing it up on its own terms. (In the first schematization of reproduction, the future divided on its own terms the present's category of expansion.) Deleuze says as much in the same paragraph: "The first synthesis concerns only the content and foundation of time; the second, its ground;

but beyond this, the third assures the order, the set, the series, and the final goal of time" (125). In other words, the future not only orders the uses of the past, it also converts past and present *into* usage, and it thus turns past and present into dimensions within the future. In the final analysis, past and present only *exist* because the future posits them. We will see this logic again in a later chapter: in the three stages of actual history (the primitive, the statist, and the capitalist/post-capitalist), the last stage is the only one whose historiography lays out the three-stage series whose last stage it will have been. The future, to put it simply, is the "goal (*but*) of time".

(iii) THE THREE SYNTHESES OF DESIRE

Describing the future in terms of goals emphasizes that the noetic medium of the future is desire. When we distinguish past, present, and future as forms of desire, we are finally defining the future in terms of the future itself (not just as metamorphosis in a future-oriented present or as choice based on a future-oriented past).

It is not easy to follow the flow of the argument through this long section of chapter 2 in *DR*. But a careful reading simplifies the structure of the text. Pages 128–34, starting with the paragraph beginning "Biophysical life implies . . .", discuss futural desire insofar as it appears in the organic synthesis of the present. Pages 134–46, starting with the paragraph beginning "The virtual object is essentially past", and highlighted by the paragraph beginning "We have thus encountered a second beyond the pleasure principle, a second synthesis of time . . ." (143–5), discuss futural desire insofar as it appears in the synthesis of the past. Pages 146–53, starting with the paragraph whose second sentence is "On the contrary, we have entered into the third synthesis", discuss futural desire insofar as it appears in itself, i.e. in the synthesis of the future. Finally, page 153 to the end of the chapter develops consequences, based on the synthesis of the future, involving the "dark precursor". (Even with this outline, properties of one synthesis are frequently recast as dimensions of another.)

To preview: (a) the desire of the present is narcissistic, bound to the ego, defined by the pleasure principle (128–9), and aesthetic (144); (b) the desire of the past is defined by the reality principle beyond the pleasure principle, yet disguised in the unconscious, hence revealed by analysis rather than by aesthetics (143–4); (c) the desire of the future is libido freed from the ego, hence defined by the death drive that disturbs the pleasure principle by affirming chance (146–53). We will follow past, present, and future within this overall futurist category of desire. On my construal, Deleuze organized the chapter so that we would find three subdimensions within each of the three dimensions of what is overall the third dimension:

(a) Desire of the present (the future in the present):

> The narcissistic ego repeats once, in the mode of the before or the defect, in the mode of the *Id* (this action is too big for me); a second time, in the mode of an infinite becoming-equal proper to the *ego-ideal*; a third time, in the mode of the after, which realizes the prediction of the *superego*. (146)

    (aa) (The present of the future in the present): the first desires of the passing present are the mobile pleasures on the surface of the desiring body, the Id.

    (bb) (The past of the future in the present): pleasures become a Pleasure Principle when they are "bound" to a stable ego, i.e. when they become narcissistic, when "the contracting synthesis is raised to a second power" (129). As long as one remains wrapped up in the Id's pleasures, one can get split into so many fragments that none of them have any energy. But by enjoying the ego's pleasures, one can become a totalizing narcissist, so that everything appears to exist for one's own benefit. For the Id, either the world is too big, and there is nothing one can do; or the world is too small, and nothing is worth doing.[2] The way out is to bind past moments to the present, but not too closely. The pleasure *principle* has to generalize from the pleasure particulars, so as to include pleasurable memories in the present. The "binding" of pleasure has several effects. The first is the recognition that the same person has several pleasure centres, hence several partial egos. The second is the recognition (the Reality Principle) that an ego can delay its pleasures yet still be the one to enjoy them (130–1). The first binds Id to ego; the second binds the ego as a persistent ego-ideal. We could call this a storehoused Ego. But simply becoming equal to one's pleasure does not differentiate pleasures.

    (cc) (The future of the future in the present): the ego that remembers is thereby capable of acting in a future when it will still remember itself. The ego posits a form that transcends what it can now see of itself: a superego. The future of the desire of the present takes the form of the "superego: the action = X" (146).

    In short, (aa) the present of present desire is pleasure; (bb) the past of present desire is the ideal; (cc) the future of present desire is action.

(b) Desire of the past (the future in the past): once there are possibilities for action distinct from present experience, desire is opened to pure possibility, i.e. by the synthesis of the past.

(aa) (The present of the future in the past): "The second synthesis of time [is] in the unconscious itself" (143). While the future of the present had to be posited in the superego, the future of the past is hidden in the present unconscious. Possibilities exist in events that did not contain such possibilities at first glance. Objects of desire are disguised and displaced, and only analysis of what desire has repressed in its own unconscious can touch on them, in a discourse that as everyone knows is itself full of disguises.

(bb) (The past of the future in the past): so the objects of desire are pure possibilities, in "a second, passive synthesis that gathers up the particular narcissistic satisfaction and relates it to the contemplation of virtual objects" (144). It is not unrealistic to desire past objects that never were present, to desire objects that never appeared other than as disguised, to desire the past to have been more than it could ever have been. After all, when an event enters into the storehouse of virtual possibilities, it enters into a realm of meaning, even if the event as such was not fully actualized. Events that were on the *verge* of occurring in history, effectively become a part of history. Napoleon lost the final battle, but he came so close that the success of Bonapartism, and the extension of rights from the citizens of France to the rest of the world, became legitimate objects of desire. If one contemplates something long enough, and compulsively enough, it becomes a part of one's real affective past.

(cc) (The future of the future in the past): deriving the future of desire from its past risks returning obsessively to the present. When we project a long-term future, and think 'What would it be like to be an X?', or '. . . to see X again', we picture a scenario, then picture continuations, until we have a way to draw the future into the past. It is tensed as future, but deferred by a past that won't give up working. When we *project* a future, we treat it the same way as we would a past or present scenario. So how can we treat the future *as* future? How do we see the past as chance, not as fixation?

The twin dangers are that the options thrown up by the past be co-opted by mythical prototypes, and that desire be lost in aimless cycles (145). It is this aporia that the desire of the future is intended to break. The circular line that recycles the same points needs to be replaced by the straight line leading towards the unknown. In "the third synthesis . . . one could say that time has abandoned every possible mnemic content, and thereby, has broken the circle into which Eros was leading it" (147).

In short, desire of the past is (aa) unconscious, (bb) virtual, and (cc) circular.

(c) Desire of the future (the future in the future):

   (aa) (The present of the future in the future): how does the future break the circle of desire? It begins with the death instinct (147). The vocabulary of death resonates with the issues of "biophysical life" that the desire of the present began with. The present is life; the past is living other people's lives; the future is Eros without the bother of life. Deleuze distinguishes two conceptions of death (148–9): (i) death as the return of life to inanimate matter, the annihilation of the individual; and (ii) death as the disengagement from matter, the impersonal state in which it no longer feels like time must be filled with some particular life course. Death makes us contemplate "free differences when they are no longer subject to the form that an I or an ego gave them" (149). The first conception takes the future as the end of present life; the second accepts the annihilation of presence that it produces, yet still lives the present of that future. For Deleuze, the second type of future can break us of our sense that desire is under our control. The death drive frees us from our fixations on the immediate demands of life in the present tense. The future is the death of our self-control, it "promises and implies, 'for all times' the death of that which is one" (152). The price to pay for this breakthrough is that desire is depersonalized. The gain is that objects of desire become available even if they had been inconsistent with the desirer's life project. Deleuze calls this "the desexualization of Eros", or "neutral and displaceable energy" (149). The "complementarity of the narcissistic libido [the present] and of the death instinct [the future] defines the third synthesis" (150), at least its present dimension.

   (bb) (The past of the future in the future): "Eternal return is the power of affirmation" (152). We think of life as our existence, but if life is what we must deny ourselves in order to stay whole, then life is self-denial, and the way to have a future is to affirm precisely what was not in one's life plans. Setting out to construct a future affirms not the plan but the future. Affirmation puts will before content; *whatever* happens is what one desired. A "bad" result is only bad in relation to what one wanted; it cannot be bad in relation to the future qua future.

   Deleuze's ethical writings often cite the Stoic motto that you should try to become worthy of whatever happens to you. The time of the "whatever" affirms the future "for all times", "once and for all" (*une fois pour toutes* (152)). And to affirm the future *in* all time is to affirm "the empty form of time" (148, 150). These phrases, hallmarks of the pure past, define the past dimension of the future of the future, when time itself is the instinct to pass through the full range of temporal possibilities. In the framework in which *all* time is oriented towards the future, time as a totality (i.e. the past dimension) is not just the set of all co-existing times, and not even just the recombination of the events of all times, but the drive to cover more and more time. The past within the future is, as it was supposed to be, the compulsion to make time searchable. In fact, the arguments of the third synthesis of time solve not only the problems of the second synthesis, but also those of the first. The synthesis of the present promised to explain the continuity of temporal flow; but the resources of the present – perception, imagination, and habit – cannot be sure to capture every last one of the infinite moments in the flow of time. Only with endless search and re-search, i.e. only with the future, can the temporal continuity of presents be guaranteed. With these points, we enter the last paragraphs on the temporal synthesis of desire. What is the conclusion to the problem of temporal searchability?

(cc) (The future of the future in the future): "The eternal return is the power of affirmation, but it affirms . . . everything of chance . . ." (152). The concept of chance, and its consequences, constitutes the solution of chapter 2 of *DR*. It is not enough to play a game and let chance decide whether one wins; the champion of chance leaves the very rules of the game up to chance, and leaves to chance the question of whether one plays, and what it means to play (158–9). (aa) Death as desexualized libido, plus (bb) affirmation as love of time, yield (cc) the player.[3]

As we move on to the consequences, we have to acknowledge that the problem that introduced the third synthesis of time has not really been dealt with. The third synthesis was supposed to explain how the pure past could be penetrated, lived, and searched. Perhaps desire does suggest how the past can be lived, and perhaps taking a chance suggests how it can be penetrated one effect at a time. But one cannot say that the issue of searchability has been dealt with fully. It is true that a formal theory of time cannot be expected to do what a concrete study of history does. To know how the future concretely searches the past, one would need to know, for example, how modern economic societies re-use structures of despotic states; or how Oedipal relations re-use traditional kinship patterns; or how Luther sees Paul. In a formal study, one can only say that the future will assemble contingencies, not which specific ones will be useful. Yet there are structures of the actual histories of desire, of production, of concept-creation, and so on, which do provide search-patterns applicable beyond their typical regions, and a fully developed theory of time will eventually have to lay out the topology of ontological regions in the historical universe.

(iv) THE THREE DIFFERENTIATORS

The three co-existing temporal syntheses are different from each other, and each of the three has its own version of how they are different. Each has its own explanation of why *it* is the synthesis that explains the other two. "There must be a differentiation of difference, an in-itself functioning as a differentiator" (154). Deleuze's last main question in the chapter is, "Under what other conditions does difference develop this in-itself as a differentiator?" (154). The theory of time needs an account of how each of the three syntheses provides a meta-theory of time. Such an account should not posit an extra-temporal logic, or even an overarching temporal logic, but should show how the different types of time themselves each differentiate temporal structures.

(a) The present as differentiator of past, present, and future "The first characteristic seems to us to be organization in series. A system must be constituted on the basis of two or more series, each series being defined by the differences between the terms that compose it" (154). Every present experience contains two or more series, each composed of differences – including the various experiences taking place in the present, as well as various series of memories and anticipations. The present as a system is defined by the differences across those series. The system of the present lays out all "first degree differences" (perceptions, memories, choices) alongside one another, as distinct simultaneous phenomena. This explains the differentiator from the standpoint of the synthesis of the present: "The syntheses of the Psyche incarnate in their own ways the three dimensions of the systems in general. For the psychic binding (Habitus) carries out a coupling of series of excitations . . ." (155).

(b) The past as differentiator of past, present, and future

> If we suppose that the series enter into communication under the action of some force or other, it appears that this communication relates the differences to other differences, or constitutes the system of the differences of differences; these differences of the *second degree* play the role of "differentiator" (154).

Deleuze calls this "internal resonance" (155).

"The major difficulty remains: is it really difference that relates the different to the different?", and not some self-same principle regulating difference (156)? Yes. "It is the in-itself of difference or the 'differently different', that is, the difference in the second degree, the difference with itself that relates the different to the different by itself" (157). This second degree difference, tied to the synthesis of the past, explains the difference between the series of present, past, and future, precisely by not simply laying the three syntheses alongside each other in experience, but instead by splitting the three forms of time into three psyches (the habitué, the rememberer, the desirer) co-existing independently. The past differentiates the three series by keeping them *in*different, and therefore autonomous. To be sure, the premise is that "we suppose that the series enter into communication". The past does translate itself into the present (by contracting) and into the future (by becoming searchable), but its meta-theory of time tells its own complete story, without dialoguing "amicably" with past and future (189). The past does not force a supra-temporal theory to arise . . . but the future does.

(c) The future as differentiator of past, present, and future When it is the future that differentiates the dimensions of time, differentiation is a "forced movement whose psychic amplitude exceeds that of the resonating series themselves" (155). Deleuze has various names for this differentiation: "death instinct", "intensity", "event" (155), and "thought" (156). The future defines an event *not* in the time-frame that it is in, but in another time-frame. The future is not the co-presence of different flows of time (the way the present is), or the co-existing autonomy of in-different time-frames (the way the past is), but the forced communication of the present, past, and future of the same event. Futuricity is what forces a child's innocence to be reinterpreted by her/his ambiguous adulthood (and conversely), and forces a craft economy to include hints of monopoly capitalization (and conversely). It forces cracks in the stable set of past events to exhibit not-yet determinate chance effects, and conversely forces the future to have shown itself, at least darkly, in its precursors. The past and the present *include* all three syntheses of time as internal dimensions, but the future forces its two internal dimensions to appear on its outside – not as dimensions but as three genuine syntheses. The future as differentiator on the one hand externalizes the three syntheses; its temporality thus expresses threefold temporality in its fully expressed form. As Deleuze says, it is "repetition for itself of difference in itself" (126). On the other hand, by expressing the kinds of time that it does not include, the future (and only the future) *does* include the very outside that it does *not* include. Such paradoxical (or dialectical) statements are typical of these pages of the text. Movements across series "exceed" the series and yet are immanent in them. Futural transversals are the "differently different" (157). Finally, the future is the synthesis in which the theory of the three syntheses of time can be fully expressed, as the immanent co-existence of co-existence and temporal differentiation. "The essential thing is the simultaneity, the contemporaneity, the co-existence of all the divergent series together" (162). This is what time simply *is*.

THE DARK PRECURSOR

The future is forced movement, and this introduces the "dark precursor":

> What is this agent, this force ensuring communication? Thunder explodes between different intensities, but it is preceded by a *dark precursor* (*précurseur sombre*), invisible and imperceptible, which determines its path of advance in reverse, as if in its inner recesses (*en creux*). (156)

At one level, there is a "dark precursor" in every temporal process. For there never needs to be a visible agent turning a past into the future; there is only some concrete past and later a concrete successor. No precursor can be anything but dark, and no successor can avoid lighting it. Since there is nothing to see in a precursor except what it is, and it is not yet its successor, the future is not given in the past.

At another level, the term "dark precursor" designates not just any temporal process, but the particular cases of non-typical ruptures in the present, and undecidable gaps in the plenum of the past. The dark precursor denotes something before the rupture, namely its futurity, which permits the rupture without providing its sufficient reason, and retrospectively provides a peg for pinning novelty back on to the temporal continuum. From the standpoint of the present, there are only luminous precursors, since anticipations immanently contain their successive fulfilments. From the standpoint of the past, there are no precursors, only what we might call intercursors, since every possibility, rupture or not, is already in the temporal plenum. Only from the standpoint of the future do we know that the precursors in our past were dark when they were present.

Deleuze does not construct a complete mechanism of how dark precursors work. The very term suggests that we get to a point where theory will not explain how time passes, a point at which we must throw the dice and make time pass. The best I can do is to list Deleuze's hints as to how the dark precursor contributes to theories related to time:

1 The idea of the differentiator provides what could be called the communications theory of the dark precursor. Genuine communication with the future can be an unwanted learning experience, but that cannot be helped (215).
2 That the dark precursor becomes visible only retrospectively with its effects suggests the quantum physics of the dark precursor (158). The dark precursor in *DR* is a contemporaneous precursor of the "quasi-cause" in *LS*.
3 Since the dark precursor is the moment when explanation fails, it "has no other place except that from which it is 'missing' " (157). Its analysis requires the psychoanalysis of the dark precursor.

4 The linguistics of the dark precursor covers the way puns can switch entire meaning-contexts by switching single letters, as well as the way "strange stories" (or "strange histories", *étranges histoires*) create "epiphanies" out of resonating differences (159). "Linguistic precursors" (160) include such well-known Deleuzian stories as Judge Schreber's bird–girl assemblage, the wasp–orchid assemblage, the nomadic jewel–stirrup assemblage, the Paul–Luther assemblage, as well as all historical neo-archaisms. The future meaning looks like nonsense to the predecessor, but as a pair they make up a "refrain" (*refrain* (161)).

5 Mimetics provides the most important science of the dark precursor. "One wonders how to take account of the phenomenon of 'delay', that is, of the time necessary for the infantile scene, supposedly originary, to have its effect at a distance, in an adult scene that resembles it, and that is said to be 'derived' "(162). In the synthesis of the present, of course, childhood is originary; but from the standpoint of the future, the scenes search each other out as moments of choice: "The childhood event . . . is the dark precursor, which puts the two basic series into communication, that of the adults we knew as a child and that of the adult we are among other adults and other children" (162–3). A dark precursor is not a prototype copied or clarified later. It is a question of "two divergent histories that develop simultaneously" (163). The past child does not cause the adult to repeat it, and the future adult's symptoms are not responsible for his childhood traumas; the two narratives are overlaid. When we try to understand each one, the other defines it. It is the difference between them, not their resemblance, which turns each into what it becomes.

The dark precursor is, in a sense, the very event of which it is the precursor. Later in *DR*, Deleuze calls it a "fragment", a singular that is both the whole and the part (373). It is the event itself, wherever it fits in the succession of presents and the architecture of pasts; it is the event *as* that which has been searched, that which is its own future. So "there is no space in which to wonder how the childhood event acts only with a delay. It *is* this delay, but this delay itself is the pure form of time which makes the before and after co-exist" (163). Whereas the past makes events co-exist in the form of levels, the future makes events co-exist in the form of delays.[4]

Because a successor scene makes its precursor, qua future, simultaneous with interpretations that could not have belonged to that precursor qua present, Deleuze says, finally, that "These differential systems with disparate and resonating series, with a dark precursor and forced movement, are called simulacra or phantasms" (165). They demonstrate "the power of the false" (167). In a later chapter of *DR*, schematizing the three syntheses yet again, Deleuze says that from the standpoint of the present, it is only "good sense" to live in the present, since the past just sounds "improbable" and the future

The Third Synthesis of Time

is at best "probable" (290–1). But from the standpoint of the future, the goal is precisely to create the improbable out of the present. It is not an accident that *DR*'s chapter on time ends with the power of the false.[5] To some extent, this is what one has to say if there is to be a concept of the future at all. If the future were simply the best continuation of the present, it would be a deduction from the present, and not an independent temporal scheme. If the past were simply a pre-existing Ideal, then the future would have only to "select good images" in order to express it (166). But if the future is genuinely not-yet, then it is not exhausted in relation to what is true about the past.

What remains of the future as search engine? To put my conclusions bluntly: (a) Deleuze's analysis of the first synthesis of time shows the indispensable role of succession in a theory of time that nevertheless subordinates succession to co-existence; (b) his analyses of the second synthesis are rigorous and persuasive, but we need to refine them until they are absolutely conclusive; (c) Deleuze's analysis of the third synthesis of time in *DR* is filled with important ideas, but the theory of how co-existence has a future is not adequately worked out in this text. The idea of dark precursors will continue to function beneath the surface of his philosophy of history in later works, e.g. in his conceptions of contingent history, thresholds, and revolutionary temporal politics. But there is a reason why the chapter on time in *DR* feels like it ends with an assortment of insights rather than a systematic conclusion.[6] Revolutionary politics has to be part of a theory of time.[7]

In the last pages of *DR*, Deleuze indicates that the concept of history is precisely what is at stake in the synthesis of the future:

> But what is the content of this third time? . . . We have tried to show that it concerns the simulacrum, nothing but simulacra. Simulacra imply essentially, under the same power, the object = X in the unconscious, the word = X in language, and the *action* = X in history. (382–3, my italics)

If the "object = X" means that a new trait will unexpectedly belong to an earlier object, an "action = X" means that a historical agent may suddenly start acting again centuries after she is dead and gone, just because of the way that time is synthesized. Deleuze's later texts do not speak much of the "action = X"; but they do develop the theme of history in the future.

The next thing we need to do in order to construct Deleuze and Guattari's philosophy of history is to designate the temporal location of political events, given that time co-exists in levels. To explain how pasts search out their futures, we need a theory of dates and their destinies.

NOTES

1. In *NP* (54), after asking his usual question, "How can the present pass?", Deleuze concludes that, "the eternal return is thus an answer to the problem of passage". Deleuze cites Nietzsche's *Thus Spoke Zarathustra* III, "On the Vision and the Riddle", but the interpretation is rather a stretch. Cf. Simont (1997, pp. 310–12).
2. Of course, temporal categories are not moral. It is not always bad to be fixated on a mother substitute. For that matter, a lot of art comes from seeing oneself, or one's enemy, or one's childhood sweetheart, everywhere – from having too much time on one's hands and no sense of the future.
3. Ronald Bogue (2003, pp. 38–53) draws a parallel between the three syntheses of time and the three periods of Western music: Classical music, with its principles of time order, succession, and the organizing point; Romantic music, with its lone hero's subjective memory; and Modern music, whose waves of force and intensity transform matter into cosmic vectors. Bogue describes the type of becoming produced by the third synthesis of time as "a sort of infinite rubato unmarked by any organizing pulse, a free-floating time" (p. 34). Infinite rubato doesn't quite sound right, but the idea of deterritorialized time as pulseless intensity is interesting.
4. Wait for my next book, *Simultaneity and Delay*.
5. *C2* also makes the transition from time to the power of the false, between chapters 5 and 6.
6. Perhaps it is unfair on my part to conclude that a certain chapter of a book does not solve the problem that it set out, without analysing its following chapters. My procedure is to focus on Deleuze's direct analyses of time and history. But no doubt one could find aspects of the problem of history in the subsequent chapters of *DR* dealing with thought and sensibility.
7. In different ways, this is also the view of Éric Alliez (1991, 1999), Antonio Negri (1981), and Guy Debord (1967).

5 Dates and Destiny: The Problem of Historical Chronology

Virtual events, and not just factual changes of state, are "dated".[1] Indeed while factual changes of course occur at determinate points in chronological time, they do not really have dates until they are extracted from chronological succession and reoriented on a virtual plane where all events co-exist. This is an admittedly unusual use of the term "date". But it is crucial for Deleuze and Guattari's philosophy of history. It is not enough for a philosophy of history to argue for a temporal level at which events co-exist; it must also be able to date such events, even if they are in a sense simultaneous. The theory of dates is the first test of whether Deleuze's theory of time can be developed into a theory of history.

Another test involves comparing Deleuze with the philosopher of history *par excellence*: Hegel. In the usual story, Hegel is the philosopher of progressive development, and Deleuze the philosopher of simultaneous transformation. But neither of these statements is true. Hegel is as much a philosopher of timeless events in thought, and Deleuze of irreversible distance. To solve the problem of the date, we will reverse their usual places.

A date marks a historical event in two ways. It assigns a singular moment to an event, and it situates events in a common era. The first function of the date gives the event a determinate location relative to other past events and to the present; the second makes all events available at once to memory and to interpretation. The first posits events in succession, the second in co-existence. For Deleuze and Guattari, detaching the event from its original chronological territory, in order to place it on the fluid plane of contemporaneous availability, is not only a psychological, but also an ontological difference. Both functions of the date are clearly genuine phenomena. But insofar as we consider events in their contemporaneity, their meaning as events in succession has been removed. This is the issue I want to focus on: what sense of succession can be reconstituted in a general context of co-existence? If Joan of Arc is an effect that can surge up at any time, and at the same time Napoleon is another such effect, and Caesar another, in what sense do these effects still carry references to epochs, social contexts, in short, to their dates? Is there a kind of distance between events not defined by chronology? The problem of how to select which past to make the present become, is, for both

Hegel and Deleuze, the problem of "destiny". This is our problem: do dates have destinies?

DELEUZE AND GUATTARI

A theory of the date is scattered throughout Deleuze and Guattari's "Postulates of Linguistics" Plateau (*MP* 95–139), but I construe a four-stage argument: (1) the date extracts an incorporeal feature of the event; (2) it embeds this incorporeal feature in a body; (3) the event thus becomes variable; (4) the hinge-points across variations constitute a diagram of dates that is non-successive but differential.

Incorporeal enunciation

The first stage of the argument demonstrates that, for linguistic reasons, "history cannot get rid of dates" (*MP* 103).

"Postulates" begins by claiming that the elementary unit of language is the *mot d'ordre* (95), an "order-word" backed by social pressure. Any speech-act has effects on potential and actual listeners. By circulating language previously in use, every speech-act in effect is "indirect discourse" (97), passing along something that some other speaker said. Every time X says 'P', she might as well be saying, 'I've heard it said that P'. Enunciations are thus "collective", and specific forces of assemblage transmit them across the social field (99). There are at any moment many voices being passed along redundantly, even in a single enunciation, and a given voice may either reinforce or countermand another. Therefore, each relay makes a choice, and language is "*free* indirect discourse" (101). Freedom in turn makes the act "incorporeal" (102). Deleuze uses Husserl to show what whereas bodies are connected physically, senses (or meanings) are connected intentionally (*LS* 22–35). For example, theft is corporeal, and so is the punishment of the criminal, but the judge's declaration of the defendant's guilt is a speech-act that puts an end to the first corporeal act and begins the second. It is a word that orders compliance, and may become a slogan that commands obedience. States of things become objects of possible reference when an incorporeal thought-content transforms spatio-temporally related physicalities into meaningfully related events. To have a theory of the date, we have to connect the incorporeality of a meaning's enunciation with the temporality of events:

> The incorporeal transformation is recognized by its *instantaneity*, by its immediacy, by the *simultaneity* of the enunciation that expresses it and the effect that it produces; this is why the *mots d'ordre* are strictly *dated*, hour,

minute and second, and take hold the moment they are dated. (*MP* 102–3, my italics)

The claim that sense-giving enunciations are instantaneous seems to mean that they take place without historical continuity. A series of physical states, and a separate series of thoughts or linguistic acts, would converge at an instant. Physical processes would not *gradually* take on meaning; they would suddenly receive a meaning when an enunciation gives it to them. But reading instantaneity as suddenness does not suit the theory of language-relay. As we know from *DR*, instants imply multiplicities (*DR* 103–6).

Instead, what makes the enunciation of a new meaning instantaneous is that when it is performed, it contracts past enunciations into its own interpretations. When Lenin says that the Soviet state exists, it *makes* previous enunciations into precursors, turning antecedents into what Oulipo calls "plagiarism by anticipation".[2] We call this instantaneous, not because it is without history, but because it remakes history with a new focal point. Instantaneity makes whole systems of succession converge not just at points, but also in rhythms. As a bodily occurrence, an event takes place only once; but as an incorporeal enunciation, as soon as an event takes place once, it sends its spin-offs systematically across time. Simultaneity is quantitatively a whole–part relation, qualitatively an interactive intensification, and temporally a contraction of differential time-lines.

Of course, there is also the obvious meaning of "the simultaneity of the enunciation and its effect". At the very time when Lenin says something just happened, it just did. The performative interrupts a continuity of similar occurrences, and it establishes a new continuity across time-lines to make the event take hold. "This is why the *mots d'ordre* are strictly dated, hour, minute and second, and take hold the moment they are dated" (*MP* 103). It is not just that occurrences take place at certain times or that people can look at their watch when they happen. It is that event-configurations change the direction of a succession. The enunciation brings back to life the whole range of past events: archaic revolts resurge, yesterday's revolutionaries unexpectedly look like collaborators, the number of years in a five-year plan becomes strangely uncountable. Simultaneity means that the time-lines that events are placed on are all problematized at once. Dating the event is what puts it into history; events are dated not by accident but essentially. An occurrence cannot be an event without being dated, and every date implies an event.

There are two sets of problems here. Does the continuity of succession depend on implicit date-enunciations taking place all the time? This would seem implausible. If only those events that are enunciated have dates, then it becomes unclear whether we should even say that there are dates between any two significant events, between 1776 and 1789, for example. If the dating enunciation marks the 'just now' of an event, from what standpoint do events take place before or after others? Can installing a calendar substitute for explicit date-enunciations? If each event contracts a whole history into its point of view, dates must be more than proper names of pages on a calendar. They must designate focal points sensitive to serial distances.

The second problem is simpler. What does it take to express a date? Is naming the year sufficient? Or do we need to add the day or the second? Can imprecise temporal expressions count as dates, as, for instance, when *QP* (8) speaks of "this hour, *entre chien et loup*" when a philosophical life begins? The examples in "Postulates" involve dates with years and days: such as 20 November 1923, when the German government decreed a change in currency (*MP* 103–4), and 4 July 1917, the day Lenin declared that the Soviets were no longer the source of power and installed the Party in its place (105). Both dates name days, but not "hour, minute and second". In fact, there are already two different criteria defining a date. One is that the event is marked by the enunciation. On this criterion, the event is dated by the second when the utterance is over. The second criterion marks the taking-hold of an enunciation, which might take years to occur (as in Deleuze and Guattari's usage: " 'One heard more talk of vampires from 1730–1735 . . .' " 290).[3] On the taking-hold criterion, dating can backdate events as well as postdate them.

The most direct uses of dates in *MP* are in the titles of each Plateau. Two Plateau titles name day, month and year; seven name single years; one names a span of 657 years (though the table of contents shortens it to the year at the beginning of the span); two round off large numbers BC; one names "year zero". Deleuze discusses these dates in an interview (*Pp* 34), where he says an event is assembled from the circumstances of a concept's where, when, and how (39). The firing of fast-moving precision weapons needs dates down to the second (40). Slow procedures need relaxed, indefinite dates.

The flexibility of the circumstance-assemblage solves (by relativizing) the problem of the date's durational scope. But in so doing, it disconnects the date from any single model of measuring the passage of time. "The dates [in the Plateau titles] do not refer to a unique homogeneous calendar but to space-times (*espaces-temps*) that must change each time (*fois*)" (*Pp* 52). This is why Deleuze says the Plateau titles contain "fictive dates" (40, 51). This raises three issues.

First, there is no uniform calendar; different cultures have different dating schemes.[4] Second, tying the date to a convergence defines the event more by "force" than by instant (*Pp* 52). Deleuze and Guattari suggests dating enunciations in the form "Werewolves swarming 1730" or "Jules to come 5 p.m." (using the infinitive[5] as an indefinite temporal modifier). Third, if each schizoanalytic phenomenon arose at a certain moment, then the dated titles of *MP* would map a history of (post)modernity. But instead, dating the Plateau titles, rather than "linking" the Plateaus (which the interviewers in *Pp* ask about), removes the common calendar. Each date makes its own temporal world. A date may mark an event as individual or multiple, backward or futuristic, depending on how it unfolds. Dates function within some sort of map, but allow for heterogeneous dating systems for the same event. Indeed, knowing how one event has been dated does not tell us how the next event should be dated.

The question is, does a date still put an event on a map, indeed is a date still a date, if we cannot tell what time comes after it? Perhaps it is. We say without disquiet that the *present* can be dated even though we do not know what will come next. Can we speak of the past in the same way? Insofar as historical events act at a distance, we do sometimes detach events from the issue of what comes next.

If historical causality at a distance confounds the map of proximate events, perhaps some simple numerical time-line, where events are just counted off ('Event-1, E2, E3'), would preserve it. But even here, as Deleuze argues (e.g. *DR* 299–300), the problem is that numbers can be continuous or discrete, extensive or intensive, ordinal or cardinal; some events might need to be dated with irrational numbers, or ratios, or nodal lines, or "numbering numbers" (as the "Several Regimes of Signs" Plateau refers to the rapid reorganizations of nomadic warrior groupings). One of Deleuze's explanations of Borges' conceit that the strangest labyrinth is the straight line is that a straight number line is filled with irrational numbers. It is not just that time is infinitely divisible (making it hard to date befores and afters in short time-spans), or that times only approach the limit of locatability (making dates fuzzy sets). The problem is that there are irrational numbers on the time-line that, while subject to calculation methods that are not at all vague, have no actual quantitative value.[6] We start a century and end it, but do not know how many times there were in between, or which intermediate times came at which time.

The density of numbers has implications for which events are worthy of dating. Deleuze and Guattari did not write Plateaus dated 1789, 18th Brumaire, or May '68. Their Plateaus are dated 7,000 BC, 1227, 28 November 1947 (nothing more recent). The dates of schizoanalytic history are neither before nor after the 'big' events of world-history, but wedged in between. Because of these choices, it becomes unclear what a datable event is. We need an ontology of what it is that has a date.

In "Postulates", it is the *mot d'ordre*, the event-enunciation, which has a date. But in the "Conclusion" to *MP* (637) the date is predicated of an "abstract machine". In the "Becoming-Intense . . ." Plateau, the haecceity is dated (*MP* 318). In *CS* (189) Guattari says that striations and irreversible "phase transitions" on a plane of immanence are "dated"; "fractal stages" on a "processual phylum" are "dated" (*CS* 194). (Guattari's books, unlike those of Deleuze or Hegel, are rather difficult.) The date is not just an event of social history, but any local transition in the flux of being.

Predicating dates of abstract machines suggests a second way of reading Deleuze's claim that dates are "fictive". The first reading was that one may choose any occurrence and date it, performatively making it into an event, lining up a new calendar around it. The occurrence could be purely imaginary, false histories could determine actions, and imaginary futures could define the present. A date would set down roots in a dark precursor, whether or not the latter is able to ground the new event's claims.

The realist ontology of fictive dates hangs on Deleuze's Bergsonian analysis of "images", according to which an image is not in a perceiver, but is the vibration of an object through other objects. Thinking of a date as "fictive" can thus mean that each event provokes real, but differentiated, dating responses in the organisms it comes into contact with. This interpretation accepts divergent dating schemes, but does not detach chronologies from reality.

This entails that the event is dated precisely because it is *not* just part of the neutral flow of occurrences. A recipient extracts the event from the flow at, and by, some particular date. And once the event is taken out of the homogeneous time-line, and placed into a network of differentiated timelines, it is no longer circumscribed within a single point of time. Dating makes events repeatable, in three specific senses.

First, the dated event becomes the "instant zero" (*MP* 103) for measuring subsequent time-lapse, a marker against which future (and past) events will be defined as variants. So "2005 AD" means "2005 years after Year 0". A date does not usually tell how much time has lapsed from the beginning of the universe, but from the rupture of the birth of a Revolution or the death of a god. One religion retroactively dates the saviour's birth, another recycles a millennia-long calendar, another counts backwards from the non-event of doomsday; one revolutionary renames the months of the year, another creates a revolution simply with the enunciation, "Today's the day!" (as everyone says of Lenin). A date tears the event out of homogeneous time and places it in a culturally specific time segment.

Second, a date is a re-usable formula. Once a significant event is dated "July 14", all sorts of occurrences on that day in subsequent years will resonate as variants. Tuesday is poker night, and events roll around in a ritournelle. "May '68" does not just make an anniversary out of a particular event; it keeps it from being contained in the particular duration in which it occurred. Far from delineating the temporal scope of the event, the date "May '68" affirms that "The Events" exist at many different discrete times. In a similar way, a big year (1914, 1968) pulls all sorts of apparently unrelated occurrences into the same event.

Third, the dated event's content is repeatable. For dating an event not only locates it but also names it *as* something. "1812" is a numeral and not a date until it takes the form: "the war of 1812". Naming an event implies that it has a date, and citing a date implies that something nameable happened on it. But we can name and date an event without describing what precedes and succeeds it, and this implies that the date names the event abstractly, as a war, as a *type*. By singling it out, we make the *particular* event a *universal* type that can be instantiated more than once. Subject to multiple predications, it becomes a topos. Michelet, for example, says that, "We have dated our injustices; this has allowed us to praise men whom later it will be necessary to blame . . . How many men in one single man!"[7] When would the "names of history" live, after all, if not in dates of history, "beyond the reasonable calendar" (*AO* 29)? Finally, if the event can be *thought* independent of before and after, it can have *effects* independently of its predecessors and successors, and so it can *exist* independently of them.

In short, the incorporeal date removes the event from the flow of bodily states of affairs. But then it puts it back.

Attribution

We will need the distinction between expression and content.[8] Deleuze and Guattari oppose what they call postmodernism's linguistic reductionism. For Deleuze and Guattari, a date is a linguistic expression; a dated state of affairs is a non-linguistic content. The expression of a historical event has form (e.g. meaning) and matter (voice); its content too has form (e.g. social function) and matter (human and other bodies) (*MP* 109). If there were a simple dichotomy of expression vs. content, and of idea vs. material reality, then the date-expression would represent, but not affect, the event. Indeed, the dichotomy seems natural as long as we think of expressions in formal terms and contents in material terms. But in Deleuze and Guattari's scheme, both expressions and contents, i.e. both dates and events, have both form and matter. Expressions do not merely represent contents epiphenomenally; rather, expressions and events interpret each other at the level of form, and interact causally with one another at the level of matter.

The forms of expression are syntactic, semantic, and pragmatic; forms of content are spatio-temporal. The form of the dating expression includes *implications* for understanding time; the form of the bodily content includes *causal* forces. Obviously, a logical implication can be a cause for a being who understands it. Deleuze and Guattari include not only cases where an expression motivates a material thinker, but also cases where social meanings and social material conditions interact. For example, implications among expressions (e.g. the fact that announcing a currency change implies a redefinition of bankruptcy) can produce a change of form in causes across contents (as the closure of banks causes panic withdrawals). What makes a date real is that it transforms forms of content (fast or slow social changes) into forms of expression (dense or sparse calendar divisions), and conversely. Date-expressions "insert" themselves into contents (*MP* 110). As performatives, they "anticipate, downgrade, slow down or speed up, detach or reunite, or divide events up otherwise" (110).

When is the time right to insert a date into the flow of real occurrences?

Deleuze and Guattari pose two ancient puzzles, citing "the sense of dates according to the Stoics" (110). First, "beginning at what moment can one say that somebody is bald?" Such a date is supposed to fix a discontinuous point on a continuum, but as everyone knows, there is no answer. Date-insertion is a perpetual, if unavoidable, problem.

The second puzzle is: "in what sense does an enunciation of the type 'there will be a naval battle tomorrow' constitute a date?" (110). Are there future dates? Of course, the calendar names the days following this one, but are potential events datable qua potential? Are there potential dates that are not actual dates? "Tomorrow" can refer to a vague future, or to a specific hour, or both (when an editor clears page one for a special edition tomorrow). Again, the problem is to cut a discontinuous virtual point into a real continuum.[9]

Inserting dates into bodies requires that forms of expression and forms of content each be divided into pieces (*morcellement*, 110) and rearranged. Dating an event by the day a battle starts, for example, requires *not* thinking of every aspect of what a battle is. The inclusive sense of a battle, with all its ramifications, would prevent it (like baldness) from being dated at any given moment. The date only succeeds in marking off an event if some fragment of the description is separated out. This single part is re-inserted into the content when the general gives the word to charge. A piece of language becomes a free matter. Conversely, the battle as a whole gives no foothold to language until a wounded soldier falls into a doorway, or a weapon arrives with operating instructions, at which point a content fragment locally tears off a linguistic context. Questions in the form "from what moment?" can only be answered by means of such divisions of totalities into "sign-particles" (110). History depends on "variability", the capacity of systems to absorb and be affected by fragments.

In sum, a sign cuts into a body, not as a tattoo draws language on a body, but as a recipe is a component in producing a meal. Dating an event (e.g. deciding whose birth date gets marked) may shift the natural calendar of bodies (by census) to a social calendar (by royal lineage), which in turn preserves natural content (recording the prince's health). In a given case, the social calendar may become relatively independent of the natural calendar (celebrating bank holidays more than harvest festivals); elsewhere, it may decline (once Saints' Days cease to arouse fear and trembling). The notion of intervention implies the relative separability of expression and content. In a given case, interest rates (content) may be more volatile than government policy (expression), or vice versa. Each fragment can either territorialize or destabilize the other, depending on the skills of the participants.

We do not need contrived cases of swords with words on them or books made in funny shapes, but we do need a theory of the neutral particle operating as a hinge-point, "the same X" (110) relaying signs into bodies and vice versa.

Variation

Variation involves detachment, system, and secrecy (111–26).

Does the date of a given event vary? Are "1914" and "1939" variants in the same sense that the Goldberg Variations are? Obviously, different stages of an event occur on different dates. But is the event itself in flux around a number of (possibly distant) dates? Clearly, the same date-enunciation can apply to different events in different ways ("1968" can name either a springtime or a decade; "the twenty-first century" often named the twentieth; "BC" sometimes names a time and sometimes a theologico-political condition). The same date-expression ("1776") can refer to event-content from different times (1775, or 1976). Some dates vary independently of what actually happens, as in the form: "the Revolution happens every day". Other dating forms use determinate content, as when a flag-raising announces July 4. The physical object is not a mere substitute for the linguistic date. When the stars and stripes set the date to marching time, the properties of content are translated into properties of enunciation. Here, the date is a technical procedure for mass-producing time-images.

The theory that dates are variables is more than nominalism, in which one expression names many objects; and it is more than perspectivism, in which one expression has different references according to context. It is strictly variationism. Its opponent is the theory that language is founded on "structural invariants" (syntactical rules, lexical consistency, or truth conditions, 116). For variationism, an expression cuts into every series to which it has a potential reference (119, 126). As soon as a date refers to one day, it potentially refers to the next, and also has a potential reference to discontinuous moments across temporal distances. The same story may be political in Monday's paper but gossip in Sunday's, since the date is an "alloy" of headline and deadline, print technology and public relations, advertising and the 40-hour work-week, *The Times*' prestige and procedures for transporting small objects across town. Of course, a dating expression may not succeed in entrenching itself in its referent if the social content does not undergo its own metamorphosis. Naming a given day in 1968 as "1917" may or may not do anything. But in general, whatever the most obvious reference of a date, other variants circulate around the population of language-users. Variation is "inherent" and "systematic" (118).

Therefore, just as there is no "standard" version of a language, every date variant is in the minority (117–20). In Canada, the American year "1776" has a secondary, minority reference to 1812; each Christian year conceals a Jewish year. When minority cultures are forbidden to mention the dates from their history, they may conceal dates within non-dating expressions. In various ways, a date can contract and relax temporal distance around a social plane, as when the Pharaoh Pepi announced that he had just defeated an enemy that in fact the Pharaoh Seti had defeated hundreds of years earlier.

When we wonder whether the twenty-first century has yet got out of the twentieth, we are caught in the same bind. It is not just a question of whether power structures of the twentieth century are left behind; the problem is the way secondary dates repeat themselves even as the next date arrives.

The minority variation is generalized in "secret" dates (122–5) concealed in gestures and jargon and stuttering and merchant's cries and animal behaviours that do not appear to be linguistic at all. Whether a given sign can serve as a date, e.g. whether a ritual is an observance, will depend on its context. Yet the idea of the secret date is that the larger context is precisely the perspective from which the date is hidden. The secret of each expression is not that it says one more thing than it could say, but that the "sober" variation (125) says one fewer thing than it could, it holds back from committing itself to a single anniversary date in order to retain the power to vary its origins. In practice, any day of the year is the anniversary of something (though anniversaries are forgotten, and birthdays arrive and end too soon[10]) that suits a group's desire to justify a present-day act.

No doubt the most salient dating expression at the time of writing of this book is "9–11". It is not yet known whether this numerical expression will produce anniversaries, like the 3–11 Madrid bombings, or, alternatively, cut off successors. 9–11 is sometimes treated as a day of infamy that will last a thousand years, but sometimes as the day the earth stood still. If the slogan that nothing will be the same as before, or the same as anything, is correct, which it may not be, then while it feels today as though 9–11 is a date *par excellence*, it may only be half a date, a date with no possible anniversary.

But if a series of variations on when things actually happened is not a totality, what order does it have? If we make dates too variable, will it cease to matter which date we assign to which event? Deleuze and Guattari say that we can "trace the virtual lines of infinite variation" (121).[11] This brings us to the final aspect of the theory of variation, namely the "tensor-point" (126) of transitivity. It is designed to explain cases like the slow but radical transition from tonal to atonal music, "across a long period in the XIXth and XXth Centuries" (121). Despite being infinite, a variation should be determinate and analysable. Each element should act as a convergence-point and a divergence-point, condensing, or tensing, a series around that point. Tracing requires that points have relative (if not essential) locations (126). The potential flux from one point to another should be mappable. A line of traceable variation has to exhibit some kind of "transitivity".

At the end of this section of text, Deleuze and Guattari use cummings' verse "he danced his did" to indicate the extent of variability and the folly of translating a variable into a standard form like "he did his dance". Are Deleuze and Guattari implying that by analogy, there are ungrammatical dating expressions like "May 35th", or "they 1929'd their desire"? Can any point in an expressive series tense up around any other? How do we explain the "transitivity" whereby one point "reacts" to its predecessor on a "chain" (126)?

Dates and Destiny: The Problem of Historical Chronology 81

The problem of transitivity is central to the theory of non-successive dating. With all the variations on the date, what remains of the sense in which Lenin starts something, in which a date is determinate and irreversible, in which Caesar is before Napoleon?

Diagram

Again, we need some technical vocabulary.

A "diagram" maps variations, whereas structures like indexes, icons, symbols, and axioms map relatively fixed fields (176–83).[12] On "strates", contents and expressions are separated and "substantialized"; on a diagram, they are not (178). To put it simply, an event takes place in phases: as virtual potential, as activity, and as fact. We call the virtual energy the "abstract machine"; the procedure of combinatory actualization is the "machinic assemblage"; the actuality is the "strate". A diagram maps the ways a machinic assemblage actualizes an abstract machine (176–83). The diagram should describe how a date creates new potential for making strates interact, and for reorganizing structures within each strate.

What is at stake in the theory of dates are the "points" on this diagram. A purely free potentiality, where expressions had no implications for social conditions, and dates could be used without any order, would not have points on it at all. Yet Deleuze and Guattari's abstract machine is not pure being; it is the generative side *of* actual processes. This, after all, is why it must be "named and dated" (181, 178). The "Lenin-abstract machine" varies, but it has the proper name of Lenin as its hinge with concrete material. The abstract machinic name-date ("Lenin-1917") has, as its other pole, a material social strate (126–7).[13]

But if the abstract machine is prior to the factual strates, how does it determine actual events? Deleuze and Guattari say that the abstract machine's diagram "is not outside history, but is always rather 'before' history, at each moment when it constitutes the *points* of creation or of potentiality" (177). Yet at the end of "Postulates", they say that once matter is conceived diagrammatically in terms of force rather than form, "it makes a body or a word that stops at no precise *point*" (138). What is a point?

It looks like there may be a way to tie variable dates down to a single point in time, based on the way the proper name "Lenin" can substitute for the date "1917" (127). In general, the question "when does the Russian Revolution subsist?" can be answered: "whenever the Lenin-machine drives a revolution, a party, a speech-act, or a counter-revolutionary". But the date called "Lenin" is the starting point, the relayable backward-referent, the potential for variation, and the limit-point. The proper name at least looks like a limit-point in that the named person is limited by date of death

(135–39). But of course the Lenin-machine does not cease operation when the man dies. As in *DR*, even death turns out to be a variable with "revolutionary potential" (*MP* 139).[14] Death is a limit-point, not as a constraint on variation but as a convergence of focus, a cry of alarm. But if revolutionaries have only revolutionary deaths, it seems once again impossible to localize points on a diagram. The force that creates variations is too abstract to explain which phenomenon is a variant of which. Although Deleuze and Guattari insist that the undetermined and the determined are always interacting, the abstract machine may be too undetermined to have anything to do with the determinations of the machinic assemblage. It may never be sufficiently clear whether or not the Chinese Revolution is one of the machinic assemblages of the Lenin abstract machine, and hence whether or not 1949 is a variant of 1917.

Now, one interpretation is to say there are two kinds of history, corresponding to actual events and virtual potencies. Deleuze says that concrete history pertains to the determinate relations between points, the assemblages; pure becoming pertains to the force of passage, the abstract machine (*F* 49). This makes it sound as though while the abstract machine generates virtual variations, only the machinic assemblage has determinate dates. But how can the assemblage remain dated for more than one moment at a time if the abstract machine is always reshuffling before–after relations? If dates are excluded from the level of abstract machines and diagrams, they will remain merely empirical, and not machinized. Yet Deleuze and Guattari insist that it is the abstract machine that is dated. The danger is that if the diagram does not have points, the theory of the date might simply dissolve.

We get one more chance to solve the problem, if we can develop the hint in *F* that diagrams can "succeed" one another (*F* 51, 91). A diagram constructs a grid of "spatiotemporal multiplicity" (42), it "produces a new type of reality", it institutes a series, it "makes history" when it "constitutes *points* of emergence or of creativity" (43). Up to now, we have said that expressions (or contents) can succeed one another on a strate; in contrast, the diagram that introduces a dating calendar was presented as an instantaneous thought-transformation. But if diagrams can be mapped historically relative to one another, there might be a procedure for dating the creations of procedures of dating, in all their controversies and all their twists and turns.[15] Such a diagram would have to be both an entire grid and a specific point on that grid. Each date would have to be the undetermined point of creativity that makes other dates determinate relative to it.

If, for example, one diagram maps a given history as a series of battles, and another maps the same history as a series of theories about human nature, there will be a combination-diagram that maps wars fought for theoretical reasons, as well as one that maps the military-educational complex, and so on. While diagrams are *a priori* models of history, they are constructions of the forces that cross variables, so they themselves also have histories. "Forces in relation are inseparable from the variations of their distances or of their relations" (*F* 91). There will always be ways to commence histories out of other histories. The presence of other diagrams will put each atemporal diagram into temporality. Non-chronological becoming will be "immanent" in chronological history (*F* 44).

This will finally explain how the diagram has points, though we will have to add some vocabulary of our own.

A single diagram does not have points. There is no getting around the fact that one can extract and date any duration one chooses, as if a lottery were to decide the order of events in time (*F* 92). But once a first-order diagram selects among the flux of movements, a second-order diagram can select among the singularities that the first-order diagram picked out. When a second-order diagram maps the passage across two first-order diagrams, the transverse line makes the two converge at a single point. At the convergence point, the abstract machine is dated. So for example, the Revolutionary abstract machine is a potential within every act, with no more relation to one actual revolution than another, and has in itself no particular date-points. But when it diagrams psycho-economic, techno-mediatic, or rhetorico-sexual assemblages, it crosses these series *at* points, and these points are both stabilizers and synthesizers.

We thus now have three levels of dating. First, at the level of strates, two occurrences, whether two bodily states or two speech-acts, exhibit a straightforward, datable, causal succession. Second, on the level of an abstract temporal expression's attribution to content, a date is an instantaneous transformation, a decision to map events a certain way. Third, we can map ways in which one diagram intervenes in another. The date of the point of contact between diagrams is a meta-event whereby two unmeasurable dates cross at a single point. It measures the unmeasurable point at which things become measured.

Examples of all three would work in the following way. On the level of strates, sequentially, we will say with common sense that by 1917 economic conditions had worsened gradually since 1914. On the second level, instantaneously, in 1917 Lenin enunciates the sharp beginning of a new era. For the third level, we will have to build a theory of intersecting diagrams. Following what we could call an "interstrate" (*F* 91) diagram, we will say that in 1917 the biology of hunger becomes a causal factor in social discourse. Following what we could call an interdiagrammatic intertemporal diagram, we will say that in 1917, the 1917 Revolution converges with a 1789 Revolution, a 1949 Revolution, and so on. There is no date until there is a triple date of this sort. Each date supplies the principle for measuring how distant its own enunciations are from the others, and so each is a diagram that measures the passage between diagrams. It is within the date "1917" that 1917 becomes the successor of 1914.

The first, second, and third characteristics of the date – the instant, the line, and the turning-point; the quality, the quantity, and the relation; the enunciation, the variant, and the diagram; the year-date, flux-date, and cross-date – are all required for a theory of continuous yet determinate dates.

But there is one more meta-problem of date and distance. The theory of intersecting diagrams is thin both on the very large and the very small scale. On the large scale, is there an overall sense in which 1917 is after 1789? To be sure, many of the ways that 1917-assemblages intersect with 1789-assemblages take place in terms of memories, or monuments, which immanently refer 1917 to an earlier date. But in an assemblage in which a 1917 phenomenon (e.g. proletarianism) explains a 1789 phenomenon (the rights of man), why can we not say that 1789 is *after* 1917? If there is no overall irreversibility *within* which time-order varies, does there remain any determinacy to the variations? Why does the simultaneity of the convergence not make all succession vanish?

The difficulty at the large scale makes us wonder whether the time arrow might be the responsibility of small-scale micro-processes instead? Guattari hints at the small-scale date by suggesting that the "Lenin-effect" is a "fractal" (*CS* 261). A fractal begins with a timeless formula, but once applied, it creates a "surplus value" of "irreversible diachronic ruptures" (*CS* 233). It dates events irreversibly by inserting a small-scale difference into a large scale (*CS* 202–4). All geometrical formulas map distances, but fractal formulas amplify the density between points, so that the next point is delayed. The very difference in scale might generate a time arrow. Guattari's suggestion is obscure, but if increase is the destiny of the micro-date, then a diagram might after all make non-sequential history irreversible on a large scale.

I will return to the concept of increase after reading Hegel on progress. But first, a word about Derrida.

FIVE DIFFERENCES BETWEEN DELEUZE AND GUATTARIAN DATES AND DERRIDIAN DATES

Derrida's *Schibboleth*, published six years after *MP*, analyses the concept of the date through the poetry of Paul Celan.

Some similarities:

1   Like Deleuze and Guattari, Derrida begins with the fact that a date refers to an event that happens just once (*une fois*), yet can refer to it in countless reiterations. The possibility of the second time is a presupposition of the first (*S* 12). As in *MP*, Derrida's argument is that it is *because* an event happens only once that it is repeatable; to be once-only is to be "cut" out of the temporal flow and this is what allows it to become the object of subsequent celebrations. Derrida's example is the date of a circumcision: it happens only once, and is therefore celebrated annually.

Dates and Destiny: The Problem of Historical Chronology 85

2 The date is an I–Other relation, a "co-signature" (*S* 20–1). One February 13 resonates with other February 13s, and with other dates that a given culture associates with February 13 (42). As in *MP*, dating attracts the voices of others: "Is there any other desire than that of dating?" (73).
3 Something about a date has to be effaced in order to be reiterated (31). Like *MP*, Derrida distinguishes territorial "calendar time" (41, following Heidegger's critique of the calendar[16], which Derrida in other ways problematizes) from deterritorialized dating time.
4 The date begins by enunciating an "ideality" (65), as in *MP*'s incorporeal transformations. It then passes through "bodies" (106), introducing "infinitely small differences" into a temporal field of event-variations (109). Finally, the date "re-opens" history (110–12), making history within history without deriving from history (112), much like the way *MP*'s diagrams make history from an immanent outside.

There are six differences:

1 In Derrida, something written on a certain date has another date *to* which it is written (21), a "*destinataire*" (107), a destiny, a "secret meeting" at another date to which it "allies itself" (24). Derrida concentrates on recipients; Deleuze and Guattari on composition. This is a difference between phenomenological and transcendental analysis. Of course, even for Derrida, we cannot determine the "proper" *destinataire*. But for Deleuze and Guattari, the date seems more impersonal, and perhaps more available. (Part of our problem is getting Deleuze, Derrida, and Hegel to be destinations for each other.)[17]
2 When a poem includes a date at the top of the page, Derrida says that the date "wounds" it (36). On the one hand, the date marks the event for good. The date itself "cannot be dated": the date cannot go out of date (32). But on the other hand, the mark is "a date of what does *not* come back" (37). For while dating an event is a code that tells successors what context to put it in, it omits features of the event that were not part of the dating-context, and those lost features haunt (as a "spectre" (37), or as "cinders" (40)) its subsequent reception. The question of loss is not a typical Deleuze and Guattarian theme.
3 How hard is it to "read" a date (70), given its uncontrollable number of referents? "July 14" will name the dates of all revolutions, including dates that are not July ("July is not July" (64)). For Deleuze and Guattari, multiplicity is not generally seen as a risk. For Derrida, it risks a tragic alternative: either the date gives specific meanings to a small number of people and times, "encrypting" the event within an inaccessible tomb; or else it gives no specific meaning, in which case the event waits for no one in particular, and no one needs to revive it.
4 Who is in a position to interpret a date? "Schibboleth" is a password:

when the Hebrews heard the Ephraimites pronounce it, they knew who was who. Derrida is interested in the almost unnoticeable, untranslatable difference in vocalization. And he is interested in the personal quality of having been chosen for, or excluded from, something. The date, he says, is the "memory of the not-chosen" (90); unlike *MP*, he says that a date affirms an unchosen burden. Since this is also what it means to be Jewish, "formally, at least, the affirmation of Judaism has the same structure as the date" (90). It is always difficult to decide who is the stranger and who has been chosen to receive a certain date. For Derrida, the date, even when available, is more foreign than hermeneutics can handle. In *AO*, foreignness is a segregation machine, an exclusive disjunction that repels certain interpretations. But in *AO*, it is also possible to overturn segregation by an inclusive schizo synthesis, a minoritarian becoming-foreigner available to anyone. For Derrida, one cannot simply switch in and out of the thrownness of being-foreign. Can a theory of relative distance account both for Derridian non-communicability and Deleuze and Guattarian common diagrams for non-dialoguing series?

5 The *destinataire* of a date is highlighted, in *Schibboleth*, by the role of the rabbi (*S* 108–9). As in *MP*, transmission depends on passing through small differences; but in Derrida, the rabbi, not a calculus, is the intercessor. Differences do not take the form of particles that fit anywhere, but of Talmudic readings that penetrate a particular passage. Derrida seems a particularist relative to Deleuze and Guattari's univocity of being. But with respect to embedded expressions, Derrida seems a holist relative to Deleuze and Guattari's atomism. This is oversimplified, but the problem is the way in which the relay across two dated events introduces thirds. In neo-Platonism, the first event introduces a dated gap between a finite being and Being, and from that moment, subsequent contingencies follow; the first finite event is a gap that time falls into.[18] The first is Being, the second is finitude, the third is the interpretation of Being throughout the rest of time. The third (indirect discourse) is the interpretant (the rabbi) who passes the date along. Because there must be an interpreter, the first and second are rendered foreigners to each other. For Derrida (like Hegel's priest-intercessor in the *Phenomenology*, paragraph 228), the rabbi's role is to point to the failure of his role as interpreter. Therefore, the receiver of the date searches for something in it that is not there. Ritually cut off from its context, "the circumcision of a word is not dated in history" (112).

Our question is what happens between the original dating of an event (when Lenin dates 23 July 1917) and our affirmation of it (when *MP* in 1980 invents the theory of the "Lenin-abstract machine"). Do assemblages need intercessors?

6 Derrida says that (a) an event is dated; (b) it is not dated *in* history; and (c) its date *opens* history. Deleuze and Guattari say something similar, but

what is the status of the date "oustide" history that intervenes in history? Perhaps each event begins outside history, then becomes historical. But why would it? If history comes into the picture too late, after events are defined, then dates will not structure the events themselves, which both Derrida and Deleuze and Guattari are aiming at. Instead of saying that dating is outside history, perhaps it would be better to say that it transforms a historical sequence from its inside. For Derrida, dating grounds history in a Husserlian paradoxical way: it subjectively grounds history as an objective being in the world. For Deleuze, dating grounds history in a Hegelian paradoxical way: it accidentally actualizes a potential and makes time the necessary essence of events. Deleuzian Hegelianism might help us to interpret Derrida's statement that the very issue of dating becomes an issue *at* a certain date in history (31). History itself becomes historical at a certain moment of history. This is obviously Hegel.

HEGEL

For Hegel, while it is better to know how to date history than not to know, the date is only a stage in historical consciousness. Dates are ultimately obstacles both to the science of history and to human progress. At a certain date, history passes out of dates. Yet Hegel's anti-date argument will help us solve Deleuze's problem of date-determinacy.

I will analyse seven topics in Hegel's theory of dates: (1) Arguments against dates; (2) Pre-dating civilizations; (3) Cross-cultural dates; (4) Death; (5) Modernity; (6) Repetition; and (7) Destiny.

(1) Arguments against dates

Hegel has two arguments that dates are unphilosophical.

First argument: "philosophical history" takes up contingent events and exhibits their rationality (*PH* 29). It is interested in the Idea in an event, not the "day" it happens. Events have dates, but knowing them has little value. The modern age – Hegel calls it the "new time" – is beyond dates. Hegel's *Philosophy of History* cites surprisingly few dates; indeed, for long sections it contains surprisingly little history. The text often describes social structures rather than events, more as spiritual topology than history. However, Hegel wants to say not only that the Ideas of events belong to "eternal reason", but also that a world-historical event occurs "in" its time (52). To reconcile these two theses, there must be temporal *distance within* eternity. Hegel has the same problem explaining historical distance as does Deleuze.

Second argument: history is the narrative of what happens, and not the simple fact of what happens (60). On this argument, events do not even have single dates; they span the temporal distance between dater and dated.

(2) Pre-dating civilizations

Pre-historical cultures have no state (no unbiased records), no prose (no demythologized history), no Law (no judgment of precedent) no abstraction (no measure of time), no historical self-consciousness (no distinction between dater and dated), and no future (no drive to a new now) (60, 111, 161).

It was a major advance when ancient civilizations started recording dates in annals. The first great advance in record keeping introduced a "fixed era" (164) beginning at Year 0, often tied to a mythical event – the founding of a city, or the creation of the world. Adding speculative imagination into the annals in this way may seem more creatively interpretative than merely recording factual king-lists (165). But when a culture does not narrate its own names and numbers accurately, it is left to another culture to do so on its behalf (164). And cross-cultural intervention in dating is time-warfare.

(3) Cross-cultural dates

Hegel's *PH* names 62 dates. (I counted.) Most are given by year, but some designate stretches of time, and others are relative expressions like "at an earlier date" (230). When Hegel says that Alexander's beauty "has not been seen a second time" (273), something like a date is implied. Twenty of Hegel's explicit dates refer to the founding of civilizations (secular or religious); thirty-three to wars (including peace treaties) or other acts of violence; nine to cross-cultural explorations. Three refer to the "modern age". All of these categories are cross-cultural. It is not just that dates designate violent changes. They designate the specific violence of crossover points between cultures. Dates are for this reason inherently disputable (298). In a few cases, Hegel gives two alleged dates for the same event (117, 165, 186), or dates an event by both Roman and Christian calendars (298).

"Periods" define explicitly what dates refer to implicitly, namely that a culture's history is its interaction with others. Each culture passes through three periods: a period of emergence, a period of overcoming its predecessor, and a period of engendering its successor (224). The period suggests a Hegelian solution to the determinacy of dates. Events are ordered not by dates in annals, but by their order in the spiritual development of Mind (though Hegel admits that primitive and advanced civilizations can get chronologically out of synch). This appears to provide a time arrow and give each local event in each culture's history a destiny. The date becomes purposive, not just instantaneous. Whatever problems there might be in matching up calendars, if the philosophical historian understands that world-spirit moves in the direction of self-conscious freedom, she will know what happened before what.

(4) Death

Periodicity is historical because cultures die. "The Persians are the first historical people; Persia was the first empire that passed away" (173). Spirit has to free itself from its own traditions, to recognize its freedom by letting past stages fall into the past (221). Constitutional unions are "modern" precisely because their fragility lets them decompose when it is time for a successor[19] to destroy them. Dating events by their transitions has a retroactive time arrow. Persia was historical not so much because its own people knew that it would pass away, nor because we know it, but because its neighbours knew it. For Deleuze, the date turns death into a variable; for Hegel, it turns the neighbour into a killer.

If the date of Persia's death begins history in the full sense, a second death ends history: the death of the Church. With the end of the Crusades, Hegel says, "we may date the commencement of self-reliance and spontaneous activity . . . Christendom as a whole never appeared again on the scene of history" (393).

In addition to pre-dates, annal dates, and death dates, we now add the act-date. This is the deed-act of absolute idealism set to history. A declaration of the form "starting now, we act spontaneously" is even less driven by content than "starting now, the Soviet Union exists". It dates nothing but its freedom to inaugurate. It is a date for-itself, the only case when the narration of the dated occurrence coincides with the occurrence to be dated.

The positions of Hegel and Deleuze have reversed. Hegel's theory of periodicity seemed a way of keeping dates in order. But the new date, the modern date, cuts itself loose from content and from precedents. Every modern affirmation affirms the same pure freedom, whether it takes place in 1204 or 1791.

(5) Modernity

In Hegel's *PH*, all world-periods have geo-cultural proper names (Oriental, Greek, Roman, German) except for "The New Time" (*Die neue Zeit*). Only modernity is designated temporally. It is as though time does not fully exist in certain places, and as though time fully exists only at certain times. This means that history is not the succession of world-cultures starting at the beginning of the past. Rather, all of history is about the modern present constituting events as spontaneous moments in the eternal self-definition of reason.

While Hegel's chapter on the new time discusses events that are not at all vague (the Reformation, the Revolution, and the constitutional debates "with which history is now occupied, and whose solution it has to work out in the future" (452)), there are only two dates cited in the chapter. One is 1780, the date of the last witch burning, a throwback (427). The second, the only actual date in modernity, is 1791 (444), the year of the "*Droits de l'homme et du citoyen*", the year when the rational became real. There is no need to name or date additional examples. Every free act from now on is an expression of the rights of man, and every date from now on is superimposed on to 1791. The very moment when history becomes fully temporal, and ceases to be geo-cultural, is the moment that time switches over from succession to co-existence. It is the only truly temporal event, and already the first, and the only, post-historical event.

(6) Repetition

The proviso to the thesis that there is only one fully historical date is that historical events depend on repetition. Speaking of Caesar, Hegel says:

> In all periods of the world a political revolution is sanctioned in men's opinions when it repeats itself. Thus Napoleon was twice defeated, and the Bourbons twice expelled. By repetition, that which at first appeared merely a matter of chance and contingency becomes a real and ratified existence. (313)

A revolution that takes place once is not a revolution: it is an abstraction that no one follows. Only when asserted for the second time does the event take bodily form, and transform chance into destiny.

Of course, there are many types of repetition. The type of repetition in the middle period of Rome is revolutionary. But at the beginning and the end of Rome, we find counter-revolutionary repetitions and destinies. At the beginning, Roman repetition is "an iron power", "crushing destiny" (277), repetition reduced to tyranny. In the last period of Rome, we find image-worship repeated long after people should have known better (Emperor Leo banned it in 754; Irene restored it in 787; the losers were beaten annually (340)). Revolutionary repetition ought not to have iron law as its first stage and stagnant images as its last stage; it ought to remain revolutionary throughout, a repetition of spontaneity without an image. Caesar is evidently not a pure case of this. But to the extent that the destiny of Rome is not to crush its enemies but to revolt, Rome will figure as the category of repeatability in all revolutions, the figure that leads Napoleon to picture himself as Caesar.

(7) Destiny

"Fate" is a Greek idea involving the outcome of passion. "Providence" is a religious idea involving the unfolding of a seamless whole. "Destiny" is a modernist idea involving the new life of the names of history.

On the names of history, Hegel says:

> It is as much an act of thought – of the understanding in particular – to embrace in one concept an object which comprehends a concrete and large significance [or "rich content"] (such as Earth, Man – Alexander or Caesar) and to designate it by one word – as to *resolve* such a conception – duly to isolate the conceptions which it contains, and to give them particular names. (68)

Reason apprehends that "Caesar" is not the name of a person, but the name of a "large significance" with a multiplicity of virtual components. Caesar becomes a name of history when spirit contemplates Caesar as one of its destinies (73). Spirit becomes all the names of history as co-existing species of spontaneity.

Hegel distinguishes three eras in history (75–9): the era of Chronos, in which each regime (*Reich*) falls to its successor against its will; the era of Zeus, the "political god" who "constrains time" (76) by giving each nation its proper spirit; and modernity, whose past is its "eternally present" destiny (79). The destinies of spirit are not constrained by time: "nothing in the past is lost for it . . . The life of this ever present spirit is a circle of progressive embodiments, which looked at in one aspect still exist beside each other, and only as looked at from another point of view appear as past" (79).

"Progress" is stranger than we usually think. We often read Hegel as saying that Persia leads to Greece, which leads to Rome, and so on. But that kind of sequencing is what Hegel calls "succession", precisely the opposite of progress. When Hegel says that "nothing in the past is lost", the present has not so much overcome the past as simply made a single co-existence out of past and present. Again, we often think that for Hegel each culture represents one stage in world-history, but Hegel no more individualizes cultures than time-periods.

On the very points where Hegel and Deleuze are usually contrasted (including by Deleuze), they are in fact using opposite terms to do similar work.[20] What Deleuze calls the "pure past" does what Hegel's "eternal present" does. What Deleuze calls the "body without organs" is what Hegel calls "embodiment". What Deleuze calls the labyrinth of the straight line is what Hegel calls the circle of progress: both oppose the teleology of satisfying lacks and compensating for losses, and both affirm the omni-directional diagram in which all pathways lead through one another in thought.

Indeed, the theory of periods does not provide a hermeneutics of succession after all. We lose chronological distinctions when we arrive at modernist destination-points. We can now return to the blunt question: in what sense is Caesar before Napoleon? Deleuze seemed first to say that it is not before. Then the diagram point seemed to say it is before. But Hegel showed that the date-point cannot save succession. And this seems to mean that destiny is an eternal present with no before-after. But now, finally, it is just this anti-succession argument in Hegel, which frees the names of destiny from any succession of images, which will allow us to use Deleuze's account of destiny to solve the theory of dating.

DESTINY, DELEUZE

Deleuze says in *DR* that "successive presents each play out the same life at different levels. This is what we call a destiny (*destin*)" (*DR* 113–14). As Hegel says,[21] it is the destiny of Caesar to live out the same life again in Napoleon at a different level. In this passage, Deleuze articulates irreversibility without succession: "What we live empirically as a succession of different presents from the point of view of active synthesis, is also the always increasing (*grandissante*) co-existence of levels of the past" (113). How can we interpret this increase as a directional arrow in a context where all directions are at play at once?

We might be tempted to say that the more things that have happened in the past, the bigger the present. It is common sense that Napoleon knew of Caesar but not conversely. Yet we do model present events just as well on anticipations of future generations as on memories of past events. If increase in the influence between past and future events is mutual, then the quantitative increase in what historical characters know about the past will not generate irreversibility.

To explain irreversibility, we need to add to dates and destiny, the concept of "delay" from the third synthesis of time. The context in *DR*, as we saw in chapter 3, concerned a childhood fantasy having a delayed effect in the adult. Instead of the childhood event being the origin of the adulthood event, Deleuze conceives of the two as mutual constructions in the same unconscious. "There is no room to ask how the childhood event acts only by delay. It *is* this delay, but this delay itself is the pure form of time which makes the before and the after co-exist" (*DR* 163). The essence of the delayed effect across strictly co-existing series is that "it is not possible to consider the one as originary and the other as derived" (163). Delay contains *both* the irreversibility of before and after, *and* the simultaneity of the two: a delay is a two-termed co-existing serial distance. How can this be built into chronological dating?

Using the critique of origins and copies (in "Nietzsche and Saint Paul, Lawrence and John of Patmos", *CC*) Deleuze discusses various assemblages of names of history with their *destinataires*, from "Nietzsche and Saint Paul" (*CC* 36), to "Nero = Hitler = Antichrist" (37), to "Saint Paul, a kind of Lenin" (51), each with its own temporal schematic. Deleuze distinguishes two ways to interpret "destiny". He calls the Jewish model of destiny a "postponed destiny" (*destin différé*); it awaits something new (though it is not always free of *ressentiment*). Christian destiny programmes a return based on an original coming that it has already seen; it takes its past as a model for its future; it reverses itself in a circle. In contrast, Jewish history moves irreversibly in a diagrammatic straight line that returns to its past in the form of a difference.

Co-existent temporal seriality defines two events in each other's terms; yet it defines each by the transversals necessary to cover its distance from the other. In *PS*, Deleuze defines "transversals" as passages between two worlds functioning as multiplicities (*PS* 152–3). "Distance" is "incommensurability as non-communication" (156). By transverse lines, we might then say, the Joan of Arc effect functions emotively and iconographically on our bodies, but due to distance, it is too detached to communicate her motives to us. In contrast, when the Bush effect infiltrates our bodies, it does communicate his motives to us, whether we like it or not. This might explain both how names of history in general operate on us, and also how some but not all names of history are distant from us chronologically. "Time signifies nothing other: this system of non-spatial distances, this distance proper to the contiguous itself, or to the content itself, distances without intervals" (156). Whereas *temps perdu* "introduces distances between contiguous things", *temps retrouvé*, *DR*'s pure past, "installs a contiguity of distant things" (157). Time is neither succession nor simultaneity alone, but the transportation of differences across both space and time. The preservation of seriality in Joan of Arc's story is "the *space* of time" (157).

By rejecting the origin-copy model of priority-posteriority, we can now solve the problem of irreversibility. When one event has an irreversibly posterior relation to another, it is precisely because the posterior event is repeating something that has *not* happened.

We wanted to characterize a commonsense phenomenon usually interpreted in terms of succession, but this time in terms of distance in a logic of co-existence: namely how one event comes before another. It might have seemed that the relation between a model and a copy is an irreversible relation, but that is the circular relation. In contrast, a repetition that has nothing to repeat takes something other than itself as its predecessor. When one event takes another event *not* as a model, then it takes it as something to increase. Hence, Napoleon comes after Caesar just to the extent that Caesar never took place, or to the extent that Caesar takes place simultaneously with, and not before, the Napoleon that replaces it. Let us emphasize this point: Napoleon is after Caesar only if Caesar is not before Napoleon. Of two dates, the prior is the one that is most in flux for the other. If what one wants is to repeat a virtuality and not a model, it is easier to repeat a future event, which is by nature indeterminate, than to repeat a previous event whose facts are given. The earlier event has to be made earlier by the force of its successor's attempts to resist identifying with it.

We can schematize the situation this way. Authentic repetition makes an irreversible past out of an event whose virtuality it actualizes. But an agent who thinks he repeats a past by copying its model performs more authentic repetition on the future than he does on the past. Conversely, revolutionaries (schizos and world-historical individuals) know that the pure past is virtual material, so what they authentically repeat as past *is* the past. This means that while non-revolutionaries claim they know that Caesar is before Napoleon by common sense – by date numbering or by content accumulation – in fact they keep circling back to the same old Caesar and in spite of themselves have no sense of the time arrow. Only the revolutionary knows that time moves forwards.

As long as we try to define earlier and later in terms of causal impact, or content-similarity, or formal date-enumeration, we are unable to protect date-determinacy from the fluctuations of variation-diagrams. Date-distances are determinate only at the moment when two events are put into contact with one another, as the delays immanent in the date-transversal. It is only once we push the flux of event-dating to the limit, varying even date-points in the co-existence-point of modernity, that we can rediscover a kind of date-measure at the purely virtual level. We solve the problem of date-determinacy, thanks to the way Deleuze's concept of increase completes Hegel's concept of progress, after Hegel's concept of modernity completes Deleuze's concept of simultaneity.

NOTES

1   An early version of this chapter was published as Lampert (2002).
2   François Le Lionnais (1973, p. 23).
3   Deleuze and Guattari offer several vague dates as well, as when they refer to the Scythian development of writing "towards the fourth and third centuries BC", and to Danish monumental inscriptions "in the ninth century AD" (both at *MP* 500). Most explicit references to dates in *MP* involve language in one way or another.
    In *FB* (66–7), Deleuze says one can "date the diagram of a painter, since there is always a moment at which the painter confronts it most directly". "Moment" suggests instantaneity, but van Gogh's moment "starts from 1888".
4   Deleuze and Guattari date their Plateaus by the Christian calendar. Their reservoir of case studies contains many non-European events, and their theory of minorities has implications for cross-cultural analysis (including the discussion of "Black English" in "Postulates"). Employing non-Christian calendars should have value for schizo-dating.
5   In the "Conclusion" Plateau (638), Deleuze and Guattari list four "tensors of expression": "indefinite article, proper name, infinitive, and date". On dates and proper names, see *Pp* (51).
6   In *QP* (57), concepts are said to emerge at dates. If the same concept emerges at different dates, we can say equally that there is (a) one concept at two dates, or (b) two different

and discontinuous times making up the same date, or (c) the creation of a new date that is neither the first time nor the second but a new kind of time (and a new kind of number) that did not exist before: "Each concept is a *chiffre* that did not pre-exist" (73).

7   Jules Michelet (1952, p. 290).
8   The distinction between expression and content is one of the most important in Deleuze's work. It structures the relations between sense and things in *LS*, between the sayable and the visible in *F*, and between thought and extension in the Spinoza books and *P*; it is essential to many Plateaus; it is named in the first chapter of *Kafka*, who is named on the first page of *F* precisely in relation to enunciations and contents. It offers the only hope of understanding anything at all in Guattari.
9   Sartre (1943, p. 73) talks of having a date with one's future. Facticity is dated, but choice is not (p. 122). He accuses Bergson of letting the past "remain 'in its place' at its date for eternity" (p. 152). (Deleuze in *C2* (106–7) says the opposite of Bergson regarding dates.) Sartre accuses Husserl's retentions of the same thing, i.e. of "maintaining [acts of consciousness] at their date" (p. 152). Instead, dates should "turn the flow of 'nows' backward" (p. 155). They should let us be (not have) our past (p. 157). Sartre shares with Deleuze the idea that dating breaks an event into two parts, one of which stays in the past while the other is set loose to become "simultaneous" with the present (p. 165).
10 Hélène Cixous (1998, p. 69), discussing Derrida's theory of dates in *Schibboleth*, cites Stendhal's remark: "I am suddenly already to be fifty."
11 In *NP*, Deleuze uses the term "trace" to refer to the teleological ("Hegelian") history that subordinates activity to a pre-determining past and future. "Trace" is contrasted with "map" (as in *MP*, "Introduction") and "diagram". But in "Postulates", "trace" is associated with diagram.
12 Deleuze and Guattari start with Chomsky, and then develop their own categories. The "generative" property of a regime of signs begins with the generation of sentences, but sets of sentences then generate mixed regimes – sentences that vary beyond the rules that seemed to define them (*MP* 140f.). The "transformational" property of the regime of signs concerns the mutual "translation" of regimes. The "diagrammatic" property extracts sign-particles for free use. The "machinic" property assembles potentials.
13 "The abstract machine is like the diagram of an assemblage. It traces the lines of continuous variation, while the concrete assemblage treats the variables, organizes their very diverse relations in function of these lines. The assemblage negotiates the variables on this or that level of variation, following this or that degree of deterritorialization, in order to determine those which enter into constant relations and obey obligatory rules, and those on the contrary which serve as fluid matter of variation" (126–7).
14 This point is emphasized by Jean-Clet Martin (1998).
15 "What a curious and twisting line was 1968, the line of a thousand aberrations ..." (*F* 51).
16 Heidegger, *Being and Time* (1927), s. 79: "The 'now', the 'then', and the 'on that former occasion' thus have a seemingly obvious relational structure which we call '*datability*' [*Datierbarkeit*]. Whether this dating is factically done with respect to a 'date' on a calendar, must still be completely disregarded."
17 For an excellent treatment of similar issues in Benjamin, see Françoise Proust (1994, pp. 26–35), "Dates et lieux, allégories de l'histoire".
18 See my "Origen on Time" (1996). This would be the neo-Platonic theory of the date.
19 In this passage, Persia dies at the hands of Greece. But in the chapter on Egypt, Egypt is the synthesis of Persian and Eastern civilizations (*PH* 198). It is not a problem that the same civilization is appropriated by a plurality of successors. It is odd, though, that Hegel locates Egypt after Persia (116; see my "Hegel and Ancient Egypt" (1995b)). In any case, spirit-dates take precedence over calendar dates.

20 A small number of commentators have worked out points of contact between Deleuze and Hegel. Particularly good is Juliette Simont, along with Pierre Verstraeten and Veronique Bergen, as well as Catherine Malabou.
21 Deleuze criticizes Hegel for having a merely teleological conception of "destiny" (*QP* 91), but their usages are similar.

6 Quasi-Causes and Becoming-Causal

In the previous chapter, I considered how incorporeal enunciations engage bodily states of affairs. In the third synthesis of time in *DR*, I touched on Deleuze's concept of the "quasi-cause" – the schema whereby the event of the future searches through the past in order to satisfy desire, without being causally determined by it. *LS* connects incorporeality with quasi-causality. I am interested in how historical causality is quasi-causal. But while *LS* deals very concretely with a few of its topics (certain literary texts, and certain Lacanian motifs), its treatments of history, and of quasi-causality generally, are rather abstract. As a result, my treatment of quasi-causality is on the abstract side as well, though at the end of this chapter, I set the stage for some concrete issues concerning quasi-causal history from Deleuze's *F*. My next three chapters raise concrete issues of history.

Even though quasi-causality must be a virtual effect independent of causality, it must in some sense engage particular bodies and particular social situations, and so it must in some sense be found in causality. It is said to "counter-effectuate" causality, i.e. to produce events with the power to de-reify themselves. But on my interpretation, counter-effectuation has to be *effective* counter-effectuation. The idea of a quasi-cause is already paradoxical: a cause that is not causal. I will refer to non-causal quasi-causes, which are causally non-causal, as "becoming-causal": virtual causality at the level of actuality. My goal is to use this notion to explain how actual history obeys quasi-causes, and to ask whether causal history is deterritorialized by a history of quasi-causes.

Following the path of *LS*, in the early part of this chapter it will seem that quasi-causality is strictly opposed to the concept of history. But we will find that *LS* uses the notion of "strange objects" (like the "strange histories" in *DR*) to create a quasi-causal sense of history, which I will call serial simultaneity. Indeed, the whole of *LS* is, on my reading, divided into two parts. The first part, Series 1–26, demonstrates the incorporeal quasi-cause; the second part, Series 27–34, describes the corporeal bodies that incorporeal enunciations have their quasi-effects on. Like all of Deleuze's texts, *LS* has many simultaneous agendas; I will focus uniquely on the one I have just described.

At various points in *LS*, Deleuze suggests that the theory of quasi-causes has ethical implications for deterritorializing power relations. I will say a few words about the ethics of counter-effectuation, using problems raised by the beat poet Ed Sanders on how to avoid "sleazo inputs".

Finally, as a running motif, I will use the trope that *LS* begins with: Alice in Wonderland drinks a potion that makes her become larger and smaller at the same time. This simultaneity of contrary processes is a model of counter-effectuating, simultaneous sequentiality. I offer 13 interpretations of what Deleuze could mean by this trope, each of which adds something to a definition of quasi-causal history.

The first lines of *LS*, under the heading, "Paradoxes of Pure Becoming", present the Alice in Wonderland theory of history:

> In *Alice*, as in *Beyond the Looking Glass*, there is a category of very special things: events, pure events. When I say, "Alice gets larger", I mean that she becomes larger than she was. But thereby, she becomes smaller than she is now. Of course, it is not in the same time that she is larger and smaller. But it is in the same time that she becomes so. She is larger now; she was smaller before. But it is in the same time, in one blow, that one becomes larger than one was, and that one constitutes oneself as smaller than one becomes. Such is the simultaneity of a becoming whose property is to elude the present. Insofar as it eludes the present, becoming does not tolerate the separation or the distinction between before and after, past and future. It belongs to the essence of becoming to move and to pull in both directions at once: Alice does not get larger without getting smaller again, and vice versa. Good sense is the affirmation that in all things there is one determinable direction [or sense, *sens*]; but paradox is the affirmation of two directions at once. (9)

Alice becomes larger and smaller at the same time. Madness. In programmatic terms, this is possible because language introduces virtualities that counter-effectuate bodily states. Language, particularly literature, *selects* enunciations to be expressed in events. Literature, therefore, is ethics. Ethics *distributes* divergences along series of events. Ethics, therefore, is history. History permits incorporeal quasi-causes to *propagate* as if causally. History, therefore, is deterritorializing power. Madness, literature, ethics, history, and power, therefore, are defined by the quasi-cause.

The effect of bodies on bodies is causal; the effect of statements on statements is semiotic; the effect of statements on bodies is quasi-causal. Quasi-causality is an effect of the interaction of heterogeneous series. How can incorporeal events have an impact on corporeal entities in general?

I am interested not just in the general question of how senses attach to states of affairs, but also in why some particular sense attaches to some particular thing. The theory that explains general quasi-causality makes specific quasi-causality problematic. The former depends on bodies being unstable, so that a sense can be either attributed to (in static genesis), or emerge from (in dynamic genesis), the swirling part-objects in the depths of a body. Similarly, general quasi-causality depends on senses being neutral as to which bodies they might apply to. But if bodies are unstable and senses are neutral, then it would seem that any sense can give meaning to any state of things, that any enunciation, without effort, produces any result desired, and that quasi-causality is indeterminate. This is not the conclusion Deleuze is aiming at. On the contrary, he says that events must be selected, that events are precisely what prevents states of things from overflowing without measure (173). Indeed, we will find, getting lost in the "grand mélange" of bodies is what makes us susceptible to sleazo inputs.

What are the mechanisms of selection of a quasi-cause? The problem has three levels: how bodies *prepare* to be quasi-caused; how events *select* bodies to quasi-cause; and how sense events *communicate* with one another. The level of preparation will be explained by castration; the selection of bodies will be explained by incompossibility; communication will be explained by immanent destination. What is at stake is a concept of history, namely the performative that makes an occurrence into a historical event, and the virtual effects that make an event return in other times and places. How do quasi-causes, for example, explain why the Joan of Arc effect arises in some bodies but not all? Of course, one could claim that they do not explain it, that once quasi-causes take effect, causal history simply becomes a chaotic field of shared time in which anything can be the cause of anything. But this would not do justice to the specificity of the politicians or the schizos who identify themselves with the great warrior of history, or to Deleuze's careful mappings of machinic assemblages. What we need for a theory of causality at a distance is neither a tracing of successive states nor an indeterminate flux where all events are crushed into one. Like any revolutionary, what I want to know is: why is this happening to me now? And I want to know how to experiment with causality.

The argument for quasi-causality in *LS* presupposes the three-part theory of time in *DR*, which is formulated in *LS* by the two-part distinction between Chronos and Aion. In a nutshell: there exist events in a temporality defined by contemporaneity rather than succession.

Given that theory of time, we can now start to analyse Deleuze's case study: Alice becomes larger and smaller at the same time. Already in Series 1, this can mean three things.

First, the commonsense meaning is that if something *can* become larger, then it can also become smaller. In principle, any species of change is neutral (also 46), in that change can occur in either direction. As we saw in chapter 1, this is a principle of classical physics, and only thermodynamics and nonsense literature provide counter-examples. Žižek reads the passage this way: becoming larger and smaller at the same time means that the outcomes of an event are indeterminate.[1] The present is equally consistent with one past and future as with another. This is a plausible account on its own terms, based on coexisting future possibilities. But to interpret the text, we need to say not only how Alice can have different potentials at the same time, but also how she can become different things at the same time.

Second, it can mean that becoming is an indifferent flux. There are occasionally reasons to interpret Deleuze as saying that becoming is undifferentiated – an interpretation associated with Badiou. On that interpretation, flux is never measurable or definable, hence neither large nor small. Here, the reversibility of larger and smaller does not follow from a whole that includes both, or from a potential that allows both, but from an indifference to both. But this interpretation entails that Alice, at the moment of becoming, is *neither* larger nor smaller, rather than both, which is what Deleuze says. Flux interpretations of Deleuze never work.

Third, it could mean that once something changes size, then there is one time at which it is larger than it is at another time. Though the different sizes are actualized at different times, the durational series as a whole includes both of those times. The past and future are included in the duration of becoming, hence, following Bergson, becoming qualitatively includes both the larger and the smaller phases. So insofar as we grasp the whole time of becoming, Alice is *both* larger and smaller at that same time. On this reading, there is a time arrow to Alice's change of size, but it is contracted into simultaneity (see Argument 1a of *DR*, my chapter 3). But this interpretation only says that over a stretch of successive moments, becoming includes larger and smaller states. We need to explain how Alice actually becomes larger and becomes smaller simultaneously.

The relation between succession and simultaneity is always difficult to sort out. At first, it seems obvious that the realm of corporeal causes operates according to succession. (Alice becomes larger and smaller in turn, not simultaneously). In contrast, incorporeal senses (or noemata, or meanings) co-exist. However, what Deleuze says in Series 2 is that causality produces the mélange of the present, whereas it is becoming that divides into past and future. That is, causality for Deleuze is a homogeneous series of states of things that mix into and generate alterations in each other, totalizable in principle as one whole occurrence over time; whereas sense-effects are singular meanings that draw states of affairs from distinct times into a common interpretation, retroactively attracting precedents towards the meanings that result from them (in the way that the meaning of "Guilt", in Kafka's *The Trial*, retroactively attracts the actions of the defendant towards the verdict). The idea that a single sense gathers states of affairs from different times into a common becoming is as crucial to the definition of quasi-causality as the idea of incorporeal enunciation. But with this in mind, contrary to first appearances, it is the causal series that sounds like simultaneity, and the series of senses that sounds like a succession of past-future. Of course, both must be both: a succession of causes co-exists in that the order of bodily states is homogeneous; the simultaneity of senses is successive in that it pulls heterogeneous series into communication.

This produces a **fourth** interpretation of Alice becoming larger and smaller simultaneously, no longer as a fact about the size of her body, but as a fact about sense, i.e. about the way her body can be expressed in language. Senses determine the meaning of, and in that way quasi-cause, what there is. Anything of which largeness can be said is something of which smallness can also be said. Therefore, senses quasi-cause a body to become larger and smaller simultaneously.[2] The series of bodily causes is a series of one-term entities (body causes body); in contrast, the series of senses is a series of two-term entities (one sense expressing a body interprets another sense expressing a body). Causes generate causes, but senses quasi-cause both causes and effects. In other words, the series of causes and quasi-causes are not symmetrical. It is not that causes generate effects and effects realize causes; the sense-effects in question cannot cause anything – they are just the content expressed in propositions, and they cannot push bodies from one place to another. Obviously, it is not the increasing size of Alice's body at present that causes it to shrink later; but it is also not merely that the meaning of the word "large" implies the meaning of "small". Neither body alone nor sense alone causes this simultaneity. But realizing what it means to have become large may be the hinge between body and sense that pushes Alice to try to become smaller again.

Hence, the first articulation of the quasi-cause, namely as the non-productive expression that attributes meaning to bodies, is replaced by a second, which takes the non-parallel structure of the two series into account. The attribution of sense to bodies consists not in describing bodies in words, but in assembling series of bodies and words in such a way that an element from one switches to the other in mid-series. In Series 27–34, dynamic genesis explains how bodies generate senses, but static genesis, in Series 1–26, starts with separate senses and bodies and asks how the former attach to the latter. Static genesis begins with "strange objects" (Series 6–9).

There are three conditions of a hinge-point between senses and bodies (54). First, both need to be variable. Second, variation needs to "orient" some direction of continuation. But while variation and orientation allow for circulations within each series, "communication" between the two requires, third, that each series includes built-in transit-junctions, or empty place-holders. Within a series of successive causes, a moment indifferent to succession – a time not filled with time-content – makes before and after circulate at the same time. The quasi-cause is this empty or neutral moment of time. Alice becomes larger and smaller at the same *time*, in a **fifth** sense, just because strictly speaking there *is* no such time; i.e. because variation can be pushed to a paradoxical point, an "event".

How do floating signifiers and ramifications constitute an oriented history?

Deleuze says that "structure includes . . . a whole history that is internal to it" (66). We might think of a quasi-cause as the moment at which Joan of Arc becomes a phantasm that anyone can live through. Such a moment begins with a particular Joan of Arc action, yet operates by way of variability. Qua phantasms, hinge-events co-exist at all times, without regard to their original manifestation. But how is this a "whole history"? What can Deleuze be referring to as the history of quasi-causal events?

The relevant passage in Series 9 says that, "If the singularities [points of converging or diverging variations] are the true events, they communicate in one and the same Event, which never stops redistributing them; and their transformations form a *history*" (68). In one way, each sense is a distinct quasi-cause that expands into particular ramifications; in another way, every quasi-cause is the same one. For the empty square that allows a sense to attach itself to a body also allows other senses to attach to the same body, and allows senses to pertain to each other through that body. The black box on the causal series makes all parts of the body subject to quasi-causality.

As in Kant, quasi-causality depends on there being loose points in the causal chain. There are four things we generally say about causality: that it is rule-governed, that it follows mechanical sequences, that it builds parts into wholes, and that it yields results. In fact, none of these is meaningful unless each singular point can diverge variably. There are no rules unless there are multiple applications; no mechanisms without surrounding inputs; no parts without divisibility; and no results without further results. Therefore, even normal physical causes are grounded not in the particulars of a situation but in a virtual system. A causal relation operates in bodies precisely when the cause is not exhausted in a present fact, or in other words, when what is present is only a "sign" of the cause (78) – when the real cause is a sense and not a body, a virtual multiplicity and not a proximate entity; in short, when the ground of the cause is a quasi-cause. At first, the concept of quasi-causality seemed almost a misnomer, having little to do with causality. Now it appears as the force of variability behind all particular causal relations. But as a consequence, we have to account quasi-causally for what causality is usually called upon to explain, namely how one thing happens after another – in short, for history.

Now, if communication across events is carried across an empty present (one of Deleuze's definitions of Aion), then causal force is not a mechanism, but pure variablility, or pure temporality. Clearly, a mechanism could not make a body expand or contract unless there were a time in which the change could occur; but once there is time, then no local chronology can circumscribe the limits to the impact that a past event can have upon the present and future. Aionic temporality is not only the form by which senses quasi-cause event-divergence; it is the force behind the operation of quasi-causality. Alice (in the **sixth** sense) becomes larger because each movement extends into a more than maximal time, and smaller because each movement subsists in less than minimal time (75). On this reading, the story of Alice becoming larger and smaller is an allegory for larger and smaller temporal contractions.

The neutral hinge explains some things about how events are assembled in time. But what of the histories of those assemblages? It seems we cannot ask about normal, successive time-order at the level of quasi-causes. Determinate sequences of bodily causes are not represented at that level; they appear only once a limited noematic sense has already been selected and a field of entities measured. Yet there has to be a selection of senses, the kind of search engine that *DR* implied, whose ordering we can ask about. To put it bluntly, even though a temporal hinge-point can attribute an Alice phantasm to my body, as well as a Joan of Arc effect and a Lenin abstract machine, in any order, it should still make a difference in which order it enacts them. Even if each event is its past as well as its future, it should make a difference which is which. Further, even if what is quasi-causing the event is not the historical individual but the conceptual persona of Alice, Joan, or Lenin, the fact that Joan of Arc activates a sixteenth-century assemblage and Lenin a twentieth-century one should be relevant to the way that they communicate in a singularity.

To develop a theory of history governed by serial simultaneity rather than succession, we need to introduce the immanence of the quasi-cause.

While the quasi-cause is virtual instead of physical, cross-temporal instead of perishing, it is nothing like a Platonic form; it is the divergence-point of an assemblage. The coordination of a series emanating from an "immanent cause" (88) is expressed by the proper name of a sense-effect. *LS* uses the same explanation as *AO* to explain the "Joan of Arc effect". The Doppler effect exists in reality nowhere else than in those occasions in which noises approach observers, yet the effect exists innumerable times whenever it repeats a corporeal series from a certain starting point. The "Joan of Arc effect" repeats a serial sense-effect that combines a religious move, a gender move, a military move, and so on. And what Deleuze calls here the "Carroll effect" (88) is a meta-repetition enacted every time an expression combines a sense-effect with a body.

The paradox of the proper name like Doppler is that no individual is rigidly designated by it. This is why Alice loses her name (Series 1) at the moment that she operates the Alice effect, and it is a **seventh** way in which she loses her largeness when she becomes large. If the proper-name effect means that "I is another", then, being schizo, a person can become larger and smaller, since some of her personalities become one thing while others become something else. It is not just that her consciousness becomes larger while her unconscious reduces to childhood; all of her is a pre-personal transcendental field subject to proper-name effects (120). Events are immanently quasi-caused by divergence on an underdetermined field, but of course, everything that actually occurs is causally determinate. Thus, Deleuze describes a "double causality" in which causes are real and quasi-causes are "fictive" (115).

The crucial question is, once the quasi-cause designates the sense of a corporeal state, has the power of the quasi-cause been exhausted? Once the empty square of signification has been filled, is it still empty? Deleuze says that each specific sense "inherits" the power of the quasi-cause. It "makes of the product something of a producer at the same time as it is produced" (116). The power of the fictive is not exhausted by territory. Other accounts of the relation between virtuality and actuality would lead either to too much stratification or to too much flux: power without variation or fiction without power. For example, if a virtual potential were uniquely represented in a particular event, then the facts of that event would harden into transcendent significance: Joan of Arc would fulfil human destiny in, and only in, its proper time. On the other hand, if a virtual potential were only accidentally instantiated in a particular event, then no affirmation would have any relevance to any other: Joan of Arc would be powerless historical fiction in her own day as much as in ours.

This is the essence of quasi-causal history. For a sense to be quasi-causal, it *really* has to effectuate itself on a causal stratum; and at the same time, it *really* has to remain in its pre-effectuated status. It has to produce a situation that effectively counters its own effectuation, a sense-effect without effect. It must do so not by producing a vague state, or an uncommitted personality, but by producing the causal efficacy of those possibilities *not* selected by its production. By selecting one possibility, the quasi-cause must preserve, at a distance, but with no less reality, the power of the possibilities that that selection excludes. This is the meaning of Deleuze's thesis that "incompossible worlds become variants of a same history" (138).

The argument that incompossibles co-exist is surprisingly simple. If two series converge, that is a real feature of the world; if one series diverges into two possible series, that is just as real. What makes the Joan of Arc effect a virtual power is not abstract "energy" (150), as if anyone could call herself Joan of Arc on a whim, but that someone who most assuredly is not Joan of Arc should assemble a Joan of Arc path not taken. On an **eighth** reading, then, Alice's becoming larger and smaller does not just refer to Alice at the pre-selection moment when she still has the energy to become either; it literally means that after Alice becomes larger, the becoming-smaller that she did *not* enact retains a force to cause her future moves. Counter-effectuation does not just mean that even after something determinate happens, it is as if no decision had yet been made. It means rather that when one determination happens, other incompatible determinations *really* happen along with it – not factually, of course (the whole point is that incompossible worlds cannot co-exist in fact), but "theatrically" (150).

It is theatre, but not a game when, as actors, we will to contradict ourselves; it is ethics. At first, variation-ethics seems to glorify the grand mélange where every event is equally good (156). But irony undermines any hope for such a totality (Series 19). What remains is to will something local with respect to a non-locality within it – not as one recognizes the whole through the part, or divines the future through the present, but as the actor detaches a theme from a performance (176). At first, morality seems like the responsibility to treat each event as a theme that ought to be "worked through" (*opérer*, 172) and represented in as many other performances as possible. Ethics is "to will the event as such" (167), to represent becoming's line of flight in a precise action. But "the event is not that which happens (the accident), but the pure expressed *in* what happens" (175).

This is an obscure passage. It makes ethics sound like taking responsibility (whatever that means) only for one's interpretations, not for the consequences of one's actions. But something more concrete is at stake. To will the event is to will *both* that a state of affairs exhibit a theme, and that the theme be represented in that state. The quasi-causal will brings bodies and senses together – not just because limited bodies need to be freed by will, and abstract will needs to be determined by bodies. A quasi-cause is revolutionary in relation to how events occur at all. A revolutionary wills that an event actually express *itself*; she wills that the event be too big for itself. The non-revolutionary feels either too big for life, when his effectuations fail to satisfy what he thought was his potential, or for the same reason he feels life is too big for him. He worries when he strays from the mean. In contrast, the revolutionary makes the event bigger, not herself. As in *DR*, the too big/too small scenarios result from tying the future too closely to the past. Alice, for the **ninth** time, becomes too large and too small in relation to the same inadequacy of her body to contain her revolutionary potential in time.

In short, to counter-effectuate, virtuality must make the actual make the virtual. It should not make actuality vanish in an unfulfillable ideal, but make actuality into *becoming*-actuality. It wills the bodiliness of the expressed in an event, even though expression can never itself be bodily; it wills the causality of that which can *only* be quasi-causal. Only in this way can the theory of quasi-causality avoid idealism, and avoid smug self-interpretations posing as revolutionary.

This is the problem of Deleuzian counter-ethics, what we might call quasi-ethics. Once actuality is cracked at the surface, how can we on the one hand preserve our beautiful souls from having their freedom limited on the guillotine, and on the other preserve our love from the blur that drinks it away? Counter-ethics must avoid both over- and under-effectuation, under the authentic humanist slogan: "Do not let being be". In short, it has to avoid the sleazo inputs.

I take the concept of "sleazo inputs" from the beat poet Ed Sanders, whose investigation of Charles Manson[3] asks how the glorious sex and drugs of beat culture (the revolutionary virtual), appropriated by the hippies, could have ended with Manson (the sleazo effectuation). In a word, it happened because in the 1950s everybody knew that poetically man dwells, but then the line of flight fell into the black hole of whatever, hence Satanism in Haight-Ashbury, sleazo inputs, Manson. California Satanism is one part reduction of freedom to facticity. (Manson tells you what your freedom means you do. In fact, that is how performatives work: free indirect discourse transmits the despot's order words (*mot d'ordre*) into your own mouth. The puzzle is not why people obey orders; everybody always obeys orders. Every cult leader who ever demanded followers got them. The puzzle is why more people don't give orders.) And it is one part reduction of the productive force of the active to a productive force of the reactive. (Manson hands you a gun and invites you to kill him. When you decline, he tells you that means he can kill you. It is the "Kill me, kill you" routine.) Finally, it is one part the neglect of poetry, since poetry is investigation.[4] Sanders frequently cites the poet Charles Olson's *Special Theory of History*: "Know the new facts early."[5] To avoid sleazo inputs, we have to know the new facts so early that we know them before they were facts, when they were still, in Deleuze's terms, quasi-causes. But at the same time, we have to know them as facts, just as we have to know "the total details of the old facts, at whatever personal cost".[6]

For Sanders, poetically knowing the new facts early leads to investigating ancient versions of Nixon as well as beatnik era Sapphos. This presupposes both the retention of quasi-causality in effectuation, and the history of quasi-causal traces. Of course, ethics through literature alone, expression without content, archive without power, fails. Which literary favourite succeeds in their line of flight: Kafka's caged animals, Fitzgerald, Biely? Expressions must find contents that are as free as they are. Knowing the new facts early is only revolutionary if cause and quasi-cause, fact and counter-fact, have a common destiny.

Series 23 thus argues that causality depends on quasi-causality, and vice versa. The causal chain as a whole is distributed throughout the mélange of bodies, but each actual causal sequence depends on distinguishing the parts of that mixture, and on measuring alterations. But the measured division into parts is a subversion of body (Argument 4a in chapter 3). It might look as though body is stable before the past and future dissipate it, before divergence contradicts it, before sense interprets it. But body would have been from the start an undifferentiated mass unless discontinuities were already subverting it. The smooth time of simultaneity and the measure of rigid succession co-exist as soon as there is a mélange. The quasi-cause is the unstated presupposition in causality, a differentiation of meaning that will have been operating before anything can have become present. The presence of quasi-causes in regular causes is what allows the Stoic sage to "identify with the quasi-cause even though the quasi-cause itself is lacking from its own identity" (196). The quasi-cause lacks identity precisely because it becomes causal the moment it divides up a body.

This argument that quasi-causes are embedded in causes is followed in Series 24 by the converse: that the quasi-cause must keep a distance from itself by way of causes. The premise, once again, is that senses operate between language and bodies, and communicate with one another by getting effectuated from one body to another. It is only through bodies that the quasi-cause operates as a "system of echos, reprises, and resonances" (199). The "positive distances" between a quasi-cause's effectuations subsist in the intervals between bodies (202). When incompossible bodily states diverge, two parts of a sense move apart from one another. It is not that quasi-causes are merely the reflections of what can and cannot happen to bodies. But they are the resonating voices that have no sense to offer unless bodies hold their shapes and distances over time.

Incompossibility is in this way the active force whereby two events communicate "by their difference" (201). Leibnizian events may communicate by intensifying different perspectives on a world they all reflect, but Nietzschian events communicate by struggling for the right to be distinct (203). Health, for example, seizes the right to have a body by wrestling the weak states to a distance. So Alice (**tenth**) becomes larger by repelling her own tendency to shrink. This is not the tautology that becoming larger means becoming less small; it is an ethics of earning the right to lord one's largeness over small enemies.

Deleuzian philosophy is not a connectionism in which everything is identified with everything. Quite the contrary, quasi-causalism affirms synthesis through self-distantiation in direction, degree, and decision. Of course, Alice does in an **eleventh** sense become larger just as long as her fellow characters are becoming smaller faster than she is, as her body represents the coordination of relative differences. But in general, what causality brings together, quasi-causality stretches apart into difference.

There finally emerges a sense, then, in which quasi-causes have a history in their immanent self-externality, that is, through the differences that they effectuate and the second-order diverging differences that they counter-effectuate in those effects.

But we still need to bring together the determinate side of quasi-causal intervention, namely how an individual at a given moment can "seize an event as another [distant] individual grafted on to him" (208), with its chaosmic side, namely how the distance between events is "paradoxically" interiorized in each. "A causes B" is to be read as an externality generated internally. In order to explain how the quasi-cause lays causality out as the externality by which it temporalizes itself internally, we need to say what is internal to causal bodies.

Series 27–34 returns to the first topics of *LS*, this time to show the genesis, or the "history" (217), of sense emerging from body. The first run-through of topics in *LS* argued for the independence of incorporeal sense. The second run-through argues that independent incorporeality pre-exists in the guise of corporeal sexuality. In particular, Series 27 on "Orality" (making subversive use of Lacan) argues that sense comes out of the mouth – the first sexual organ. Deleuze is not conceding that body is the cause of sense; he is rather asking what the body was doing to prepare, so that a sense could quasi-cause it to speak. History has to prepare, so that events will be able to erupt within it.

Alice (**twelfth**) becomes larger and smaller orally. As soon as corporeality is broken into particular bodies, each body is a part-object. The body's identity is a mere sign of ideal unity. The unity of meaning is thus from the start already lost and the body already wounded. The body has the Oedipal "good intention" to reunite its lost ideal (father) with its own wound (mother), its sign-function with its body-function. The good intention is the will to make the body become the event of body–sense convergence. The fact that this necessarily fails at the level of body means that the body has no choice but to manifest itself as thought (242). The failure in the body is depressing, but the sense of the failure, luckily, is the "castration-effect" or the "death of the father-effect" (245: what else indeed is the "Joan of Arc-effect"?). Because it defines the body as symbolic, "the phallus plays the role of the quasi-cause" (246). The quasi-cause is a castrated cause, sexual difference sublimated as phantasm (250). Thought is the play of surface phantasms *without* the good intention to reunite a family of resemblances. In turn, phantasms recur topologically rather than causally, eternally recommencing the cycle of expression effects on the body (256).

This explains what we were looking for earlier, namely the way effectuations preserve counter-effectuating power. In order for sense to attach to body in the first place, a quasi-cause has to incarnate itself by regenerating the entire genesis of oralization, symbolization, castration, cerebration, and topologization. Quasi-causality takes hold on the surface of bodies by germinating in their depths, so that by the time they become thinkable as incorporeal senses, senses will already have been invested and enveloped in corporeal causalities. This is why Deleuze claims that the quasi-cause is a "concrete counter-effectuation . . . really inscribed in the flesh" (258). The fact that sense and body run through each other in cycles without ever closing the gap between the two series means that each particular stage in the psychogenesis of meaning-in-action is a kind of madness: psychosis on the way to body, sublimation on the way to sense, and neurosis during the rotation (258–9). If the phallus stands for the madness in which each moment is either too much body and not enough sense, or vice versa, then Alice's (**thirteenth**) obsession with size is the problem of the phallus. Becoming larger and becoming smaller are not two directions on the same continuum; the large and the small (the repair and the return) are completely independent species. Hence, Deleuze says that "the whole problem is: how does the phallus make series resonate" (266). The conclusion of *LS* as a whole is that the phallus is the sense-invested, bodily zone of reiteration in which "the cause of the symptom passes to the quasi-cause of the work" (277). The formula is that castration is the intervention of language into body; cycles of symbol-making repeat again and again the history of quasi-causal effectuations, counter-effectuations, and reiterations (247).

But *LS* ends not with a formula but a problem: "the event is too soon recovered by everyday banality, or, on the other side, by the sufferings of madness" (290). Madness is ultimately not a quasi-cause; it is a sleazo output. And the fact that literature lets itself get covered over by the mere causality of madness-symptoms implies that the logic of sense is not, finally, a solution to the problem of quasi-causal history. Something else is needed in order to preserve the power of counter-effectuation in causal history and the history of concrete divergences within the quasi-cause itself. Soon after *LS*, the theory of the phallus takes a different turn in Deleuze's corpus. Interventions of body and sense need more historicity than *LS* provides. They need more than cycles of ramifications and reinvestments, of madness and poetry, more even than flows of desiring-production; they need a post-Foucauldian theory of resistance and memory.

Let us recommence the analytic cycle once again, this time recasting sense, communication, and phallus in terms of strategy, power, and fold (drawing from *F*), to add historicity to the quasi-cause.

Foucault's "greatest principle of history", according to Deleuze, is that "everything is always said in each epoch", though a subsequent listener has to know how to hear it (*F* 61). History is the process of extracting the expression from the content, which is difficult because each enunciation has "variable speakers and *destinataires*". Each epoch has its own diagram of meaningful possibilities, and the history of these different diagrams is the trans-diagrammatic diagram describing the way a *destinataire* receives a variation *as* an after-effect. The problem of history is thus, "how is non-relation a relation" (*F* 72)? The answer is that causality is a relation of exteriority (*F* 73). *F* analyses distant-event causality, following three categories: exteriority, the outside, and the fold. Causality by exteriority requires (a) that forces outside those operating in an event can be made to intervene in it, and (b) that a predecessor creates a forced movement in a successor, ordering the latter to use her own resources to deal with a problem given from the outside.

In *F*, the virtual events that conjoin externalities power up a region "outside" normal states of affairs, not just as empty hinges, but as "strategy" (*F* 80–2), using stratified assemblages to navigate uncharted territories. Distant events are the substance that quasi-causality uses in order to express what co-exists *in* an event. The outside is the "power" to internalize at a distance (*F* 79). Talking of an "outside" may at first sound ineffable, but Deleuze exemplifies the outside in terms of "institutions" (*F* 84). For what is at stake are such issues as whether prisoners can exercise the power of speech outside the walls, or whether Manson has stepped too deep into the Joan of Arc effect. *LS* can explain power-exchange and diagram-shift in terms of divergence-points, but it cannot explain how an actuality carries the memory of the line of distances that it was traversing. Adding strategy to sense – i.e. adding power to knowledge – begins to explain how "time is auto-affection" (*F* 114–15). But to turn auto-affective time into history, we need to add the third category of outsideness, namely the fold, the "inside *of* the outside" (*F* 104).

Diagram-shifts are not just strategies of causal transfer, they are also strategies of causal "resistance" (*F* 95). Force/externality is a quasi-cause intervening in bodies; power/outside is a quasi-cause communicating by intervals with another quasi-cause; resistance/fold is a quasi-cause becoming-causal, which is the structure we wanted to end up with.

When one event affects another not just by connecting externally with it, but also by introducing a germ around which another event can crystallize, then it becomes the *self*-causality of another. Topologically, it is a fold; phenomenologically, it is "memory" (*F* 105); temporally, it is simultaneity at a distance; ethically, it is care of the self. Quasi-causality turns the external causality of one event into the self-causality of another. Naive historiography treats an original event as one that emerges on its own steam, and a second, copycat event as one caused by a foreign epoch. But of course, the second event has to generate the conditions for its own occurrence, without relying on the context of the event it repeats, which *ex hypothesi* no longer exists. She who repeats Joan of Arc is even more Joan of Arc than the so-called original, since the repetition-variant is self-causing whereas the original was an accident of external conditions. To be sure, the original was already a repetition of herself the moment she began operating from her sense of herself, rather than as a milieu-ensemble. But what is important is that self-causality is quasi-causality through memory-folds.

Deleuze introduces memory to explain how Foucault, late in his career, began to write long-term, instead of short-term, histories. The long term is "co-extensive with forgetting" (*F* 115). In order to pass over intermediaries in favour of the distant past, the present needs erasing-machines. Long-term history bypasses facts of the historical milieu in order to think thematically; it must make the present forget itself in the past, and must then erase the fact that the present has forgotten much of the past (forgetting the forgetting). Investigative reporting is the science of escapology. And each hinge-point of forgetfulness is a determinate practice of experimentation. In short, historical quasi-causality is the process of event-deactivation, resource pooling, distanced re-use, and recommencement. In one direction, a causal sequence is particular and a quasi-cause extends it into multiplicities; in the other direction, a causal series is continuous and only takes shape when a quasi-cause selects a part of the mélange as a data cluster to represent a particular theme.

What we call historical causality is thus the "practice" of "conditions" (*F* 122). There is no conflict between cause and quasi-cause once we think of time as a fold for writing events into each other's problems. Like *LS*, *F* solves the relation of body and sense under the category of "thought", but whereas the former defines thought as phantasm, the latter defines it as experiment (*F* 124). A phantasm is successful on its face, whereas an experiment succeeds only if it manages to re-chain itself into assemblages of power. Each event tests whether it can resist its own effectuation. The causality of the event is solicited from within, but what it has within it is self-resistance.

The Deleuzian historian wants to do three things. First, she wants to observe the sense-effects that are omnipresent but impotent in things. Second, she wants to be the revolutionary who reorganizes bodies into war machines, whose mad science successfully attaches minds to bodies. To do this, she needs, thirdly, to know how and when a quasi-cause like the Joan of Arc effect, or like capitalism, attaches itself to particular kinds of bodies, and how to determine which quasi-causes are at work in a given assemblage. Using the theory of self-causality through memory-resistance, she needs to assess what actually quasi-causes what.[7] There are thus three tasks of quasi-causal historiography, namely to describe divergence (in relation to the present), resistance (in relation to the past), and counter- [and counter-counter-]effectuation (in relation to the future). In the next three chapters, I will work out how these categories can be applied to the question of why capitalism (as desiring-production, neo-archaism, and revolution, respectively) emerged when and where it did.

The first task of locating a quasi-causal impact involves measuring the proximity of diverging variations, mapping territories that form, collapse, and re-form around sense-effects.

The second task involves seeing how quasi-causality makes causality the effect of distance as such. It is not Joan of Arc *per se* who intervenes in me, but the difference between us. The Joan of Arc effect is the interiorization of the exterior forces emitted by it, whence the odd formula that X quasi-causes Y if and only if everything *except* X *per se* is internalized in Y. X quasi-causes Y just in case X is the intensified focal point made distant from Y by *everything* else. The real cause of Y is the one thing in Y that operates as its empty point, the one and only thing in Y that becomes mad in it. In other words, the quasi-cause is what is still making the event diverge, that in the event which resists capture. We isolate it precisely when we find what in the event persists as a non-localizable essence.

The third task is that counter-effectuation effects of causality must be seen as counter-effects and not just as counter-causes or counteractions. While the counter-effect prevents the effect from becoming *merely* a cause (though it does become cause), it must also be a real practice of resisting both bodies and senses, and even in a way resisting temporality.[8] Isolating a historical quasi-cause is inseparable from constructing divergences from it. The knowledge of quasi-causal history is the power to become a "master of one's own speed" (*F* 130), to be able to slow down the pace of history long enough to have a life, or to speed it up fast enough to have another's.

A full theory of quasi-causal history would need to pose concrete questions. Are quasi-causes cumulative in the same way that causes are? For example, if the Joan of Arc effect is enacted on a body twice in one day, is the echo strengthened? Are quasi-causes transitive? If Napoleon expresses the Joan of Arc effect, and we express the Napoleon effect, do we therefore by resonance express the Joan of Arc effect? Can Mill's methods of inductive reason distinguish the roles of several quasi-causes in the same mechanism? Has quasi-causal production changed since the Greeks? Could Joan of Arc, or capitalism, have arisen at a different time and place than it did? Such questions are possible only on condition that quasi-causality becomes-causal, if Deleuzian philosophy of history can give an account of actual historical events.

There are a number of functions that quasi-causality seemed as though it might play in a philosophy of history, which on my interpretation, it does not. It might have seemed to be a kind of free will that intervenes in causal historical sequences. It might have seemed to represent pure becomings in thought operating alongside causal history without interfering, and thus to have nothing to do with the philosophy of history. It might have seemed to refer to inexplicable eruptions of flux due purely to chance that change the course of history, or mysterious resonance effects across history – as if insufficient conditions were sufficient to cause events. On my interpretation, quasi-causality is both more concrete and more abstract than those possibilities. On my reading, actual events capture and release senses that extend beyond their normal conditions. Such procedures assemble the time-relations of events. When we talk of historical causality and its twists and turns, we are not talking about a force, or alternatively a chaotic lack of force, defining their connections. We are talking about a kind of time that folds events simultaneously into each other's processes, a universal history of machinic abstractions that lets actual events become larger and smaller at the same time.

NOTES

1. Slavoj Žižek (2004, p. 10).
2. The idea that Alice can become larger and smaller at the same time manifests the main theme in *LS*, namely that nonsense precedes sense. The basic argument is that any significant expression, e.g. "X becomes larger", presupposes that there are other possible expressions to select from. If one were to put the sum of equally possible significations into the same expression, the result would be nonsense. So analysing the construction of sense is to classify forms of nonsense.
3. Ed Sanders, *The Family* (1970). See also his *1968: A History in Verse* (1997).
4. Ed Sanders, *Investigative Poetry* (1976).

5   Edward Sanders, *The Z-D Generation* (1981, p. 1).
6   Ed Sanders, *Love and Fame in New York* (1980, p. 166).
7   Žižek (2004) thinks the Deleuzian historian ought not to ask how quasi-causes quasi-act on actual history. Citing Badiou, he distinguishes (the good) Deleuze's early concept of the virtual as "Sterile sense-event" (OwB) from (the bad Guattari-influenced) Deleuze's later concept of "productive becoming" (BwO). Žižek prefers the former (p. 30), because it is elitist and apolitical. He says that Deleuze is at an impasse between the two, and retreats into the latter in *AO* ("arguably Deleuze's worst book", p. 21). My argument for becoming-causal in *LS* aims to undermine the division. Having said that, there are superb passages in Žižek's book. At certain points, he too makes the virtual into a becoming-causal: "Virtualization and actualization are two sides of the same coin: *actuality constitutes itself when a VIRTUAL (symbolic) supplement is added to the pre-ontological real . . . actual reality is the real filtered through the virtual*" (p. 84).
8   For Zourabichvili (1998, pp. 342–4), a visionary, seeing the intolerable, first seizes on a pure potential "independent of all space-time coordinates"; second, he invents a way that space-time can be "redistributed otherwise"; third, the intensity of the potential is exhausted in its actualization, so that the new space-time is dissipated again in the intolerable.

7 Why This Now? The Problem of Actual Historical Events: the Theory of Beginnings

INTRODUCTION

I have considered what it means to order events chronologically, and what it means for events to have causes. I now consider what it means for there to be an actual historical event. To get at this, I will consider what it means to ask why an event occurs when it does.

Three texts of Deleuze and Guattari contain almost identical passages:

1 "When Etienne Balazs asks: why was capitalism not born in China in the XIIIth Century, when all the scientific and technical conditions seemed nevertheless to have been given, the response is that . . ." (*AO* 233). And later in *AO*: "Let us return to this eminently contingent question that modern historians know how to pose: why Europe, why not China?" (265).
2 "Why philosophy in Greece at such and such a moment? It is just as it is for capitalism according to Braudel: why capitalism at such places and at such moments, why not in China at some other moment, since so many of its components were already present?" (*QP* 91). And shortly afterwards, "Why capitalism in the West rather than in China in the IIIrd Century, or even in the VIIIth?" (*QP* 93).
3 "Whence the impression that historians have when they say that capitalism 'could have' been produced from that moment – in China, at Rome, at Byzantium, in the Middle Ages – that the conditions of it were given, but they were not effectuated or even effectuable" (*MP* 564).

In the next three chapters, I will analyse Chapter III of *AO*: "Savages, Barbarians, and the Civilized"; Chapter 4 of *QP*: "Geophilosophy"; and Plateau 13 of *MP*: "7,000 BC: Apparatus of Capture". These three texts deal with many of the same issues, political and ontological, involving the origin and mutation of world-historical events. The texts include only a few pages each on what I call the 'Why now?' questions, but I will thematize this question throughout in developing a philosophy of history. Each text discusses "universal history", but also many issues that I will not have time to

The Problem of Actual Historical Events: The Theory of Beginnings 115

develop (including details of Marxist economics and Freudian analysis[1]).
There are many features to discuss in the passages above.

1. All three texts begin with contingency: "Universal history is not only retrospective, it is contingent, singular, ironic, and critical" (*AO* 164, 265); "There is no universal history except of contingency" (*QP* 90; *MP* 537). We will discuss "universal history". But how there can be a 'why?' question if history is radically contingent? How there can be a 'why' question in an ontology of pure becoming?
2. Asking 'why' a historical event occurs can ask about pre-existing contexts; or about the sufficient conditions of a punctual event; or about the threshold at which gradual processes come to fruition; or about what problem an event solves, or what project it aims at; or about how the event comes to have meaning; or about a proximate efficient cause, whether simple or complex or chaotic, material or ideal or virtual. The passages above differentiate between listing pre-existing conditions of fact and extracting a new force.
3. Some phenomena exist first in minor forms, then get extended and systematized. 'Why now?' sometimes means 'what is the difference between local and systematic versions of the same phenomenon?'
4. The question 'why at such and such a place (*lieu*) and time (*moment*)' puts the focus less on causes and more on space and time.
5. There may be a difference in principle between 'why then?' and 'why now?' questions.
6. The form "why at *such* and such a moment?" (in the *QP* passage) is more vague than 'why at that particular time?' though more concrete than 'why does that kind of event happen?'
7. Asking whether capitalism could have occurred elsewhere implies the use of hypothetical conditionals. When social systems anticipate, fear, or delay their successors, they deploy hypotheticals in action.
8. Deleuze and Guattari pose some 'why now?' questions in their own voices; others are posed in the voice of "historians" who have the "impression" that there is a 'why now?' question.
9. To what degree do Deleuze and Guattari intend to solve the 'why?' question? The relevant chapters of *AO* and *QP* end with the idea that every historical event is a "problem", and the text from *MP* ends with "undecidability". I will argue that 'why' a historical event occurs is answered precisely by problematizing its relation to conditions.
10. The rise of capitalism is the primary case for asking 'why then?' in all three texts. *QP* asks, in parallel, why philosophy began in Greece. In *AO*, the parallel is whether Oedipal relations have always existed, and if not, why they emerged when they did. Can any historical event be the subject of a 'why then?' question, or do different senses of 'why now?' pertain to different kinds of events?

11 What defines "event"? These texts deal with the origins and combinations of social regimes: the primitive territorial regime, the despotic state regime, and the capitalist schizo regime. Each has a kind of beginning, as well as a kind of atemporality; each has its own way of retaining, anticipating, and yet co-existing simultaneously with, the others. I will examine these temporal-historical structures. But a large part of Deleuze and Guattari's point is that transformations from organized territories to state leaderships to chaotic systems can occur as a singular breakthrough event at a certain time (the first arrival of a despot), or as a small-scale transformation at a micro-level (the occasional expulsion of a scapegoat from a town), or as a repeated occurrence at very different times and places (the acts of traitors no matter when). A philosophy of history needs to account for the advent of both large-scale events and small-scale occurrences, both singular crises and repeated variants.

12 The three regimes in Deleuze and Guattari's social history do not all have the same structure. Each has its own way of signifying occurrences and their relations, origins, and powers; therefore, each regime has its own account of what history is. And since every society contains some degree of all three regimes (even if each expresses one regime more prominently) – like the way every event includes all three syntheses of time in *DR* – it follows that there are three kinds of history in everything that happens. So every 'why now?' question requires not one answer but three. And each of the three has an account of how the other two can be combined with it. Can there be one overall account of the three accounts of historicality? Or is an event nothing but a series of diagnoses along differentiated lines? Which, if any, of the three historical views of history that Deleuze and Guattari *describe* is the one they *use* in their own analyses of historical events. Is the third account of history, the one specific to the (post-) capitalist stage of history, the only one that posits "universal history"?

Before proceeding, we need to decide whether the three social regimes are supposed to count as stages of history.

PRELUDE: PLATEAU 5 "587 BC–70 AD: ON SEVERAL REGIMES OF SIGNS" AND THE ARGUMENT AGAINST THE SOCIAL EVOLUTION OF REGIMES

In some texts, the territorial, despotic, and capitalist regimes are only minimally identified with real historical events. They are said to co-exist and not to evolve (*MP*, 147–50), they are described as "idealities", as merely "logical" transitions (259). Some scholars of Deleuze and Guattari's idealized portrayal of historical nomads criticize it for being empirically inaccurate; others praise

The Problem of Actual Historical Events: The Theory of Beginnings 117

it for keeping the discussion on the virtual level.[2] But as Foucault says, even "structuralism" takes history into account, as long as "history" is understood to vary with the multiple structures of time.[3] Deleuze and Guattari clearly do not think the historical regimes are exclusively ideal. Nor is it out of place to ask whether actual world history can be divided into periods. The text says at the very least that a given regime may "dominate" in certain "historical conditions" (152), and we want to know why. I use the "Regimes" Plateau to ask whether the three regimes are, or are not, historical.

This plateau sets out the three regimes: (1) The primitive territorial regime, in which each person and place is assigned a position on the earth. A social position is not an essence (it is pre-signifying) but allows leaps whereby a person can magically identify with other persons, places, or gods. This regime includes the pluralizing effects of nomadic warrior collectives. (2) The despotic regime, in which an authority arrives suddenly on the scene. The despot cancels (or deterritorializes) all familial and economic relations and presents himself as (or reterritorializes as) the centre of all significations, the face behind the law, the father of all children, and the creditor of all debts. It may include a priest who interprets for, or against, the despot. (3) The post-signifying regime, in which significations are universally exchangeable, either by subjective desire or by uncontrolled production. This regime can yield revolutionary emancipation, or can be constrained by capitalist "axioms".

In other texts, Deleuze and Guattari define the stages slightly differently. But they always resist designating them strictly as periods in chronological history (as one might be tempted to think roughly of 10,000 BCE to 1500 BCE for the territorial regime, 1500 BCE to 1800 CE for the despotic, then 1800 CE onward for the capitalist post-signifying and post-capitalist a-signifying regimes). To be sure, the question "why did capitalism not develop in China in the thirteenth-century?" suggests that the regimes originate as real historical events, but in this Plateau, the regimes are only minimally identified with actual historical events.

The text begins with an argument against social "evolutionism" (147). The proof is that we can always find mixed phenomena in which the regimes "co-exist" (149) "simultaneously" (150). Even saying that each regime is "already" in the other (a kind of preformationist evolutionism) suggests "too much temporality". Similarly, Deleuze and Guattari declare that when they say a regime "originates", or is "no longer", they do not mean it temporally; they only mean that regimes stand "in opposition" (160–1). Mixed regimes exhibit the activity of an abstract machine on the plane of immanence, which is extra-historical (165). By regime, in short, they insist that they do not mean "a moment of history" (149); though they acknowledge that there are "dated social systems" like Courtly Love (150). On my interpretation, while the three social regimes are not themselves chronologically successive, they constitute a map of coordinates and descriptive categories by means of which we can sort out the threads of meaning in those events that *are* historically definite. We "return" from the regimes to "historical events" (150).[4]

But if a regime is a semiotic that could be enacted at many moments in actual history, it nevertheless has to make use of the specific historical situation that exists at the moment of its enactment. So what does it mean if *ever* a historical condition lets a regime be enacted in actual history?

Deleuze and Guattari here give an example: "the most fundamental or the most extensive event of the history of the Jewish people: the destruction of the temple, which is done in two times (587 BC–70 AD)" (153). This is the case that gives the "Regimes" Plateau its date, a double date. This is not an event that takes a long time to occur, but a double date in which the singular event happens twice, with a time-gap in between, in order to happen at all. The doubled event assembles the "two great moments" in the "history of the temple". "The formula that scans [*scander*] Jewish history" is the *mot d'ordre*: "Let evil fall *back* (*retomber*) upon us" (153–4). Jewish history is a paradigm of not being confined to a single historical condition. But its particular mode of not being confined is that it is enacted in two very determinate moments, extended into a perspective that expects the same phenomenon (the evil) to repeat itself at various other times. (Evil repeats the same; the Messiah repeats the different.) The actual history of a historically unconfined semiotic takes the form of "unlimited delay" (*atermoiement illimité*) (154). But even if the final dating of a regime is indefinitely delayed, in each event in social history the historical indefinite has a determinate and specific form.

We thus now see a less minimalist relation between the regimes and history, which allows Deleuze and Guattari to say something near the end of "Regimes" concerning "when" transformations of regimes occur. The question "when the enunciations of the bolshevik type appeared" means "not just at what moment, but in what domain" (173). If this just meant that the moment is less important than the structure, then we would be back to minimalist historiography. But what is meant here is that a regime of signs affects a "people as a whole", not just a "fraction of this people" at a "locatable margin" (173). It is shortly after this that Deleuze and Guattari say that abstract machines are "dated" (178). Asking "when" a regime takes hold requires analysis of the sociality of a people, the structure of anticipation and retention that that people has at that moment, and the way that its sense of history determines its speed or delay, its continuity or flight, and its openness to the spirit of the times, to other models of history, and to subsequent actual history.

Why, then, do actual historical events, like capitalism, happen when and where they do, and not at some other time and place when the conditions seem ripe? I will use *AO* to set up the problem, *QP* to intensify it, and *MP* to solve it by making it worse. The rest of this chapter focuses on *L'Anti-Oedipe*.

The Problem of Actual Historical Events: The Theory of Beginnings

INTRODUCTION: UNIVERSAL HISTORY AS RETROSPECTION

The opening paragraph of the "Savages, Barbarians and the Civilized" chapter of *AO* reads:

> If the universal is in the end, bodies without organs and desiring production, in the conditions determined by seemingly triumphant capitalism, how is it possible to find enough innocence to do universal history? Desiring production is also there from the beginning: there is desiring production as soon as there is social production and reproduction. But it is true that precapitalist social machines are inherent to desire in a very precise sense: they code it . . . Capitalism liberates the flux of desire . . . *It is thus right to understand retrospectively all of history in the light of capitalism*, on condition that we follow exactly the rules formulated by Marx: first, universal history is one of contingencies, and not of necessity; of breaks and limits, and not of continuity. For it required great chances, astonishing encounters, which could have been produced elsewhere, previously, or might never have been produced, in order that fluxes escape coding, and, escaping, would constitute no less a new machine determinable as a capitalist socius, thus the encounter between private property and market production . . . In a certain way, capitalism has haunted all forms of society, but it haunts them as their terrifying nightmare . . . In another way, if it is capitalism that determines the conditions and the possibility of a universal history, this is only true to the extent that it has something essentially to do with its own limit, its own destruction . . . In short, *universal history is not only retrospective, it is contingent, singular, ironic, and critical.* (*AO* 163–4, my italics)

The classical idea of "universal history" is that all events are contained in a single context, and can be interpreted together, but only once history has come to a certain point that can look back on itself. Deleuze and Guattari commit themselves to this idea,[5] though with provisos.

Universal history is "retrospective, it is contingent, singular, ironic, and critical". It is ironic, since it knows that it sees phenomena from the final standpoint of capitalism, yet also knows that this standpoint is not final.

Universal history is critical because universality unleashes desire, and desire is always a critique of social structure. A theme in history, no matter how systematically it theorizes about the universality of desire, will always be one step behind the next emancipation of desire.

Universal history is singular because of the contingency of historical encounters between processes (e.g. between specific forms of wealth and labour). It charts desire-related events wherever they surge up, but does not say that all events express the same human condition.

The contingency of universal history is extremely complex. In this passage, it refers to two traits: (a) that events are the intersections of independent series (encounters); and (b) that events could have happened differently, previously, or not at all. In other passages that I will consider, history is said to be contingent in the sense that (c) events occur in flux, or chaotically, catastrophically, or without determinate conditions at all; (d) different events occur in incommensurable rhythms or temporal streams, and so do not have measurable causal efficacy on each other; (e) events depend on milieu-conditions, which themselves depend on conditions, ad infinitum (contra (c)); (f) events depend on minority effects, not on the large-scale conditions that historical causality depends on; (g) events are irreducibly indeterminate or ambiguous, making it impossible to isolate their defining factors. (See section entitled 'Capitalist History' on page 132.)

Finally, universal history is retrospective. Marx says that universal history, i.e. the recognition that all history is the history of class struggle, is possible only once proletarian class consciousness arises explicitly during the capitalist age.[6] For Deleuze and Guattari, only once the decoding of desire is universalized can the particular decodings of prior times be recognized as such. In previous ages, decoding was experienced as anarchy or delirium, not as the universal history of desire.

The idea of universal history read backwards from its endpoint makes us think of Hegel. For Hegel, actual events in history are not caused by antecedents; in order for modern agents to be self-determining, *they* have to be the causal force behind their own predecessors. In Deleuze and Guattarian terms, a present event introduces a rupture into the continuity of time; the retroactivity of history spreads a phenomenon existing now into the totality of past time, and this is what will answer a 'why now?' question. Universal history is a virtual effect of the event.

The other side of retrospective history concerns what dark precursors look like prior to the standpoint of the end. After the long opening paragraph of the chapter, Deleuze and Guattari introduce the history of the Oedipal complex, where a similar question of retrospectivity arises. Oedipus is defined structurally as any situation where an individual is detached from social desire and productivity, is reconstituted as an individual with a private organ, and senses the absence of others; this all leads to desire for a father-authority, a mother-unifier, and an infantilized self. All of this is associated with capitalism's interest in having individuals desire their own isolation and repression. Deleuze and Guattari ask whether the Oedipal structure exists prior to capitalism. The short answer is that all societies have had family traumas, but not all societies have separated the individual from the group in the modern way:

> What *remains* in order to make Oedipus? The structure, i.e. a non-effectuated virtuality? Must we believe that universal Oedipus *haunts* all societies, but exactly as *capitalism* haunts them, that is, like the

The Problem of Actual Historical Events: The Theory of Beginnings 121

nightmare or the anguished presentiment of what would be the decoding of flux . . .? (168)

The flip-side of the retrospectivity of our historical analysis of the past is thus the past's presentiment that we will be doing so now. The flip-side of universal history is universal waiting. Structuralism finds Oedipus in all cultures and times; the presentiment theory allows that pre-modern versions of Oedipus are different either by degree or by kind from modern familial psychopathology.

To see how presentiment works, we need to consider the actual stages of history.

TERRITORIAL HISTORY: NEGATIVE LIMIT (BEGINNING) – SURGE AND CUT

Deleuze and Guattari's discussions of primitive[7] territorial society (170–227) focus on its economic scheme of debt-distribution and its psycho-familial scheme of filiation, inter-family alliance, and incest. Its kinship relations are constantly being destabilized and rearranged by marriages. In contrast to Hegel's notorious claim that Africa had no history (*PH* 99), Deleuze and Guattari argue that there is not only history, but historiography, in territorial regimes:

> If one calls history a dynamic and open reality of societies, in a state of functional disequilibrium or oscillating equilibrium, unstable and always compensating, comporting itself not only through institutionalized conflicts but also through conflicts that generate changes, revolts, ruptures and scissions, then primitive societies are fully in history. (*AO* 177)

Such a society constantly surpasses itself from within, rearranging and re-evaluating itself, managing the wagers that its members make for their own advancement, and the rise and fall of fortune and power. It puts power relations into flux, but organizes a territory in which the flux is controlled. Territorial history means oscillation.

Just after introducing the three (quasi-)historical regimes, Deleuze and Guattari add a sixth feature of "universal history": "negation"[8] (180). They remark upon historical negation under categories of phenomenology, conflict, and temporality. The first role of negation is that if traditional society were to look forward to the capitalist free play of wealth and labour, it would see in capitalism the negation of the very idea of history:

> If capitalism is the universal truth, it is in the sense that it is *the negative* of all social formations [i.e. it negates them by decoding them] . . . It is not

primitive societies that are outside history, it is capitalism which is at the end of history, it is the latter that results from a long history of contingencies and accidents, and which makes this end arrive (*advenir*). One cannot say that the anterior formations have not pre-viewed it – this Thing which came from the outside only by rising from within, and that they try to stop from rising. Whence the possibility of a retrospective reading of all history as a function of capitalism. (180)

It is not only that later societies dismiss earlier societies as inadequate versions of themselves. It is also that the earlier societies anticipate and try to ward off the structures of later societies. But how is it that they know what history has in store for them? A future society cannot after all introduce causal mechanisms into the past. Earlier societies must have actual but self-restrained agencies of anticipation. Deleuze and Guattari call it "presentiment". This is difficult to characterize phenomenologically. What is going on in consciousness, individual or collective, when some content is present in anticipation but not actually present to perception? The appeal to "fear" or "anxiety" (180) begs the question. From the standpoint of the later stage, it seems anachronistic to claim that earlier stages experienced it already. From the standpoint of the earlier stage, anxiety about future changes seems empty of content. If we could read retrospection *in medias res*, as the duration *between* primitive and modern, between the anticipation and its fulfilment, then we could speak of a result immanent in its beginning, the tree in the acorn. But commensurability of historicity across historical periods is precisely what Deleuze and Guattari challenge. So the phenomenology of presentiments is not sufficient to explain the negative presence of successor societies. (In *MP*, the theory of presentiments is replaced by a theory of thresholds.)

The second form of negation in universal history involves contrast and conflict. We "understand [a code] *a contrario*" when we contrast it with what the coded material would have been if it were not coded (*AO* 180). But there is no neutral standpoint from which one can say, for example, that territorial society's castes are either similar to, or contrary to, capitalist society's classes. A general comparison can always find similarities and differences (180), but both findings are superficial. The way we see opposition between two societies is not by comparison, but in the actual conflicts at their border. We see the negation of presentiment, for example, when an aristocracy represses an emerging merchant class, or when a capitalist class whitewashes its sordid past. We see actual war between historical periods, ideological, military, and economic. But the two sides of the conflict fight different kinds of war: the one, for example, fighting for more territory, the other to replace territory with property. One side fights to perpetuate history, the other to rupture it and start a new kind of history that it will then read back into the societies it conquers. This is the severity of capitalism: it does not fight fair; it uses even the phenomena that most oppose it, as part of its own mode of production.

The Problem of Actual Historical Events: The Theory of Beginnings 123

It opposes communism, until China wants to buy Pepsi, at which time capitalism announces a new axiom of constructive engagement. It asserts its distinctive modernism, but finds the history before it to be filled with capitalists. These decoding procedures are precisely what allow it to do universal history, in a way that no society committed to specific social codes could do. A coded society can only *compare* itself to other societies, or colonize them by force; capitalist society is beyond historical comparison, since it decodes differences and sees universality everywhere. Capitalism is therefore the only schema that can date events in history on a commensurable time-line. It conducts universal history not only because it lies at the end of history so far; it does so because its decoding mechanisms make retrospectivity possible. Capitalism is the first historical age, treating all precedents as its gradual becoming; and it is also the first non-historical age, since from its perspective nothing has ever changed, and history itself is decoded; and it also includes all ages, constituting history retrospectively as co-existence rather than succession. For a capitalist society to ask why capitalism emerged at a certain time in history is thus an odd phenomenon, searching for a determinate date to assign to its origin, while reaching back further and further into the past for its origin.

The question 'Why X then and not before or elsewhere?' applies to capitalist events differently than the way it applied to earlier events. For example, 'Why did a Joan of Arc arise in the fourteenth-century and not earlier?' asks about the specific conditions for a new state of affairs, whereas 'Why capitalism at a certain moment and not earlier?' asks, rather, 'How is it that all the predecessors to capitalism were already capitalist?' To be sure, every historical age de-individualizes its predecessors, but most do not do so as obsessively as capitalism.

In sum, a historical transition goes beyond the limits of what it surpasses by introducing a new sense of history along with a new social order. This moves us from conflict analysis to temporal analysis.

Territorial regimes do not have the resources to universalize time that capitalist historiography has. When territorial historicity represents to itself its own limits, it can do so only in terms of incest taboos. Normally, new families surge up with marriage, on the background of old families already traced in lineages. Deleuze and Guattari (235) call this the historicity of "beginnings" (*commencements*). As soon as a new patriarch makes a new beginning, territorial society does its best to negate the novelty by tracing a lineage as far back as imaginable. Oscillation and equilibrium combine the living present with the pure past (in the terms of *DR*). Filiation-history and alliance-history have two "memories" or "genealogies" operating at once (*AO* 183). When families strike an alliance, they affirm direct lineages to privilege their two lines of identity, but having declared that filiations are prior to alliances, they then declare filiations to be unacceptable, incestual grounds for perpetuating families. Incest taboos express the dual nature of continuous discontinuity, and they express the ambiguous desire for an authoritative genealogy that will both exhibit and conceal its mergers. This explains Deleuze and Guattari's odd argument that incest prohibitions define incest as an impossibility. Both family relations and historical events in general have to introduce flux into actual states of affairs taken to be not in flux.

Deleuze and Guattari describe three categories of incest repression: (i) the repressed representative (particular desires that are put aside in order to establish authoritative genealogy); (ii) the repressing representative (the incest prohibition); and (iii) the displaced representative (Oedipus, the figure through whom violators are identified and judged). These might be developed into three elements of Oedipal historicity that will replace the oscillations of territorial historicity: (i) contingencies put aside for the sake of authoritative history; (ii) exclusive causal explanations; and (iii) state-propagating historical narratives. The territorial historian has the presentiment of a historian from the future (a despotic historian representing the state) who will treat the past as a primitive child with unconscious motives. Territorial historicity will thus introduce a different model of historicity into its own midst, a despot who condemns its procedures. To ask whether Oedipus is universal, then, is to ask whether history has always been organized, or alternatively, whether authoritative history arises at a certain moment in history, and if so, according to what temporality.

Before we can say how a despotic judge "arrives", we need to say how a territorial regime, or any regime *at* which something else can arrive (we might say that any society at which something else can arrive is by definition territorial), is defined by its "limit". This takes us to the third aspect of the negativity of territorial historicity: temporal negation.

Deleuze and Guattari define four kinds of limits (207–8). Revolutionary "schizo-flux" is the "absolute limit" of a territorial regime. Capitalism, which would free desires but distribute their satisfaction, is its "relative limit". Presentiment, the ability to "see with melancholy the sign of its own proximate death", along with practical efforts to ward it off, is its "real limit". The incest myth is its "imaginary limit". In one sense, the Oedipal judge prohibits free desire, and so wards off capitalist schizzes; in another sense, it narrates the excess that it prohibits. Oedipal anxiety is as inherent to territorial regimes as its fear of outsiders; yet it is only imaginary, it is repressed. The limit prohibits what it articulates and hence ensures that it will not be needed.

It is difficult to specify, based on the text, which of the three quasi-historical regimes contains the Oedipal repression of desire. Deleuze and Guattari say that that there is no universal history of Oedipus, and that the "conditions" for Oedipus are "realized" only in a "capitalist formation" (209); yet Oedipus is the figure of repression *in* the territorial regime; yet again, the latter's presentiment of Oedipus anticipates the judge from a despotic regime (211). In fact, the repression of desire requires all three conditions: an imaginary threat (recognized in territorial society), an actual authority (represented in a despotic society), and a universally distributed internalization (signified in a capitalist society). The lessons of these difficult pages of the text, for a philosophy of history, is that a social phenomenon is not located exclusively in one historical age, but distributed in levels across history, and that a historical period is in turn defined by the historical levels that co-exist in it.

The authoritative mode of repression is already, but only negatively, present in the territorial mode. "If there is a primitive Oedipus, it is a neg-Oedipus, in the sense of a neg-entropy" (210). Repression functions in advance to prevent a certain future, activating that future negatively before its time. Universal history shows that capitalism at the territorial regime's end is the driving force, albeit a negative one, operating from the beginning. Further, if entropy refers to the increase of homogeneity and the decrease of energy, neg-entropy would mean that as time goes (negatively) by, the past becomes more and more heterogeneous and energetic, more and more functional. The result of function-analysis, in contrast to signification-analysis, is that historical "conditions" (changes in a state of affairs that have to precede a given change) and "limits" (structures of a precedent state that allow it to be replaced) are dependent on "field totalities" (configurations whose instability provides interstices that novel forces can intervene in).

In short, the instability that allows the territorial regime to oscillate through dynasties also makes it susceptible to a rupture in history, which it will not be able to evaluate and assimilate. Oscillating equilibrium explains all of history in terms of continuity and renewal. Rupture is another explanation of all history, co-existing with the first. Any oscillation, at whatever point in history it occurs, whether among clans or within a multi-party democracy, is primitive; any judgement, whenever it occurs, is the arrival of despotic historiography. How does the era dominated by the first give way to the second?

DESPOTIC HISTORY: THE RUPTURE OF THE ABSTRACT (ORIGIN) – SYSTEM AND CONCRETENESS

The despot "arrives" (227), always from the "outside" (226) to found a state. To the extent that every sort of state (religious or secular, parliamentary or monarchic, ancient or modern, psychological or political) has a central authority, Deleuze and Guattari say that there is only ever "just one state" (227), the *Ur-staat*. How is it that the despotic stage of history can (a) arrive all of a sudden, and (b) always have existed?

The basic feature of the despotic regime is that it overcodes the central authority as the sole distributor and referent of social significations. Its first act is to cancel debts between individuals and make all debts payable to the state; it cancels individual marriages and makes the king everyone's father.

It is paranoiac because it starts over at zero, and celibate because it keeps everyone at a distance (228–9). In territorial regimes, power "jumps" from one centre to another; the despotic regime installs a centre that cannot be reached. The despot surveys, evaluates, and re-interprets those who have preceded him. He does not just forge a stronger alliance than his predecessors. His claim is transcendent (the divine authority of kings, the inspiration of a people, the executor of inalienable rights). He is the "I think" who makes all judgements. If territorial history oscillates, despotic history is truth that establishes a rule of law without exception "from a precise moment" (231).

Deleuze and Guattari's claim that the despot arrives from the "outside" is difficult to interpret. It is supposed to mean (a) there has always been one Ur-state; (b) the despot arrives at a precise moment; and (c) the territorial regime gives itself "*its own*" death *from* that outside (226). This is why the question 'why now?' is problematic. Asking 'why?' seems legitimate insofar as events are conditioned by the past, but it seems illegitimate if events arrive from outside the previous laws of normal history? How does the logic of 'its own outside' solve this contradiction?

Consider the traditional question of whether history proceeds by gradual and normal shifts, or alternatively by paradigm shifts and catastrophes. Deleuze and Guattari's solution is not to choose either side, but to determine which regime functioning in an event-field proceeds in one way and which proceeds in another, and to analyse the particles that pass between inside and outside. (For example, Joan of Arc suddenly arrives as a messenger from the outside, then entices long-time internal rivals to pay for her campaigns, which bring catastrophic upheavals from the outside, and so on.)

To see how the outside is death from the inside, we have to see how the despot, who "supplants" territorial procedures, remains "haunted" by them (229). Using the terms of *DR*, the territorial regime operates as a living present, haunted by its future; the despot announces that the present does not pass, that his rule lasts for all time, that the rule from this instant on is the rule of the pure past, yet he is haunted by the present in his past. Each haunts the other as an intratemporal dimension. Deleuze and Guattari insist on the hermeneutical difficulty of sorting out when a society is being anxious about what its new despot will do to it, and when the despot is being anxious about whether his new subjects will resist his innovations (231). The same transformation is both a futural projection of the past's internal fear and the historical retrospection of what is external for the future. The territorial alliances cannot resist the despot, yet archaic forms of production and consumption remain a stubborn obstacle to central control (even if a smart despot figures out how to manipulate them). The before and the after of the despot's arrival are thus confused (231).

The very uncertainty about whether the despot truly arrived from outside or is simply a front for one of the old kings is what shows that the despot

The Problem of Actual Historical Events: The Theory of Beginnings 127

really comes from outside. Even if it is a former insider who founds a newly central state, that novelty makes it a rupture from the outside, and a new form of temporality. It replaces the oscillations of before and after with a confused temporality of archaic remnants and their overcoded future. The question 'why X at such a time?' can in a way still be explained with reference to what came before, but the price is that the 'before' is now equivocal. 'Why X?' means 'what does it take to affirm X in a society that could just as well still be not-X?'

Why do archaic remnants, and archaic temporality, remain? Deleuze and Guattari ask, for example, why capitalism (they could have used an example from the despotic regime here just as well) does not develop as soon as there is the first hint of centralized currency. Why, for example, did capitalism did not develop in thirteenth-century China at the first hint of economic and technical development (233)? Deleuze and Guattari answer (footnoting Balazs), in a nutshell, that in China the state turned merchants into civil servants. But we want to ask, 'why was this a fact at this time?' *Why* did the functionary class think as it did, and why did material conditions not sweep those attitudes aside? Were the forces not 'strong' enough? Did the people not 'desire' it? The point is that the difference between one regime and the next has to do with the way that the predecessor is affirmed in and as the successor, and all variants are possible. Co-existing forms are sometimes affirmed connectively (in which case the new regime does not take over), sometimes disjunctively (when the new regime disenfranchises local powers), and sometimes conjunctively (when the new regime grants local authorities the licence to represent it).

Different ways that predecessors are affirmed define the different ways that an event can *begin*. And different sorts of beginnings too co-exist. Deleuze and Guattari distinguish the "beginning" of a territorial regime from the "origin" of a state regime (235), and later, from the "creation" of a capitalist regime. The first is "concrete": a new territorial alliance re-uses the families and production techniques that had been used before. The second is "abstract": it overcodes people, redefining family members as citizens. A "beginning" is gradual; an "origin" is abrupt. A "beginning" exploits one part of society for the sake of another part; an "origin" uses the part for the sake of the whole. Any re-use is territorial, whether it re-uses metal or government agencies. And any declaration that something will never be the same again is a despotic act, whether it re-interprets cities or warfare or music, even if the governing authority plays no obvious role.

The ways in which different regimes narrate historical beginnings differently could take us to Deleuze and Guattari's extensive theory of signs: pre-signifying territorial signs, signifying despotic signs, post-signifying capitalist signs, and a-signifying revolutionary signs. I will deal only with the way despotic signifiers are responsible for the origin of "historiography", i.e. for laying out the totality of history under an authoritative interpretation (239).

A territorial regime does history by assigning each object and event its own code. A capitalist regime does "universal history" by assimilation. A despotic regime does authoritative history by keeping annals written by the voice of authority. Whether the historiography is romantic or real-political, it is the determining signifier, its thematic consistency, its record of progress, that gives it its imperial character. Its downfall is that once historiography introduces and then answers the question 'What does it mean?', it cannot prevent that very question from proliferating. Its own authority will inevitably be questioned (247). The clever despot even plays on this, affirming his autonomy yet hinting at a power he only conducts.

Indeed, when Deleuze and Guattari distinguish the three regimes of history, one wonders if they are using the same method that despotic historiography uses when it keeps track of the history of states. To avoid this, Deleuze and Guattarian historiography will not only have to avoid the signifying models of the three regimes, it will also have to avoid being a fourth, truer, type of regime above and beyond the three (since every regime, qua regime, is despotic, even if its content is not). Theirs has to be a way of deconstructing all regimes, folding them into for and against each other. Again, this will make the 'why now?' question problematic.

The reappearance of a micro-despotic moment in the most anti-despotic philosophy returns us to the problem of how any one regime can narrate the history of other regime's historiographies without reducing them to variants on its own constant semiotic. How can Deleuze and Guattari say both that the state invents historiography to organize progress, and at the same time affirm that the *Urstaat* has always been present? If despots are all in the same position of arriving from, and historicizing from, the outside, then it seems there are no radical events arising from the outside, only a series of authority figures. To use Deleuze and Guattari's distinction, the despotic state arises as an "origin", and changes everything suddenly, yet *does not "begin"*. The very perspective of despotic thinking that is able to ask when a truly novel concrete event suddenly takes place in fact, is the perspective that most prevents it from isolating such an event.

We have to consider again what it means to say that a state emerges not progressively, but "all at once" (*en une fois* (257))? At the moment at which any one signification is conferred by a central authority, all meanings are subject to it at once. The origin of the state is thus by definition forgotten, preserved only as a myth of the founders, or as the imperial aspirations of a class. So on the one hand, the very consequence of his sudden arrival is that the despot had always *already* arrived. It is "as if [the state] witnessed to another dimension, a cerebral ideality that adds itself on top of the material evolution of societies" (259). Yet on the other hand, there are determinate criteria for when it actually *did* always already arrive:

On the one hand, the ancient city, the Germanic commune, and feudalism presuppose the great empires, and can only be understood as a function of the Urstaat that serves as their horizon. On the other hand, the problem of these forms is to reconstruct the Urstaat as much as possible, while taking into account the requirements of their new and distinct determinations. (258)

Something specific has to happen in order for a state properly to exist (namely, it has to extend to the horizons), and social life has to be explained concretely in its imperial contexts. This is the paradox of despotic signifiers in historiography: every sense-creating event is radically new, and every new event already makes sense.

As always, the text draws together the claim that the state is a special case of non-progressive emergence, with the idea that the case of China tests whether progressive causes are sufficient for the emergence of the event. If we were not at all concerned with actual events, we might say by stipulation that capitalism did not emerge in China in the thirteenth-century just because "China" is the name for any overcoded state that does not become capitalist, that Europe before the seventeenth century and parts of rural America today should be called "China".[9] This would make of "China" a "name of history", like the Joan of Arc effect. I am arguing that the 'why this now?' question cannot be reduced to stipulation. But mythical self-images do after all explain some events in actual history.

Deleuze and Guattari introduce "the imperial myth" that is part of the despot's retrospective arrival from outside (259): the despot announces that his all-at-once arrival was prefigured either by prophets, or by progressive causal forces. Myth-telling separates an origin from a beginning, affirms the newness of the new, and constitutes an origin as a self-referential enunciation. The myth is the origin of originality, a new kind of beginning that is possible only once the originator declares herself to be free from the traditional course of beginnings, continuations, and ends. Yet at the same time, the myth is a way of generating a new kind of origin precisely by re-appropriating beginnings, not just a re-appropriation of this or that beginning, but of the whole sphere of causal beginnings and ends all at once. We might say (varying the terms of the *C* volumes) that myth is a time-origin rather than an action-origin. The "power of a new All", might even be called "genesis" (259).

Citing Vernant's theory of myth, Deleuze and Guattari insist that "we do not really know which is first", the factual condition under which a mythical ideal is affirmed, or the ideal that provides a new way to signify the factual conditions (260). Almost any territorial lineage can be the occasion for a myth of state origins. "The state over-cuts what comes before, but re-cuts the formations *before those* (*ultérieurs*)" (260). There is a potentially deep epistemological problem here, combining the problem of knowing whether one event comes before or after another, with the problem of knowing whether a phenomenon is virtual or factual. If we really cannot know which ontological dimension an event comes from, whether it begins or originates, then it would seem that the whole theory of events is unverifiable. But we can read not-knowing in a different way: it is precisely when there is no factual evidence whether a state began in prior conditions or in posterior interpretations, that we can be certain that the event is virtual, and is a genuine origin. The *problem* of origins is just what makes an event known to be an event.

In cases that pose particular problems for whether a regime has changed or not, e.g. the problem of whether feudalism, or democracy, belong in the category of the despotic regime, an empirical "comparative treatment" will not decide. "It serves nothing to make a list of differences" (261). Even traditional taxonomic differences like how many people are in the ruling class, or differences in the pleasures and pains in daily life, are not necessarily differences of regime. Since empirical criteria cannot decide whether a new regime has come to prominence, Deleuze and Guattari offer three structural differences between despotic and territorial regimes.

The first and most important is that the despotic state makes use of time differently:

> [The state] has its concrete, immanent existence only in the previous forms which make it return under other figures and other conditions. As a common horizon of what comes before and what comes after, it conditions universal history only on condition of being not outside but on the side, the cold monster that represents the way in which history is in the 'head', in the 'brain', the Urstaat. (261)

The despot centralizes not only the state's resources, but also its temporality. The state plots out its future destiny, and over-determines its past, all from the instant of its foundation. Its temporality is no longer successive and oscillating but systematic, spreading one event throughout a socio-historical field. It *has* a past only on condition that it returns to it indifferently under different figures. This is why the state does not exist in immature stages; it exists as a trans-historical Ur-system or not at all.

This implies a second difference between territorial and despotic events, namely that the latter are abstract (261). Even when one tries to find the origin of events in material conditions rather than in ideology, one finds a singular point extending itself by abstraction throughout a system. Hence, the third difference is that in the despotic event, history becomes "systematic". Systematization involves several stages (to schematize 261–2): the state unites separate "subsets" of people (abstracting to a common rule); it "subordinates" certain behaviours to others in a common "field"; it "invents" new codes to control anti-social loose ends; it allows the codes a life of their own, e.g. as classes; finally, these despotisms within despotism produce a meta-system, a "whole" made up of several wholes. These stages may not

The Problem of Actual Historical Events: The Theory of Beginnings 131

all be necessary or sufficient for every state process. The point is that systematization concretizes the abstract;[10] its temporal assemblage makes quasi-causes become-causal.

The mechanism of systematization is desire. The state, having extended its codes throughout the social field, returns to a central authority by means of the desire of its subjects for a leader. "System" is defined (a) by the way each part internalizes the common temporal horizon, and (b) by the way an abstracting force is transmitted all at once from member to member throughout a whole. The sudden moment when a state arises thus covers the whole time it takes to systematize. The state originates as the gradual spread of an all-at-once. So when we evaluate whether a state of affairs is despotic yet, we ask such questions as, 'Is its central authority the subject of a collective assemblage of enunciation?' 'Does it spread systematically by desire?' 'Are its future effects felt at once by every member as soon as it is felt by any one?' Or, typically for Deleuze and Guattari, 'Is it through the despotic regime that people desire their own repression?' (262).

But now, just when it appears there is a historiographic methodology for deciding what is the systematically despotic era, we have another textual problem. We were about to answer 'Why X now?' using the despotic regime's historiography. But its historiography is immediately rendered anachronistic by capitalism, and capitalism will be unexplainable by the very concept of "system" that was about to entail it. We said that the procedure of state despotism is to deterritorialize behaviour throughout a territorial field, then to reterritorialize on the desire for a despot (263). While the state is spreading out systematically, it is decoding people, objects, and institutions along the way, in preparation for recoding, and this decoding already starts to germinate the capitalist flux stage of history. There are passages in the text where it is not clear whether Deleuze and Guattari are talking about the state or the capitalist regime,[11] but they insist that the "birth" of capitalism renders the state obsolete (263). The capitalist stage of history will introduce a radically third kind of event-actualization.

Capitalism is the worst enemy to have at one's temporal border, since it negates (finally, the last sense of negation in universal history) the very identity of its predecessors, insisting that non-capitalists are stuck in ancient history, turning them all into capitalism wannabes. This is precisely what allows capitalist-era historians to produce universal history – not by superimposing its own model of authority on the past (as the despot does), but by de-valuing the question of whether societies are historically the same or different, as long as they generate working capital. It is the only age that knows how to be a successor, just because its temporality is built on co-existence rather than succession.

CAPITALIST HISTORY: DIACHRONICS (CREATION) – REVOLT AND DELAY

Capitalism can be defined on one level by typical socio-economic phenomena: private property, markets and profit, investment capital, contract law, exploited labour, and so on. But each of these technical features can exist in a despotic state without the emergence of capitalism as such. According to Deleuze and Guattari, the "big difference" is that "the despotic machine is synchronic while the time of the capitalist machine is diachronic, the capitalists arise by turns in a series that founds a sort of creativity of history, a strange menagerie: a schizoid time of the new creative cut" (264). Capitalism has no "beginning" or "origin", but a "creation"; it is absolutely deterritorializing, having no temporal territory of its own.

The difference between abstract all-at-once origin and concretely abstract creation, the difference between the synchrony and the diachrony of what happens in history, suggests once again that we have not only three founding events in history, nor simply three kinds of events, but three levels of the same event-material. We cannot ask what causes events in general, since there are three kinds of beginnings.

Whereas a state is founded by fiat, a capitalist enterprise succeeds by "contingency" (265). Capitalism is the period of history that creates a historiography through which all the periods can be characterized as contingent. In *AO*, contingency is defined by flux and encounter; in *QP*, it is defined by resistance; in *MP*, by staggered thresholds.

The contingency of encounter occurs when capitalism disengages economic life from central authority: when wealth may be owned by anyone, not only the prince; and when labour is freed from any given employment. To be sure, a despotic state apparatus can rule over a capitalist nation, yet once capitalism arises, "one feels", at least "virtually", a "new life" (265). Contingent encounters begin with the flux within social forms like wealth and labour, but they engage only once several social forms in flux are conjoined:

> Decoded fluxes, what will tell the name of this new desire? The flux of properties that are sold, the flux of money that flows, the flux of production and the means of production that are prepared in the shadows, the flux of workers who deterritorialize: it will require the encounter of all of these decoded fluxes, their conjunction, their reaction upon each other, the contingency of this encounter, of this conjunction, of this reaction, which is produced once, so that capitalism should be born, and so that the former system should die, this time from the outside, at the same time as the new life is born and at the same time as desire receives its new name. There is no history other than that of contingency. Let us return to this eminently contingent question that modern historians know how to pose: why Europe, why not China? (265)

The Problem of Actual Historical Events: The Theory of Beginnings 133

The contingency thesis is that several social forms can *co-exist without* initiating a chain-reaction from one to the other. Property can be detached from central authority without labour becoming detached from central authority, and so on. If the two independent series become attached, so that capitalism arises, they will do so contingently. In support of this claim, Deleuze and Guattari provide the empirical case of China, where, historians have argued, the relevant social forms became fluid independently, without capitalism emerging.

Stated in this empirical way, the contingency of the emergence of capitalism seems uncertain. Perhaps some empirical condition *would* show that if one social form detaches from central authority, the others must (eventually) do so as well. Indeed, free labour and free market do look like they conceal a common cause that would make their relation necessary rather than contingent. Even when a despot prevents the loosening of property law from loosening bureaucratic control, perhaps what is contingent is not the relation between the functions, but the despot's obstinacy. In the case of a society that exhibits the conditions associated with capitalism without being capitalist, must we conclude that conditions are irrelevant to capitalism?

To defend the thesis that "there is no universal [i.e. capitalist] history other than contingency" we need to construe Deleuze and Guattari as having an ontological, not an empirical, argument for historical contingency. We need to show how capitalist decoding necessarily results in contingencies. We might imagine the following construal. When wealth is detached from national currency, it is necessarily also detached from central authority, and investment choices become purely contingent; when labour is detached from feudal lords, it is necessarily also detached from craft, and its employment becomes purely contingent. Each function is neutralized; its use becomes a matter of indifference. What makes the history of capitalist activity contingent is not that its elements do not have to react upon one another; it is rather that their mutual reaction depends on each one of them being *undirected*. Since each series[12] is aimless, they interact by chance. Yet because each is undirected (labourers looking for work, speculators looking for opportunities), the two series are *forced* into a chance encounter. The encounter is contingent in the sense that the processes are undirected and no outcome is predetermined. Yet it is necessary in that each series makes the others even more undirected.

It seems plausible that contingent flux within series leads to contingent encounters across series. But once the conditions for a society based on social flux are met, why are the contingent encounters that constitute capitalism not inevitable? Why are there not certain historical conditions that make capitalism, along with its contingencies, necessary? Conversely, if it is contingent whether capitalism emerges at a given time or place, what is the point of asking why capitalism did not emerge in China?

It is time to consider what Deleuze and Guattari envisaged as possible explanations of Chinese history. The case of China[13] of course raises ontological as well as political problems for interpreters.[14] Of the several historians they cite, I will give a synopsis of just one. Étienne Balazs's *La Bureaucratie céleste* (1968) is a collection of essays on Chinese economic history, culminating in "*La Naissance du capitalisme en Chine*" (pp. 290–312).[15] In some ways, Balazs is an odd choice for Deleuze and Guattari.

Balazs begins with variations on why capitalism did not begin in China before it was introduced by European powers. One might ask, he says, why capitalism did not exist at all up until that point; or why it existed only at a "lower level"; or why it began but was stifled; or why it developed but then "regressed"; or merely why it took a different form in China (pp. 291, 296). Balazs proposes that capitalism had modest beginnings in China but was prevented from "developing". As the "principle cause" (p. 292), he cites the intransigent bureaucracy of the class of civic servants, and the entente between the lettered functionaries and the merchant class that worked to the detriment of the peasants (p. 297). Once merchants were beholden to functionaries for legal and bureaucratic backing, their own economic initiatives were in turn held in check. The easiest route to wealth was not capital expansion, but bureaucratic corruption. The root of suppression is found at the level of "desire" (p. 298): the merchants lacked "fighting spirit" (p. 299).

About half of Balazs's examples show that conditions for capitalism did exist in China; the other half, interspersed with these, show the contrary. Evidence that capitalism did begin to exist consists of the fact that there was: (1) a credit system in China in the eighth century (p. 299); (2) a printing system in the eighth century, leading to paper money in the eleventh century (p. 299); (3) usury in the seventh century (p. 300); (4) low workers' salaries in the fourteenth century (p. 306); (5) large industries (e.g. in salt and transportation) gained by the eighteenth century (p. 307); (6) monopolies by the eighteenth century (p. 308); (7) large merchants on the geographic frontiers, as in the beginnings of Western capitalism (p. 309); and (8) a frugal spirit by the seventeenth century (p. 309).

Evidence that capitalism did not develop in China consists in the fact that there was: (1) a state monopoly on paper money in the eleventh century (p. 299); (2) a rule that government orders were to be filled before private orders in the eleventh century (p. 300); (3) cities defined as seats of government rather than as market centres by the eighth century (p. 301); (4) government control of industries involving salt and military hardware, and fixed rate taxation of private industry independent of levels of production from the fourteenth century (pp. 301–5); (5) monopolies that discouraged competition in the eighteenth century (p. 308); (6) spendthrift children succeeding frugal parents, along with excessive clan solidarity in the eighteenth century (p. 310); (7) a preference, based on safety and prestige, for investment in land over production (p. 310); (8) abundant manpower, hence no urgency for efficiency (p. 311); and (9) an absence of middle-class class-consciousness (p. 312).

The Problem of Actual Historical Events: The Theory of Beginnings   135

Balazs concludes that if capitalism means market competition or free enterprise, then capitalism never did take hold in China. But if it means a credit economy, a profit system based on the surplus value of labour, along with advanced technology, then (state) capitalism did develop in China long before it did in Europe (p. 312).[16]

This conclusion may be a fair balance of empirical fact and stipulative definition, but where is the explanatory force? Is it an explanation from class desire, or from the power of the state, or from individual inertia? For that matter, Balazs is an odd choice for Deleuze and Guattari in that he is trying to show the permanence of bureaucracy in China. He wants to show how China (at all times) provides a lesson to Western society (at this time), by showing how bureaucracy tends towards "totalitarianism". His characterization of China as "proto-scientific" (p. 42) has the ring of Eurocentrism. Further, he complains against the thirteenth-century Chinese historian Ma Duanlin's "evenmental history" of "contingency"; Balazs prefers the "modern" (European) model of "evolution or development" (p. 52). This all sets Balazs's historiography against Deleuze and Guattari's. Yet even here, Balazs is difficult to construe. For he holds that Europe's own birth of capitalism in the sixteenth to seventeenth century was a " 'miracle' ", a "lucky exception, a privileged moment of history" (p. 43). For Balazs, the unanswered question is not why capitalism failed to arise in China, but how it could have emerged anywhere at all.

Deleuze and Guattari share with Balazs the last point, i.e. that capitalism arose contingently in European history. We "return to this eminently contingent question that modern historians know how to pose: why Europe, why not China?" In spite of their sardonic identification of modern historians (who are ironically a chance product of that contingency) with contingent history, Deleuze and Guattari seem to expect a direct answer to the question. The question 'why not China before?' does not ask after a threshold of conditions, but asks how contingencies are put into circulation. It asks how desires can be released from the traps in which despots aim to contain them.

The passage that concludes Deleuze and Guattari's discussion of the 'why not China?' question moves quickly to the level of general decoding:

Decoded desires, desires for decoding, they are always there, history is full of them. But here [in Europe] the decoded fluxes form a desire, a desire that produces instead of dreaming or lacking, a desiring machine, that is at once social and technical, only by their encounter in a place, their conjunction in a space that takes hold of time. That is why capitalism and its rupture are not defined simply by decoded fluxes, by the *generalized* decoding of fluxes, the new massive deterritorialization, the conjunction of deterritorialized fluxes. It is the *singularity* of this conjunction that makes the *universality* of capitalism. (*AO* 265–6, my italics)

General procedure, singular event, and universal extension suggest a kind of dialectic. But in what sense is the decoding of desire "*why*" capitalism emerged when it did? We can see why low-intensity capitalism might not count as capitalism at all. But does it not beg the question to say that capitalism emerged when the desire for capitalism emerged? The same paragraph contrasts genuine decoding from the farce that capitalism in Europe immediately became, favouring production for its own sake instead of for the sake of joyful desire. The strategy of the text is to replace the question 'why capitalism now?' with the problem of how capitalism gets reterritorialized. Yet this is not a case of philosophers dropping a question that is too hard to handle. I have been taking the question 'why X?' to mean 'how does X get systematized throughout a field?' This will allow us to see how the description of capitalism that follows is not a non sequitur to 'why capitalism now?', but a solution to it. The key point is that two series can be systematically connected, yet still only contingently related, if they belong to two different temporal layers superimposed upon one another.

We have seen that a 'why now?' question points to an encounter between two relatively independent series of phenomena. At the level of any one series, e.g. at the level of a labour pool freed from the land and from a given set of tools, or at the level of wealth freed from state control and from a given set of industries, it will always appear that capitalism, the encounter *between* labour and money, "might not have happened" (266). At the level of a single series, an event will look ahistorical, as though it combines a real phenomenon (human labourers), with chance (the arbitrary purchase of that labour by the wealthy few).

In contrast, in the temporal logic of serial encounters (unlike the all-at-once origin of the state), several conditions catch up with each other. This requires time for what Deleuze and Guattari are content to call by the somewhat misleading term "original accumulation" of capitalism. It is common to say that capitalism arises with the accumulation of wealth. Deleuze and Guattari's variation is that it takes interactions across several parameters – wealth, labour, desire, technology, communication, and so on – occurring in rhythms of diachronic velocities. Their long case study (265–85) involves the history of money, and focuses on quantitative accumulation, hence on the quantitative nature of beginnings in capitalist historiography.

Four kinds of quantification are involved in accumulative history: quanta, quantity, differential equation, and diachronic velocity.

Before capitalism, there are various forms of production, labour, commodities, prices, and coinage, all of which measure value. Loose equivalences of value at this level are "quanta" (268–9). When currency is centralized by the state, there is a generalized rule of "quantity" (269). Once money begins to regulate production, as capital, it operates like a quasi-cause, generating variety out of its own univocal, virtual mechanism. Quantification is now measured by differential equations, like those that relate changes in variable capital to changes in constant capital. Indeed, capitalism can still accumulate even when profits are falling, even while markets crash, as long as the flux of capital is still dematerializing commodities and finance capital by putting them into circulation, as long as investors still choose to put capital into flux, as long as money is still constantly being returned to abstraction.

Because it operates by differentials, the presence of underdeveloped regions is part of capitalism's global system (274). Regions where goods are recycled or unaffordable, in which waste is dumped, in which corruption or wars predominate, make objects all the more deterritorialized, and put money to new uses and counter-uses. Some regions accumulate more than others, and it is normal for the balance between centres and peripheries to shift.[17] By definition, most of the world is underdeveloped relative to the area of greatest accumulation. The more extreme capitalism becomes, the more extreme is the anarchy at its borders. The more extreme the anarchy, the more room for accumulation. In the differential field, the concrete *absence* of corporate capitalism constitutes the virtual presence of capitalist creation. Violence, economic piracy, and other pre-capitalist anachronisms (277–80) drag capitalism back through time and allow it to speed up in "ultra-modern" (544) sub-pockets, where capitalism is frenzied rather than procedural; capitalism is always both its own delay and its own avant garde.

This is the fourth type of quantity in capitalist accumulation, a temporal, "diachronic", form of quantity. The capitalist regime preserves its predecessors' codes precisely to prevent its own meanings from stabilizing, so that capital will remain free to increase beyond the moral pale. It incorporates miniature despots of industry, anachronisms in advertising imagery, and classical rhetorical personae ("the banker", "the worker"). It creates (by war, exploitation, or neglect) distant societies for whom capitalism will always be just beginning in its most raw, violent, and unlimited form. In short, capitalism uses time-differentials to keep codes changing, and to undermine moral and technical attempts to regulate the future. Diachrony is the first axiom of capitalism (277–8),[18] as well as the foundation of contingency.

Deleuze and Guattari give three examples. The first is that in the face of new inventions (like the new steam engine), old modes of manufacture (like the old ironworks) slow innovation down, "up until the moment" when the new takes over the entire system of the old (278).[19] The second is that when production exceeds consumer demand, capitalism must preserve anti-capitalist state apparatuses, centres of "anti-production at the heart of production" (280), like the military, in order to squander matériel. The third case "integrates groups and individuals in the system" (280), e.g. as patriotism allies itself to a capitalism that has already superseded nationality.[20]

It is through relations of time, nature, power, and desire that novelty schizzes throughout a field, differently yet equally in each part-object. In part, 'why now?' means 'why so slow?', since it is the drag on the new that makes the new into an event. Why, for example, was technology in the second half of the twentieth century so painfully slow? Why do we still travel on commuter airplanes, a technology of the 1950s? Why is ground transportation still based on the wheel, as McLuhan already complained in the 1960s? New technology seems to develop faster when it is resisted ferociously than when accepted gracefully.

In short, territorial beginnings are chronic and continuous; despotic origins are synchronic and sudden; capitalist creations are diachronic and two-timing. They do not so much start as undergo a series of stops-and-starts.

One might have thought that despotic synchrony would play the role of co-existence, while diachronics would count as succession. But in capitalist history, it is precisely events that are temporally distant, and expressly anachronistic, which co-exist. Accumulation might look like gradual increase one step at a time, each moment at its proper time, but in fact accumulation is the encounter of two phenomena that act outside of their own times in the time of the other. This makes capitalist events historical as such: they contain history rather than being contained by it; they do not only have a beginning and then a successor but immanently contain their own beginning, middle, and end. Capitalism does not exist until its pre-capitalist history is made simultaneous with it.

So saying that capitalism did not occur in thirteenth-century China is consistent with saying that China at that time *was* undergoing a typical history of capitalist accumulation. We can imagine situations where capitalist technical procedures exist, but leave pre-capitalist procedures alone, instead of seeding them to re-create the urgency of capitalism's historical emergence again and again. The reason capitalism did not occur in China is that the relevant states of affairs did occur, but in insufficient diachrony. Indeed, any multi-stage historiography says that an event does not really occur until it reaches its last stage. But for diachronic historiography in particular, there is still a problem: what is a 'last stage' if history itself is deterritorialized?

CONCLUSION: UNIVERSAL HISTORY AS NEW PAST

The problem for universal history is that each of the three stages within the capitalist event has its own interpretation of all three of those stages. The first stage of capitalism, namely relative decoding (when novel procedures are introduced), may interpret the three stages of capitalism as: technical progress, increased production, and uncontrolled expansion. The second stage, namely reterritorialization (when it becomes ideology), may interpret the three stages of capitalism as individual progress, liberal freedom, and the war against terrorism. The third stage, absolute deterritorialization (when a revolutionary escapes), may interpret the three stages of capitalism as machinic assemblages, axioms of control, and abstract machines. Just as the question why capitalism occurs at a certain time is ambiguous, since it may refer to different stages of

The Problem of Actual Historical Events: The Theory of Beginnings 139

capitalism, so the search for a method is ambiguous, since each stage of an event has its own historiography and each historiography has its own division of stages.

It seems that the third stage of capitalist history, the stage of revolutionary deterritorialization, is the standpoint from which Deleuze and Guattari aim to do history. But how does absolute deterritorialization allow for history at all? We may still call it 'history', yet the last stage of history is not really a stage at all, but a multi-levelled temporality. The end of history is not the beginning of a new age that will from now on last for ever, but a new level at which events are paralleled by their own breakdown, a level at which dates are fluidized.

Deleuze and Guattari side with Marx and Engel's "rereading" of history as stages in the class struggle, not to reify classes, which is a despotic act even if one sides with the proletariate, but to create classless, deterritorialized historiography. Capitalism uses the state as a war machine to get the state itself out of its way, and the revolutionary regime must do the same with capitalism. Any time one invests one's "objective interests" in an event, one limits its historicity; one turns the "historical process" into "neo-territoriality" (306). Sadly, Deleuze and Guattari admit, "we do not know too well" what causes a revolution to fall into the celebration of a state, or reactionary paranoia (310). Avoiding reaction requires diachrony without investment. Happily, in "real history" (*histoire réele*), events still have a level of becoming even when most determinate. Hence, the other side of an event's neo-archaism is its "futurism"; the other side of "nostalgia" is the "inevitability" with which it forces us to hurry up and do something; the other side of its "delay" tactic is its "advance" guard (310). But it is not simply that deterritorialization is futural and reterritorialization is historical; rather, past and future must be paired as simultaneous temporal displacements if they are to serve as revolutionary tactics.

So to say that capitalism, as system, arose in Europe, means that it arose in Europe simultaneously as paranoia against the archaic and hysteria against the future. If China blocked the accumulation of capitalism, that means that capitalism emerged there as a localized paranoia within the functionary classes, but not as a systematized paranoia with a death-wish manifest destiny, or a millenarist saviour fantasy behind a revolutionary counter-plot. It means that capitalism arose in China only for the time that the time was ripe, and did not fracture into a tripartite universal history of past, present, and future, for better or worse.

The conclusion is that the 'why now?' question has several answers at once, since each event expresses itself in several planes of time at once. The co-existence function in each event engages and disengages the time-differentials of forward and backward reference. It might have seemed that territorial, succession-oriented schemes, or despotic organizational schemes, define the historical point of view. But to have a truly historical view, where a revolutionary can become all the names of history, concretely differentiating events even while systematizing them, there has to be a co-existing fractalization of multiple self-representations desired, displayed, and produced, in and as, time.

The difference between what deterritorializing historiography calls universal history and what state historiography calls universal history, but which we would call global parochial history, is that the latter adds developments to its past, whereas the former subtracts the codification of its past, until it "has realized the immanence" of each phenomenon in the flux of modernity (311). As Hegel says, the end of history is not something we yearn for; it "has been accomplished". History is universal not just because a certain standpoint can see itself in all its predecessors, but because the free play of events has become available. Despotic regimes impose a futuristic novelty on to the past, but Deleuze and Guattari are as anti-future as they are anti-neo-archaist. Since the new is not the future, but *has been* achieved as the co-ordination across mutually available time-lines, the New is the Past.

The final paragraph of chapter 3 of *AO* concludes that "universal history is only a theology if it does not conquer the conditions of its contingency, its singularity, its irony, and its own critique" (323). This implies, conversely, that history is not theology if it does. I have taken the task of "conquering its own critique" to mean laying multi-layered temporality over the temporal structures of prior stages of history, becoming universal by rendering immanent the transverse temporality of actual events.

I will return to the revolutionary potential of co-existential history. And I want to be more specific about 'why now?' questions. But first, I will use *QP* to show how multi-levelled historicity creates a problem for diagnosing events.

NOTES

1   Eugene Holland (1999) shows how Deleuze and Guattari connect "universal history" to anti-Oedipalism. He lays out Norman O. Brown's interpretation of Freud on history: repressing the death drive leads to infantile attitudes towards infinite future projects, which leads to the concept of history as progress and to neurotic guilt regarding history. Brown translates history into psychology. Holland's response is that for Deleuze and Guattari, (i) repression occurs only at a certain point in (capitalist) history, therefore history is not reduced to psychology; and (ii) the will to power means that history is free to go beyond capitalism (pp. 8–11). So while schizoanalysis is "historically oriented" (p. 13), it "sees history critically" (p. 12) as "autocritique" (p. 18).

Holland takes Deleuze and Guattari's "universal history" to refer to (a) a generalized freedom of human forces; (b) free libido (p. 92); (c) permanent revolution (pp. 95, 105, 123); (d) contingency (pp. 109, 111); and (e) material and not just human forces (p. 111). I think it also refers to a method by which the last stage recasts its predecessors.

2   See Christopher L. Miller's (1993) discussion of this problem.

3   Foucault ("Revenir à l'histoire" (1972), in (1994)) argues that it is wrong to criticize structuralists for being anti-historical. Structuralism's preference for "change and events" over time (p. 273) emphasizes the "simultaneous or synchronic", but it does take "time

The Problem of Actual Historical Events: The Theory of Beginnings 141

into account" (p. 271). Foucault uses Dumézil to argue that myths change, but not in time. And he uses "serial history" (see my note 13) to show how gradual population growth is an event but not at a datable moment. "It is thus necessary to substitute for the old notion of time, the notion of multiple duration, and when the adversaries of the structuralists say to them, 'But you have forgotten time', these adversaries do not seem to have taken into account that for a long time, if I dare say it, history has divested itself of time" (p. 279).

4   "There again we do not make history; we do not say that a people invents this regime of signs, but only that it *effectuates* at such a *moment* the assemblage that assures the relative dominance of that regime in the *historical conditions*" (*AO* 152).

Paul Patton's (2000) interpretation is that abstract machines co-exist and have no evolution; but the "successive actualizations of a particular machine", or "particular kinds of state", undergo "historical progressions" (pp. 99–100). Forms have no history, but instances do. But Patton also shows that the forms have an internal dynamism (p. 101). Given that "the task of philosophers is to help make the future different from the past" (p. 132), philosophical history has to produce history within the virtual and becoming within the actual.

5   In *NP* (159), Deleuze uses the term "universal history" to refer only to the triumph of the reactive.

6   Marx (1993, p. 109): "World history has not always existed; history as world history [is] a result." This sentence occurs at the end of Marx's "Introduction", but is not developed. Similarly, Foucault (1966, p. 165): capital accumulation "introduces, by its very existence, the possibility of a continuous historical time". (Holland (1999, p. 140) cites this passage.) Cf. Debord (1967), chapter 5 "Time and History".

7   Deleuze and Guattari insist that "primitive" does not suggest anything pejorative, that it just means "territorial", and that their intent is to show how primitive forms like nomadism can be renewed. Still, it seems preferable to refer to "territorial" society, except where primitiveness is at issue.

8   Deleuze and Guattari normally avoid the category of negation, as everyone knows, but in these passages, and these senses, they do not.

9   "What China is Miller talking about: ancient, current, imaginary, or still some other one that would form part of a moving map?" (*MP* 29). Deleuze and Guattari may be talking about that last China as well.

10   I take this to be the sort of account that DeLanda (2002, pp. 102–3) calls for in a different context, namely "empiricism of the virtual" or "mechanisms of immanence".

11   E.g. at *MP* 558, Deleuze and Guattari open a paragraph to deal with "the very particular character of *State* violence", and begin their evidence by saying that "Marx remarked on this concerning *capitalism*. . . ." This overlapping is understandable in context, just hard to follow.

12   "Serial history" refers to a specific method of historiography in the 1950s. Fernand Braudel "Pour une histoire sérielle: Séville et l'Atlantique (1504–1650)", in Braudel (1969, pp. 135–53), citing Pierre Chaunu: "[Serial history] 'is interested less in the individual fact . . . than in the repeated element . . . which can be integrated into a homogeneous series itself subsequently capable of supporting the classical mathematical procedures for analyzing series . . .' It is, consequently, a language – and very abstract, disembodied" (pp. 135–6). For example, the study of a single shipping route, in detailing types of ships and cargoes, eventually reveals social history on a world scale. Cf. Foucault (1972, p. 277).

Deleuze (*F* 29–30) says that serial history shows how a singular point is prolonged in various directions. Deleuze says that Foucault manages this method well, but that other historians use it to overvalue continuity. Historians do not account well for phenomena that are gradual yet also radical, like the emergence of capitalism. Paradoxically, it is only when series are described discontinuously that they can be understood as wholes.

13　Questions in the form 'why in the West and not in China?' have been posed in the history of science as well, e.g. by Needham (1969). I owe this reference to Don Bates.
14　Gayatri Chakravorty Spivak (1999, pp. 107–8), for example, challenges the whole Marxist idea of the "Asiatic Mode of Production", though she says that Deleuze and Guattari use it in a less essentialist manner.
15　That paper was originally written in English as "The Birth of Capitalism in China", *Journal of Economic and Social History of the Orient*, III, 1960.
16　Fernand Braudel (1976, p. 112), cited at 265 as well, has a similar conclusion. If we define capitalism in terms of social mobility, wealth based on international trade, free market centres, and technological growth in production methods, then capitalism did develop in China centuries earlier than in Europe. But assuming, as Braudel does, that we describe a culture as a whole, we have to acknowledge that whereas Chinese history exhibits brief boom periods of capitalism, it also undergoes crises at which capitalism collapses. In Europe, capitalism somehow maintains itself through the crises. Braudel has more in common philosophically with Deleuze and Guattari than Balazs does.
17　Deleuze and Guattari cite Samir Amin (1976) regarding capitalism on the peripheries, but it is not easy to find their particular conceptions in Amin's text.
18　Étienne Balibar (1965) is one of the most important sources on co-existential history, though he uses the term "diachrony" to mean succession and "synchrony" for distributed co-existence, contrary to Deleuze and Guattari's usage. For Balibar, the apparent "diachronic" transitions between modes of production are in fact structural variations on synchronic modes. Yet while the various systems co-exist through time, their variations generate real historical moments. Balibar explicates what he calls Marx's "transformation of succession into synchrony, into 'simultaneity' " (p. 508). He also develops his own "distributive" argument for "a radical absence of centre" in history (pp. 493, 528, 548–9). "*Differential analysis*" (pp. 565–6) is synchronic, but incorporates "time lags (*décalages*)": a "period of transition" is "*the co-existence of two modes of production (or more) in a single 'simultaneity' and the dominance of one over the other*". In short, "problems of diachrony must be thought within the problematic of a theoretical 'synchrony' "(p. 554).

Judith Butler (2004, p. 66) has a similar concept of "anachronistic resurgences". "*The historical time that we thought was past turns out to structure the contemporary field with a persistence that gives the lie to history as chronology*" (p. 54).
19　Braudel (1969, p. 24) says, speaking of cargo boats, that "there is not one social time with one single and simple flow, but a social time at a thousand speeds, at a thousand slownesses, which have almost nothing to do with the journalistic time of the chronicle or of traditional history" ("Positions de l'Histoire en 1950", pp. 15–38).
20　Mani Haghighi (2002) applies Deleuze and Guattari on neo-archaism to the Rushdie affair.

8 Why this Now? Diagnosis of the Now

The "Geophilosophy" chapter of *Qu'est-ce que la philosophie?* (82–108) is in some ways a companion to chapter 3 of *AO*. The categories of relative and absolute deterritorialization are here again tied to the effectuation of virtual events in actual history. Like *AO*, *QP* asks 'Why now?': why philosophy began in ancient Greece, and why capitalism began in modern Europe. The pairing of these two particular events is used to define what it means for there to be history at all.

In *QP*, the focus is on the way philosophical concepts emerge in, yet remain free from, historical cultures.[1] *QP* is not as clearly structured by the three historical regimes as *AO*, but both texts articulate something beyond capitalism. If *QP* moves too far in extracting the virtual from machinic assemblages, our study of the "Apparatus of Capture" Plateau in *MP* will conjoin the two sides again.

"Geophilosophy" moves from why philosophy arose in Greece (82–91), to why capitalism arose in modern Europe (91–103), to how philosophy can actualize itself in various states while resisting state temporality (104–8).

CONSISTENCY

The "earth" (*terre*) is a smooth space in which concepts and ways of life are communicated without borders; "territory" (*territoire*) is bordered social space (82). Philosophy, Deleuze and Guattari say, emerges in Greece when the stranger enters the city. They present various relations between cities and states, agriculture and commerce, autochthony and nomadism, land and sea cartographies, long- and short-distance migrations, straight and circuitous lines of import/export, welcoming and hostile immigration practices, capture and exile of enemies, and so on, which prepare Greek society for philosophy. The subjective condition for philosophy is the pleasure of thought; the relational condition is sociability; the ontological condition is the plane of immanence; the discursive condition is dialogue; the virtue ethics condition is friendly rivalry. These conditions obtained for a "rather short period" before the Greeks reverted to sea-borne imperialism. But how can social "conditions" determine at all whether a concept is created?

In *QP*, nothing deterritorializes more than a concept, a thought that distributes contents and expressions on a plane of immanence. A concept undertakes the "absolute deterritorialization" of social opinions and practices. In contrast, a societal change is gradual and partial, a "relative deterritorialization" of historical practice. It can spread new concepts around geographic areas, and can determine regional "eras and catastrophes" (85). But it is never as radical as philosophical concept creation.

It may seem that "history" is Deleuze and Guattari's term for normal social succession, which stands in the way of concept creation. But the term "history" in this text refers to the way a concept's *absolute* deterritorialization inserts itself *into* normal occurrences. A concept *per se* may not strictly speaking have a history, but it can only be "thought" according to *relatively* deterritorializing "cosmic, geographic, historic, and psycho-social" relations (85). "Geophilosophy" aims to explain how history is the relative side *of* absolute deterritorialization, how history relays thought into time.

Deleuze and Guattari describe how concepts are immanently "connected" to actualities, in terms of three kinds of "consistency" (86–7). (1) Concepts can be connected by "internal consistency" to constitute a "zone of indiscernability". The text does not provide many examples, but we could say that ideas of beauty, reason and power together made up the consistent "Greek worldview". (2) Concepts can be connected by "external consistency": "bridges" are formed "from one concept to another, whenever the components of the one are saturated". For example, the Greek concept of reason was worked out so thoroughly that it spilled over as democratic politics. (3) Concepts can be "created" when their saturation is so complete that any addition results in a paradigm shift. These saturations work like social dark precursors, perhaps in the way that the overdetermination of myth by exegesis turns it into reason.

The theory of saturation sounds like a guarantee that a fully thought-out concept will find applications in the social realm, and that a thoroughly developed society will start thinking about itself. But Deleuze and Guattari insist that a social structure can never entail the origin of a philosophical concept, citing *AO*'s principle that "there is no universal history except of contingency" (90). The origin of philosophy neither comes from an ahistorical mind, nor from a politician who constructs philosophy as a useful technē. It is rather an "encounter between the Greek milieu and the plane of immanence of thought" (89). In *AO*, "encounter" referred to two social series (labour and wealth); here it refers to one social series and one conceptual series. The application of concept to actuality must be "a conjunction of two very different movements of deterritorialization, the relative and the absolute, the first already operating within immanence" (90).

The history of philosophy is not a two-term relation between concept and social milieu, but a three-term relation between pure concept (immanence), the intermediary of social thought (a facticity–immanence hybrid), and social milieu (facticity). The middle term is somewhat like a concept: a stable cultural worldview nevertheless with the potential to yield innovative consequences. Absolute deterritorialization operates twice in this account: once as conceptual freedom (the gadfly), and once as the power of thought within social construction (the history of ideas).

This three-term relation avoids both simple historicism and simple ahistoricism. Deleuze and Guattari accuse Hegel and Heidegger (not entirely fairly) of being "historicists": they "posit history as a form of interiority in which the concept develops necessarily its destiny" (91). On the one hand, they are accused of affirming that philosophy emerged fully grown in Greece, *as if philosophy had no history* other than the society that invented it; on the other hand, they are accused of tying philosophy to the *history of states*. Conjoined with their ungrounded attachment to Greece, they are led to affirm that philosophy has an "origin" in Greece.

Deleuze and Guattari's counters to historicism are typical, namely that philosophy is "unpredictable" (91), and cannot be identified with any one set of concepts, periods, nations, or social forms. But *QP* is not simply ahistoricist. A simple separation of concepts and societies would leave no room for "geophilosophy", or for asking why philosophy began in Greece. What can it mean, then, for philosophy to be expressed in actual events, but not to have a history? We need a theory of how different sorts of concepts encounter different sorts of social milieus.

"FALLING BACK INTO HISTORY"

At this moment in the text, Deleuze and Guattari ask 'why now?'

> Why philosophy in Greece at such a moment? It is the same sort of thing for capitalism, according to Braudel: why capitalism in such places and such moments, why not in China at some other moment, since so many of its components were already present there? (91)

The quasi-historiography of concepts requires that we detach history from four attributes: from necessity, so as to value its contingency; from origins, to value its milieus; from structures, to "trace lines of flight"; and from the traditional concept of history, to value "becoming", "even though becomings fall back into history" (92).

The problem of "falling back" (*retomber*) is a retroactivity problem. It is not that concepts fall *down* from the heights of abstraction into the social world. They fall back *again* into history:

> [Geo-philosophy] ... separates history from itself, in order to discover becomings, which are not from history even if they fall back into it: the history of philosophy in Greece must not conceal the fact that *the Greeks,*

each time, first had to become philosophers, as much as the philosophers had to become Greeks. 'Becoming' is not from history; today still history designates only the set of conditions, however recent, from which one redirects oneself in order to become, that is, to create something new. The Greeks did that, but there is no one redirection that works for all time. One cannot reduce philosophy to its own history, since philosophy never stops separating itself from this history in order to create new concepts that fall back into history, but do not come from it. How would something come from history? Without history, becoming would remain undetermined, unconditioned, but becoming is not historical. Psycho-social types are from history, but conceptual personae are from becoming. The event itself needs becoming as a non-historical element (92).

Becoming is non-historical because it is not entirely a consequence of previously existing conditions; but it is indeterminate until shaped by historical conditions. The identification of "history" with conditions and consequences is the way we use the term "still today" (in future we might use it differently). I count five senses of "falling back into history".

First, it means concepts need history and vice versa. Deleuze and Guattari appeal to Nietzsche's treatment of philosophy as the "ambient atmosphere" of Greek society, as if becoming is as much a milieu for society as vice versa. For Nietzsche, the concept acts like the "moment of grace" in history. This is a nice touch, but obviously, we need something more than "grace" to answer 'why now?' questions.

Second, falling back into history means continuity. On the heels of asking why philosophy began in Greece, Deleuze and Guattari ask, "Why did philosophy *outlive* Greece?" (92). 'Why then?' means 'why still?' How does philosophy survive when its Greek milieu comes to an end, so it can fall back in an entirely different medieval culture? How can philosophy express itself in entirely different concepts and still remain philosophy, and thus constitute a quasi-history of concepts?

Third, falling back means feedback. The "Geophilosophy" chapter is centred on two analogies: that capitalism emerges in modern Europe, just as philosophy emerges in ancient Greece (93); and that modern philosophy emerges in modern capitalism, just as ancient philosophy emerges in ancient Greece (94). The initial similarity of Greek philosophy with modern capitalism is that both produce conjunctions out of flux: modern Europe conjoined wealth and labour without a social hierarchy, just as Greece conjoined thought and argument without warfare. There are a number of difficult points here.

The account of capitalism begins again with the 'why now?' question (and a footnote to Balazs): "Why capitalism in the West, rather than in China in the third century, or even in the eighth? It is because the West accumulates and slowly adjusts its components, whereas the East prevents them from coming to term" (93). The very slowness of capitalism's cumulative rise in Europe allowed for a feedback loop among its parts, so that capitalism could "extend and propagate its foyers of immanence". The East treated capitalist elements as foreign; the West took itself to be a universal, so it subsumed those elements (a universal which would then subsume other cultures). Capitalism's universal exchange value is a "reprise", "under another form and with other means", of Greek "democratic imperialism", "at a level previously unknown". The analogy culminates in Husserl, tying the transcendental subject to a universal reason whose history starts with Greece. To put Deleuze and Guattari's complex analysis bluntly: slowness makes capitalism universal, just as Greek philosophy was universal. Greek universalism falls back into history when it returns as capitalism. Greek philosophy and modern capitalism are two parts of one and the same event spread discontinuously across time. 'Why now?' questions do not ask about one event at a time, but about two paired events, like the double-dated and delayed reaction events we saw in earlier chapters. Or perhaps triple events, if one territorial, one despotic, and one capitalist event belong under a single universal 'why?'

Fourth, "falling back into history" means that modern capitalism exercises backward causality to ensure that Greek philosophy falls back into history. Capitalism is not only a system of economic exchanges, but also the plane of consistency that abstracts from local and historical conditions. There is not merely a similarity between Greek and modern universality. To put it simply: modern capitalism promotes modern rationalism; modern rationalism interprets the Greeks as rationalists; therefore the Greeks become the founders of perennial philosophy; therefore there is universal history. To put it bluntly, philosophy is able to define and outlive Greece *because* 2000 years later, capitalism universalizes exchanges.

Clearly there is a circle in the argument. We were trying to explain the relation between concept and society using Greece as a test case. We explained that case by analogy with the relation between concept and society in modern capitalism. But when was the relation between concept and society explained in principle? Indeed, just at the moment the text lays out the analogy, it breaks off to re-emphasize historical contingency. But if it is in the end merely by chance that capitalist exchange universals and modernist transcendental universals are conjoined, then the analogy will not answer either 'why now?'

On the other hand, if the analogy is meant really to explain the earlier origin retrospectively by the later, it sounds like revisionism, as if to answer 'why then?' we reconstruct utopias out of past ages. Certainly, capitalist ideologists do appeal to Greeks precursors, and certainly modern philosophers bought Greek thought a second life. But is the only answer to why anything happens that modernity inscribes it so?

There are three features in the concept–society hybrid that might be used to give retrospective answers to 'why now?' questions. The first is to think of modernity's deterritorialization as the basis of historical explanation; the second, reversing the first, is to think of modernity's reterritorialization on the past as the basis of historical unity; the third, in the middle, is to think of modern minorities as the founders of minoritarian temporality and the basis of historical lines of flight (92). I will consider these three possibilities in turn.

The first of these geophilosophical options is that the concept–society hybrid is the product of utopian thought. This makes concepts the only real power in historical explanation. Indeed, there are passages throughout *QP* that suggest this construal. Instead of thinking of concepts and societies as two ontologically distinct series, perhaps we ought to think of concepts as the *only* series that powers events on the plane of immanence, and think of the social series as merely a material limitation or obstacle to the conceptual series. At some points, Deleuze and Guattari seem to side with this construal, especially when they refer to concepts as "utopias" (95). But most of the time, they want to show how a concept can "connect itself with" (*se connecte avec*) an epoch. For example, they read Butler's backwards "Erehwon" not as "nowhere", but as "now here". A utopia is not an image of the future but a declaration that there is a concept for politics "now" and "here". A utopia pulls together a social assemblage according to a meaning that the latter would not have on its own. It singularizes a society as 'the now' precisely by critiquing it. Just as absolute deterritorialization operates twice – once as pure concept and once as the liberating force within the social – so revolution operates twice – once as the atemporal maxim that each now be "fought against" (96), and once as the temporalization which takes each event "now". In utopian concept–society hybrids, "connecting with the now" is not very different from "fighting against the now".

Finally, "falling back into history" thus means "fighting against the now". The concept falls back into history each time history challenges itself conceptually. Revolutionary utopianism is the concrete attitude of becoming-now; the revolutionary attitude is a temporal attitude.

This is the second geophilosophical construal of the concept–society hybrid. In contrast with the anti-historicist construal, this ties philosophy to the internal self-critiques of actual historical societies. But when we look at what Deleuze and Guattari say about particular historical societies' philosophical self-critiques, we find another problem.

"RETERRITORIALIZING ON GREECE": ARE DELEUZE AND GUATTARI ARGUING FOR OR AGAINST GEOPHILOSOPHY?

Like everything virtual, the event occurs twice in the same occurrence: once as the "self-referential" incorporeal event, and a second time insofar as it "makes an appeal to" a new people with the will to carry it out. How does something virtual "appeal to" a concrete agent in a particular society? The references in the text to Heidegger on the "call of conscience", and to Kant on "enthusiasm", are problematic, not only because they are vague, but also because they are German.

Almost all of Deleuze and Guattari's examples of pragmatic utopianism are geo-historically determinate. Their first set of utopian examples are tied to German thinking: Kant, Hölderlin, Schelling, Heidegger, 1930s German thought in general, as well as French commentators on German thought (97–8). The next set is tied to English thought in the eighteenth century, French in the seventeenth, German in the nineteenth. Why name nations? Surely Deleuze and Guattari's assessments of the philosophical characters of nations are suspicious, of a kind with those old ethnocentric explanations of why Italy and Spain have no philosophy (98–9), and worse. Are Deleuze and Guattari actually doing geophilosophy on these pages, or parodying a discredited pseudo-sociology of knowledge.

The first variant on the concept–society hybrid, which rested on the concept, failed to reconnect with the social; but the second variant, which rests on national sources of thought, ends in nationalistic parodies of utopia. The third variant, the only way to loosen up and save geophilosophy, will be to describe nations as various ways of becoming anti-national.

When utopias are nationalized, nations insert their images into previous national ideals. "Modern philosophy reterritorializes itself on Greece as the form of its proper past" (97). This allows the concept to have "past, present, and possibly still-to-come forms" (97). The simple fact that different nations express different utopias is now split into the relational fact that nations insert their utopian dreams into previous nations. What does it mean to reterritorialize "on" Greece?

To begin with, reterritorialization cannot mean stabilization, since it can be shocking or catastrophic. The reterritorialization of modern Germany on Greece no doubt helped keep Germany from becoming revolutionary, and made Greece seem more unified than it was. But reterritorializing *on* something need not treat it as a mere token on which to pin an idealization; it need not make Greece out to be Christian or Western or even postmodern. It can instead reactivate the virtual territory of Greece. When we think of becoming-Greek, becoming-modern, or becoming-historical, we have to think of Deleuze and Guattari's logic of becoming: X becomes Y only at a moment when Y becomes Z. The becoming that X performs is not just a change in X as it becomes Y; it relays its becoming into a change in Y as the latter becomes Z. X's becoming Y does not entail Y's becoming X. When two things become, they must become other than each other. So, for example, a revolutionary must not only become free, she must make others free as well. A human becomes bird at the moment when a bird becomes song (*D* 88). Humans do not grow feathers; they sing, and become-birds in song. And birds after all do not sing (they screech); humans sing, and it is the humans' becoming that makes birds become songsters. In short, X becoming Y does not identify X and Y, but pulls both X and Y on to the plane of immanence.

We need this logic to explain how anything becomes event in history, how history can be the relative reterritorialization of philosophy, how Joan of Arc can be an effect. But what does a historical event become, *other* than itself, when a posterior event becomes *it*? Modernity's return to the Greeks cannot make the Greeks modern. When a national culture reterritorializes on the Greek past, it does so in order to free its own concepts from current affairs, and to free ancient concepts for the future. The past needs to be the storehouse of futures not yet taken, not what will already have been, but what will still be (already) to be. This is the third, temporal, reading of the concept–society hybrid.

Around *QP* 98, it is unclear whether Deleuze and Guattari are presenting this as their own, or as German Idealism's theory of modernity. The theory of the past as the present's future sounds, after all, Hegelian. But what is clearly at stake for Deleuze and Guattari is that while modern philosophy must reterritorialize on some political regime, it wants to do so with a collapsible hinge.

Modern philosophy would like to find itself in a social milieu as liberal as possible; it would like to reterritorialize solely on "democracy and the rights of man" (98). But in the absence of pure democracies, Deleuze and Guatarri say, modern philosophies reterritorialized on the next best things: national states of questionable democratic leanings. Faced with compromised nations, they went as nomadic as they could. We could think of the cogito in France as a call for individual rights; of English empiricist historiography as the contemplation of its rebellions of old; of German speculation as the intellectual desire to have a revolution just like France's. Each national character would be a way of becoming-revolutionary, a way of becoming non-national, a way of becoming-philosophical (100–1). The nation is a false category to reterritorialize upon, and the national drive is precisely to expose that falsity. Some nations are republican, some totalitarian; some are responsible for concentration camps whereas some, whatever their tendency, happen not to be (102). Even a democratic nation *per se* does not deterritorialize, for its appeal to the "rights of man" is too easily reduced to free market ideology (103), its fervour for mass communication hinders creation (104), and its majoritarian electorship suppresses resistance (104). Indeed, one of the things that helps to deterritorialize nations is that they are all up for sale. The whole business stinks of "mistrust" and "fatigue".

The alternative that Deleuze and Guattari propose is to reterritorialize not on a nation but on a minority – not on a past, no matter how fluid, but on a resistance to time. This is the conclusion to the chapter. The social condition for philosophy is that philosophers be in the minority and reterritorialize on a minoritarian past. Minoritarian philosophy is created not "for" others but "before" (*devant*) others (105). It need not be an avant-garde that thinks chronologically before (*avant*) other people; it is thought in the face of others; in the foreground for others, it brings otherness to the fore; it creates other thinking in others. When philosophy creates a concept, those who do not represent the state become thinkers. In minoritarian "double becoming" (a) a people is "interior" to the philosopher insofar as the philosopher becomes a challenge to actual thinkers, and (b) a thinker is "interior" to a people insofar as a concept "calls" a named subset of existing humans (105). Concept creation is the way that the philosopher and the people together resist death, servitude, shame, the intolerable, marketing, public opinion, each other, the present, and themselves (105).

A philosophy has a social milieu just when it turns its environment into a people with a future that resists itself. Philosophy that does not call society to repopulate itself with a new people is academic. Social revolution that does not call for new concepts is technocratic. Strictly speaking, it is a contradiction in terms to say that a philosophy exists for its time; it cannot reterritorialize on the present.

These interpretations save the counter-effectuating character of falling back into history. But does the fluid pairing of present and past, of now and anti-now, answer the 'why now?' questions? How does the mutual call to dissolution constitute the assembled field that we call capitalism? The last paragraph preceding the final example of "Geophilosophy" leaves it unclear whether the 'why now?' questions have been answered or not, so I cite it in full:

> Utopia is not a good concept, since, even while it is opposed to History, it still refers to it and is inscribed in it as an ideal or as a motivation. But becoming is the concept itself. It is born in History, and falls back into it, but is not of it. It has within it no beginning or end, but only a milieu. It is in this way more geographical than historical. Such is the nature of revolutions and societies of friends, societies of resistance, for to create is to resist: pure becomings, pure events on a plane of immanence. What History takes from the event is its actualization in states of affairs or in lived [experiences], but the event in its becoming, in its proper consistency, in its auto-position qua concept, escapes from History. Psycho-social types are historical, but conceptual personae are events. Just as one grows old according to History and with it, so one becomes old within a very discrete event (possibly the same event that permits one to pose the problem, 'what is philosophy?'). And it is the same for those who die young; there are many ways of so dying. To think is to experiment, but experimentation is always in the midst of being done – the new, the remarkable, the interesting, which replace the appearance of truth and are more demanding than the latter. What is in the midst of being done is not what comes to an end, but neither is it what begins. History is not experimentation; it is only the set of almost negative conditions that render possible

the experimentation of something that escapes from history. Without history, experimentation would remain undetermined, unconditioned; but experimentation is not historical, it is philosophical. (106)

In this passage (which repeats entire phrases from p. 92), the doctrine that the concept "is born in History, and falls back into it, but is not of it" implies that a concept has no beginning or end. *AO* distinguished types of "beginning", and it is not easy to do without some sense of beginning, if only as the beginning of resistance or dissolution, the beginning of a future interrupting a present. It is one thing to loosen the bonds of history in order to free concepts, which in turn frees historical events for thinking; but what of the effectuation of the actual historical events? When the text says, "without history, experimentation would remain undetermined, unconditioned; but experimentation is not historical, it is philosophical", why does the first clause not seem to count as much as the second? Why does "Geophilosophy" begin by asking 'why now?' questions about Greece and about modern capitalism, and at the end switch back to the "What is philosophy?" question? Can the latter be a direct answer to the former?

VARIATIONS ON THE "NOW"

QP from the beginning chapters asks us to "experiment" with phenomena, to make concepts out of birds and folds and dreams, whose avatars are found in empirical actuality. Having asked 'why now?', the "Geophilosophy" chapter naturally ends with variations on how to create a concept of the Now (106–8).

One variant is Péguy's distinction between two ways to consider an event: lengthwise in history, as the rot of successive events; or ascending, as the maturing intensity of a single event. A pair of concepts that for a long time appear stable (like "event" and "history" themselves) might suddenly come into tension and inaugurate a new problem; or a traditional topic might go stale. Nothing in the historical conditions of language or politics need change for the concept cluster to change, yet the latter calls the world into question. Such an event is "*internel*", or in Nietzsche's terms, "untimely" or "inactual" (107).

A second variant is Nietzsche's proposal for " 'acting against time, and thus on time, in favour, (I hope) of a time to come' " (107). At first, this seems to mean acting against the past, upon the present, and for the future. But acting against time also acts against present and future. It acts in favour of a time which is all in the future, and in which all the past will be present. "Acting against time", while taking seriously the time "on" which we act, suggests a third variant: the "infinite now, the *Nun* that Plato already distinguished from every present" (107). How do we act against time yet remain in the Now?

The "Now" is terminologically difficult, Deleuze and Guattari say, in that what Nietzsche calls "inactual" is what Foucault calls "actual" (107). But for both, the concept occurs in the "difference between . . . the present and the actual". A concept exists "now" only while it is "becoming-other", when it is *not present*. In other words, critiquing the present shows how conceptual events are "actual" now (108). Deleuze and Guattari say that this allows us to "diagnose our actual becomings" (108). The critique of the present will, for example, distinguish becoming-revolutionary from "the past, the present, or the future" of revolutions, and distinguish becoming-Greek from "what the Greeks *were*" (108). But with examples like these, it is difficult again to see how becomings are actual at all, as opposed to being virtual diagrams. Deleuze and Guattari recognize how hard it is "to diagnose the becomings in each present which passes".

The last lines within the example at page 108 of "Geophilosophy" return to the 'why now?' repertoire: "What are the becomings that traverse us today, which fall back into history but do not come from it; or rather which come from it only in order to depart from it?" (108). "Now" is a category from the ontology of becoming. "Today", the fourth variant on the now, is a category from the ethics of self-determination.

The last sentence of the chapter notes the importance of the "slight displacements" among all these variants, which can lead to "the modification of a problem" (108). This seems an odd way to end the chapter, but it is the unsettled variability in the relation of concept to history that *keeps* it a problem, that perpetuates its status as philosophy. Obviously, there is something unsatisfying about this ending. If we do not say *how* philosophy is in, is from, leaves, falls back into, and quasi-causes a milieu, but only say that the *problem* of the relation of philosophy to milieu defines them both, we will not be able to specify what it is about these various terms that populates the plane of immanence with becomings.

It seems correct that the evaluation of theory requires diagnosing whether a given term from the history of philosophy suits a problem "today". But this raises an additional methodological issue for interpreters of Deleuze and Guattari, and for philosophers of history generally. Does the commentator on their texts have to conduct a concrete schizoanalysis on some particular event of the day in order to have an interpretation of Deleuze and Guattarian concepts at all? Do philosophers of history have to understand current events prior to researching the past, contrary to the usual motto that the past clarifies the present? How do we even decide which becomings *do* traverse us today? How is someone trained in philosophy supposed to know how to name even one genuine event of "today", let alone analyse one convincingly as part of his book? What qualifies someone like me to diagnose it in an interesting way, so as to avoid making amateurish or pop-postmodern pronouncements? It is not interesting merely to apply their terms to particular events; philosophical interpretation ought to convert the events into concepts.

One has to admire the way a few philosophers (of the many who try) have actually succeeded in giving interesting 'why now?' accounts of the global market, the Gulf Wars, the Millennium, the 1960s, and 9–11. I am tempted to make up similar accounts of Meech Lake or Ipperwash (to cite nation-busting names from recent Canadian history), or to schizoanalyze the new Walmart at the edge of town. But through what concepts should such pronouncements proceed: the concept of community or of sensation, survival or difference, collective enunciation or abstract diagram? And what is the difference between doing it "today" as opposed to some other time? Does any case study, short of one that inaugurates an entirely new world-historical Regime of Signs, show what a historical event is qua event, or show in general how the now captures the 'why?', or how the 'why?' captures the now? Of course, a philosopher, like anyone else, is capable of researching concrete events, and perhaps of analysing them deeply while they occur. But it is not obvious from the terms of *QP* what the mechanism of diagnosis consists of. I have been suggesting that it is primarily the conception of time within events, and the concept of time that founds a theory of events, that is the middle term for a schematism of history. But to verify that diagnosing an event means analysing its temporal structure, we will need a more explicit theory of the co-existential history of temporality.

In sum, *QP* resists the history of states in order to answer 'why now?' questions, but it ends by resisting the 'why now?' question itself. It resists defining a virtual concept with reference to cultural conditions. But if *QP* succeeds in saving philosophy from the lure of historical and cultural relativism, how will philosophy and its friends ever fall back into history? If philosophy resists history too much, it will not cut through history's resistance to it. Knowing how to capture something requires knowing how to be captured by it without becoming it. We learn many things from *QP* about events with two temporal levels. But we need more theory, and we will find it in *MP*. We need to know how the Now and its history co-exist, albeit at a distance. It is good to have a toolbox for making Nows, but why *this* now?

NOTE

1   Philippe Mengue gave an excellent reading of the "Geophilosophy" chapter at a Conference on Deleuze at Trent University in 2004.

9 Why this Now? Co-existing Levels of Temporality

The "7,000 BC: Apparatus of Capture" Plateau of *Mille Plateaux* (528–91) runs again through the three historical ages found in *AO*: primitive territorialization, state despotism, and capitalist proto-schizoism. I will discuss the three ages again, but this time under different categories. *AO* concludes with the diachronics of the historical stages, but only touches on the revolutionary character of co-existence. *QP* emphasizes the revolutionary break with succession, but does not discuss at length the way actual events assemble co-existential histories. *MP*, with its attention to political economy, emphasizes the co-existence of the stages of actual history. I am not arguing that *MP* presents a synthesis but, on the contrary, that history consists not of one but three (or three times three) co-existing temporal serialities, each with independent ontological and causal principles, each with its own transverse lines across the others.

"Apparatus of Capture" continues the previous Plateau, "1227: Treatise on Nomadology: The War Machine". Fourteen "Propositions" are numbered consecutively through the two texts. The "Nomadology" Plateau's central question is: "Is there a way of warding off (*conjurer*) the formation of a state apparatus?" (*MP* 441). It shows how nomad structures, prior to and subsequent to the formation of states, confront and sidestep states and their histories. The "Apparatus of Capture" Plateau treats the transitions from nomadic (exchange) to state (stockpiling) to capitalist (surplus accumulation) regimes. The transitions show not the inevitability of each regime's triumph over its predecessor, but the three-sided battles throughout history.

I take "capture" on several levels. Politically, it is the capture of nomadic culture and its sedentary territorial spin-offs by state culture; ontologically, it is the capture of flux by order; temporally, it is the capture of events by history. The Plateau is divided into five subsections: "The state and its poles"; "Which is the first?"; "Capture"; "The state and its forms"; and "Axiomatic and current situation". But I will divide the text somewhat differently, according to historiographic categories: (1) Cultural evolution vs. co-existence (to 537); (2) Contingency as consistency (to 545); (3) Thresholds and penultimacy (to 557); (4) Release and accumulation, which includes the 'why now?' question (to 572); (5) Universal history and the "current situation" (to 583); and (6) Destabilization and revolutionary co-existence (to 591).

The most important categories for 'why now?' questions, and for Deleuze and Guattari's philosophy of history as succession-in-co-existence, are those of "threshold" (between the territorial and state regimes) and "release" (between the state and capitalist regimes).

CULTURAL EVOLUTION vs. CO-EXISTENCE

Territorial nomads are jewel-wearing, weapon-bearing warriors; the state replaces them with magical emperors and jurist kings. The state backs alliances that the warrior betrays (529–30). Both offer death and mutilation, so there is no question of progress or decline. The state finds itself preceded by nomadic "histories of war" (529), but the war machine will already have policed itself by proto-state apparatuses like community-owned weapons. In this sense, the state is "pre-existing" (*préalable*) and "unconditioned"; it is "born adult", and "surges up at one blow" (532).

As we saw in chapter 7, territorial regimes have successive histories, but these co-exist with a state apparatus that is trans-historical. In answer to the sub-titular question, "Which is first?" (533), Deleuze and Guattari describe the state not as a new stage in "evolution" (534), but as a level of overcoding superimposed on territorial society, a public "system" that co-exists with the division of territories. There are two types of social history: a successive history and a co-existent history, and the two co-exist historically. The territorial regime is to the state as succession is to co-existence.

To be sure, there are processes of various types and duration that go into a state's assertion of control over a territory (533–4). But a state can have an effect on a territorial society even before the state has reached the threshold of existence, as when a city exercises central authority over a region *as if* it were a capital, without actually being a seat of government (538). It is precisely the co-existence of variable relations that gives society a "history". In the vocabulary of this Plateau, Deleuze and Guattari are opposed to "progressive development" and "evolution", but not to "history".

The argument for co-existential history involves a twist. Those who think that the state evolves, i.e. that at one point in time it does not exist and later it does, cannot see elements of the state in pre-state societies. Evolutionism, paradoxically, denies development, by asserting what Deleuze and Guattari call "the absurd theme of society without history" (535). Evolutionism treats new events ahistorically. Only co-existing conditions allow for historical explanation. States, in particular, depend on multiple series of "co-existing", indeed "perpetually interacting", relations (536). For example, states presuppose communication, which requires co-existing mutual translations. Similarly, states presuppose trade, which requires the co-existence of primitive rural production and advanced urban markets. Whereas "economic evolutionism" imagines that hunter-gatherers were succeeded first by cultivators and later by urban traders, co-existentism shows how the needs of the city-dwellers already populated the countryside with farmers. It is not that "movements" never exhibit temporal order, but that they might occur in either order (536).

Evolutionism is proved wrong because the various co-existing components of the state can always be "made to interfere with one another" (536). When we abstract to one component at a time, it can seem that social forms evolve, e.g. from hunter to cultivator, or from warlord to jurist. But when we considered interacting series in chapter 7, we saw that apparently later forms of certain components of the state have reasons to sponsor apparently earlier forms of other components. Therefore, the apparently earlier forms are not holdovers, but up-to-date developments. It follows that a single series of events cannot be historical; only simultaneities constitute history.

Given that *MP*'s theory of co-existential history is even more explicit than that of *AO*, does this mean that the question 'Why does the state begin to appear now?' has no answer, since there has always been a state? We have to consider the possibility that the best thing to say in Deleuze and Guattarian historiography is that every event is always happening, that Joan of Arc is always at work. Yet there are some Deleuze and Guattarian ways to save 'why now?' questions.

One option for interpretation is that the arrival of the state is an exception, the unique event with no 'why now?' answer. After all, the state is the specific regime whose self-referential causality and consistency force its components to co-exist in a single apparatus. Deleuze and Guattari could still ask 'why now?' for capitalism, just not for the state.

Another option is to posit that co-existing conditions exercise backward causality to determine a point at which they will have arisen. Deleuze and Guattari complain that historiography does not follow physics and biology, where robust "backward causalities (*causalités à l'envers*) without finality" are accepted as accounts of "an action of the future on the present or of the present on the past" (537). (We might think of Feynman (1985) on quantum causality, or Libet (1981) on neurological delay.) We have already seen that the state "already acts before it appears" on the societies who try to ward it off (537).

There are two features of backward causality. First, "the state appears in *existence*" only after it has an effect. Second, "the state *pre-exists* by being the warded-off limit-point". This odd combination of existence and pre-existence defines *MP*'s conception of "*contingency*" (537). Contingency is not what simply exists out of the blue. That kind of existence is either "ideal", since it has no immanent relation to the concrete situation; or, necessary, since it emerges from its own self. In contrast, something is contingent when it is both effective fact and yet still dependent on other beings arriving later.

That it has thoroughly real, yet backwardly causal, effects, means that it really exists, yet not entirely in its own right, and this is what makes it contingent. Backward causality is not just causality in reverse order. It is "two inverse movements" (538): "before"-causality, in which anticipations drive societies to avoid possible futures; and "after"-causality[1] in which future possibilities constitute patterns into which situations before them are forced. This produces two strategies. A territorial regime can ward off the state either by the before-strategy of reinforcing its warrior class or by the after-strategy of fearmongering; similarly, the state can control territory either by the before-strategy of policing the precincts or by the after-strategy of rewriting history. All regimes must be able to "succeed one another" symmetrically, in order to "unfold simultaneously" (538). As we have seen in other contexts, simultaneity is the simultaneity of succession and simultaneity.

But we still need to know what happens when an after-cause is activated, when the state does "exist". We define existence in terms of a "threshold" of "consistency" (538).

CONTINGENCY AS CONSISTENCY

"Consistency" plays the role of "system" in *AO* and "saturation" in *QP*, but the examples here involve concrete matters, such as a consistent network of roads, and a consistent placement of soldiers, temples, translation posts, and so on along those roads. At a certain point, a quantitative and qualitative threshold of consistency is met, and a regime exists.

It is not difficult for a theory of thresholds to explain how elements of a new social form accumulate and forge a new system; mere aggregation is almost enough for that. What is difficult is to explain why a few new components do *not always* spiral into consistency (e.g. why China did not become capitalist when it had sufficient wealth and labour). We know empirically that they do not, that a society can incorporate a little bit of democracy, or capitalism, or racism, without reaching the threshold of consistency. But once Deleuze and Guattari have said that virtual systems have causal force even *before* existing as actual systems, how can they maintain that such systems do not yet exist, or explain why they do not exert their causal force consistently? To this end, Deleuze and Guattari construct an elaborate theory of consistency.

(a) "Trans-consistency" – the city paradigm (539): Consistency is not just the interaction of parts, but also the interaction across interactions. A city is not merely a centre of power, but a hub to which representatives of many cities travel.

(b) "Intra-consistency" – the state paradigm (539–42): Laws connect mixed systems (agricultural, technological, speculative), which roads alone cannot connect. They destabilize local authorities so as to "make a set of points resonate" (539).

City and state represent opposing structures of consistency, but of course they co-exist meta-consistently. The test of whether a society has reached the threshold whereby a state has superseded its cities cannot take the form of measuring whether its roads are wide enough, or its languages similar enough, or its leaders obeyed enough. Homogeneity does not test intraconsistency. The test must be a temporal measure, dealing with the way a present relates to its future and past. In other words, the virtual systems that pre-exist their actualization are consistent, but the meta-consistent level of the system in which they are involved can prevent them from crossing the threshold into predominance. Social formations can co-exist under two types of what I am calling meta-consistency: extrinsically in succession, or intrinsically and jointly, i.e. by speed or delay respectively.

As always, the tricky thing is that one of the two socio-temporal forms that co-exist is succession and the other is co-existence. When a society structured by succession co-exists with a society structured by co-existence, the previousness of the former relative to the latter (as defined by the former) is concurrent with the contemporaneity of the two (as defined by the latter).

(c) "Extrinsic" meta-consistency – the "periphery" paradigm (542–4): We have seen that in capitalism, there remain pockets of pre-capitalist society, and within these in turn are "ultra-modern" (544) super-capitalist sub-pockets with even more exploitation of labour, and even more spectacles of consumption. This might seem evidence for evolutionism, in which members of an earlier species survive into the first generations of its successor. But the pre-capitalist pockets become capitalist even faster than the capitalist regime can, unrestrained by organized consistency and free for speedy mutation. Temporally, they co-exist extrinsically.

(d) "Intrinsic" meta-consistency – the capture paradigm (544–5): This is the main topic of the Plateau: a successor turns the prior social formation into its predecessor by turning succession into co-existence, capturing historical succession. What is important for us are not "powers of appropriation" (e.g. taking over existing gold mines), or "powers to be transferred" (taking over existing armies). What is interesting for us is the kind of consistency where historical succession as such is captured by the state. I will focus on the move from territorial exchange to the state's stockpile, and on the problem of the "penultimate" trade.

THRESHOLDS AND PENULTIMACY

Deleuze and Guattari pose the problem: how can a society exchange something with another without being captured by it? How can a grain-cultivating society trade grain for an axe (or an almanac), without re-orienting itself consistently into a tree-cutting society? Just at the "limit", it has to linger at the "penultimate" exchange (546), and avoid crossing the threshold.

The threshold between normal succession and transformative event requires a theory of penultimacy. 'Why this event now?' implies an exchange that breaks a threshold. Whenever a 'why now?' question is hard to answer, it is because a society is held at this penultimate point, a Now split over two sides of the threshold, consistently incompossible. The event is split between having happened and not, between having an explanation in prior exchanges and not.

In practical terms, people can use axes for a long time without acquiring much facility. But historiographically, it is tricky to explain how societies succeed in using a technology over time, without ever giving it a wider role in social life.[2] How do societies pre-incorporate co-existence with something without becoming co-existent with it. Phenomenologically, this is like failing to recognize when something critically important has happened; worse, it is like strategically perceiving something while diverting one's glance, so that one only sees the backside it casts on familiar objects and never the profile by which it faces a new life-world. Sociologically, the temporality of penultimate exchange is what lets neighbouring cultures avoid meeting each other authentically.

A successfully consistent, autonomous society is one that is always still working on the penultimate exchange, the last new product before there is a "change of assemblage". This is "the economy of daily life" (546), like the alcoholic's last glass before the threshold of hospital care (*A*, "*B comme Boire*"). Succession sounds continuous, but it consists rather of a series of last-presents that do not reach the next: constant delay.

Once a society does go one exchange further, ceasing to import one axe at a time, and instead taking a census of its stock of axes, the succession of territorial exchange becomes the simultaneity of a stockpile, and a stockpile of simultaneities (548–9). The apparatuses of the state by which it captures and stockpiles resources include such things as consolidating real estate, profiting from exploited labour, and writing taxation policy that benefits the wealthy. Of course, the stock exists simultaneously with successive exploitations. Regime change ushers in co-existence, not as simple simultaneity, but as synchronizations of staggered successions according to the relative velocities of consumption, production, and exploitation across the earth's temporal regions. Staggered co-existence preserves a succession-effect. Deleuze and Guattari pair territorial exchange with a "Law of Temporal Succession", and the state's stockpile with a "Law of Spatial Co-existence" (549).

Defining the state as a crossover into the simultaneous measurement of territories, humans, and objects of desire, partly answers, but partly problematizes, our problem concerning 'why' the state arises when it does.

RELEASE AND ACCUMULATION: 'WHY NOW?'

If events were exclusively all-at-once affairs, there would be no 'why now?' questions. Events with staggered succession-effects have a 'why now?' hinge.

Insofar as the state is not staggered, but is the simultanization of economic functions (555), it is the paradigmatic regime, the regimated regime, whose essence is to be a code. This is another way of saying that the state originates when succession becomes co-existence. It makes even the pre-state past look like the state (as if the state of nature already had a bill of rights). On the other hand, the state's future must get "remade every day" (559), as people pay their taxes, to preserve its self-caused but fragile perpetuity. The state arises when a threshold is crossed and a multitude of states of affairs all become enactments of one event. But to this extent, the contingent question 'why is the state's emergence an event now?' is just the essential question 'why does history now have *events* in it at all?' Before state society becomes evenmental, we can ask what happened before what, but once events come on the scene, nothing before them appears to be of relevance.

It *almost* seems that Deleuze and Guattari take the no-prior-cause position, when they say that the apparent "succession" of the territorial regime by the state is "a solely logical relation" (557). Requiring a cause behind the state, they say, would require "a state behind the state, ad infinitum" (557). However, the fact that co-existence preserves staggered succession creates a number of wedge points for 'why now?' questions.

One wedge point is that while the 'why now?' is invisible from one standpoint, it reappears thanks to historical asymmetry. When the state looks for its own cause, it finds it has always existed; but when the territorial regime looks for the cause of the state, it finds plenty of culprits. Another wedge point for 'why now?' questions follows from the "violence" of state origins (558). Sometimes it seems like a metaphor to speak of the "violence" of the new against the old. But what is not metaphorical is the state's mechanism of "original accumulation" (558). This term is yet another paradox from the 'why now?' collection, as if an event is both originary and cumulative, present all along yet needing a 'why now?' answer, peaceful yet violent, sharply wedged into smooth time.

"Original accumulation", which Deleuze and Guattari introduce in scare-quotes, involves the snowballing centralization of wealth within the state that sets the stage for the capitalism that will make the state irrelevant. The state is perpetual, yet only transitional; as soon as there is enough centralization to make a state, there is already a process of capital accumulation that undermines the state. Of course, we need to explain cases (like China) where the state allows original accumulation without creating capitalism. But the state is self-originating just when its successor originates within it.

The origin of the third historical epoch, capitalism, is thus "internal" to its own processes, as the state is, but, unlike the state, Deleuze and Guattari say, capitalism "evolves" or "mutates", *accumulating* self-causality (560). This follows from the way that the state is so pervasive that it needed no "last" proximate cause to meet its conditions for existence. By recoding everything it was given to work with, its authority was only an incorporeal enunciation, and there was never anything but that to keep its components (its mercenaries, its farm workers, and its investors) from escaping. The state for this reason constantly releases free particles of wealth and labour. These escapees normally get recaptured, but until they do, they operate as proto-capitalist fluxes, which in turn release temporal particles into the third stage and type of history, which I will call the history of "release" (560).

To take some examples, the state monopolizes legal currency, but the spin-off is unsupervised commerce. It overcodes people and their roles, but thereby allows slaves to buy their freedom and employees to be fired. In general, "decoded fluxes" "escape", and people find themselves part of the "collective personage of the Excluded One" (560–1). Deleuze and Guattari's evidence that capitalism arises from a causality of release is drawn as usual from China (560–1). For capitalism to exist, wealth has to break away from ruling functionaries and attach itself to fluid labour power, liquid investments, and uncharted markets.

The causal structure is that something is excluded from the system that produced it; once released, it becomes a new paradigm. "The reason for the evolution [to capitalism] is internal, whatever the exterior factors that support it. *The archaic state does not overcode without also liberating a great quantity of decoded fluxes which will escape it*" (560). This is the moral of history: when successive alterations are *essentially* successive, the result is the rigid territoriality of traditional rule; when simultaneous situations are *essentially* simultaneous, the result is the self-justifying face of the state; but when successive lines are drawn simultaneously, free becomings escape from social regimes.

One form of flux that the state releases is subjectivity. The despot's signifier is replaced by capitalism's "subjectivation" (*subjectivation*), which sometimes frees people as transcendental subjects, and sometimes "subjects" (*assujetissement*) them to commodified self-images, even to the point of servitude (*asservissement*) (571–3). And of course the state releases its stockpile to the promise of future profit.

The state presents itself as suddenly always; capitalism presents itself as gradually always just now falling into place. *MP* recasts *AO*'s three regimes of history as co-existing poles of staggered co-existence. It is not that *MP*'s is not a historical account; on the contrary, it shows how a theory of co-existing virtual forms need not abandon historical analysis. It shows how different levels of history come to co-exist.

This analysis begins concretely, with examples from various transitional moments in history. A freed Roman slave can "double" as a functionary of the state (564), simultaneously playing one role in the new social form and another in the archaic form. But does this mean that two historical periods literally coexist? The transitional co-existence of flux and pre-flux histories returns us to the 'why now?' question that we have been tracking:

> Now, the subjectivations, conjunctions, and appropriations do not prevent the decoded fluxes from continuing to run, and from ceaselessly engendering new fluxes that escape ... Whence the impression that historians have when they say that capitalism "should have been able" to be produced from that moment – in China, in Rome, in Byzantium, in the Middle Ages – when the conditions for it had been given, but that they were not effectuated or effectable. The situation is that the pressure of the fluxes sets up the skeleton of capitalism, but that to realize it requires a whole *integration of decoded fluxes*, a whole *generalized conjugation*, which overwhelms and reverses the preceding apparatuses ... (564–5)

"One has the impression[3] that capitalism ceaselessly gets born, disappears, and resuscitates, at all the crossroads of history" (574).

The difference between proto-capitalist flux and capitalism *per se* is that the latter requires a "whole *integration* of decoded fluxes". When codes are loosened to the point where people leave their towns in search of employment, village life loses its normal progression, and an end of succession ensues. Exchanges are completed neither one at a time nor in bulk, but by accelerated trading-up, where no transaction is guaranteed in advance and the next deal is already being set up. This is a partial explanation of how co-existence only operates at certain moments of history. The conditions of accumulated wealth and labour are not the cause of capitalism. They are conditions that allow economic events to occur in free encounters; capitalism is proximally contingent on these encounters, not on the conditions for these encounters. Capitalism preserves the instability of the elements that drive it, simply by forcing them to co-exist.

In one way, it looks like the necessary conditions for capitalism are always being met, but not its contingent sufficient conditions. But in another way, it looks like there must always be contingency; and capitalism should always arise by this contingency, necessarily. Capitalism's inherent instability is precisely what is always making it arise throughout history. But in that case, capitalism is a historically contingent ahistoricity. The state's release of the co-existing fluxes whose encounter generates capitalism gives a good reason for why capitalism arises, just not of why it arises *now*.

Yet in a different way, the fact that its conditions are always ready to fall into place makes it easy to locate actual capitalist encounters at certain moments in history. Simply narrating the material interactions of wealth and labour in a particular society is the most determinate historical explanation there can be. It is completable without remainder, in a way that historical explanations that appeal to deliberative agents, or hidden causes, or long developments, could never be. For capitalism is not a new sort of decree or a new kind of engine; it is nothing but the preceding state insofar as it has collapsed into the flux of desiring-production.

This, in general, is how co-existential history works. It makes prior causes co-temporal with their effects. Conversely, it shows that one of two simultaneous layers of a society can be the other's historical cause. It makes effects self-evident consequences of their times, and simultaneously makes layers of time contingent enigmas in each other's eyes.

Deleuze and Guattari propose an analogy with axioms applied to heterogeneous fields. Some states may be easier for capitalism to apply to, but capitalism is capable of using everything from regime change to space travel, not to mention virtually every form of production. The applications describe a "ritournelle" around "models of realization" (567–70). This may not explain why capitalism arises in certain places at particular times, but it might at least explain how it arises at a different rate of speed in each realization. Realizations of capitalism are relayed temporally as well as structurally from state to state.

The interaction among states sometimes tends towards "isomorphism", in which case socialist states approximate market states; sometimes it produces asymmetrical colonization, which leads in different ways to the dissemination of capitalism. One way or another, accumulation needs the "living and passional forms" of the state in order to get realized (570). And the various states would not interact unless their stockpiles created desires across borders. This is the ritournelle: the realization of flux requires an actual state; the state struggles against its internal flux; therefore the realization of flux is the struggle of flux against itself It is a struggle, within the same collection of subjects, between its temporally layered desires (570).

Every technology under capitalism is "cybernetic" (572), in the sense of a mechanism some of whose working parts are desires. Cybernetics reduces neither to a blueprint of cog-sci wetware under an archaic model of mechanism, nor to the promise of Wild West but high-priced net-anarchism promoted by *Wired.* In contrast with the metaphor that humans in modern times are cogs in a machine, post-despotic economy uses precisely the anxieties and aggressions, the fears and dreams, the pride and rebellion of its participants to grease the cogs. This is a necessary moment in the historical transition from coding to decoding. The new figure is the "simultaneity" of the man-machine[4] (573). As in *DR*, desire keeps serial co-existence in rotation, but here not by the throw of the dice but by specific mechanisms of temporal co-production.

In the "transition" from state to capitalism, for the first time in history, the before and the after of an event are "co-existing poles" rather than "stages". Modernity's assemblage of past and future is "universal history" (573).

UNIVERSAL HISTORY AND THE "CURRENT SITUATION"

"Universal history" in this passage covers three stages, but all within the regime of the state: the archaic imperial state with its overcoding systems, the "evolved empires" with their decoding techniques, and the "modern nation states" with their recoding capabilities (573). The use of the term here does not seem to cover the pre-state territorial regime or the post-state capitalist axiomatic. But it is possible that Deleuze and Guattari intend "universal history" to cover all three stages of history, not just the three phases of the second stage. This is not just a terminological matter. The whole philosophy of universal history, the procedure that turns code into history, depends on the way the last act of the state is, and is not, something new. The ambiguity over whether only one age, or all ages, are properly historical is at the heart of Deleuze and Guattari's philosophy of history: there must be (a) one univocal sense of history, which is (b) univocalized by the last stage of history, and yet (c) distributed and differentiated throughout all stages of history.

This is common sense. History is about transitions, the moments when successive events collide in time. Universal history is therefore the universal co-existence of all successions. Co-existence therefore, conversely, is a succession of forms of transition.

Since the last stage of the state yields to capitalism, and capitalism "has never ceased to be born, to disappear, to arise again, at all the crossroads of history" (*à tous les carrefours de l'histoire* (574)), it follows that the last stage of the state is distributed evenly across all of history. Deleuze and Guattari here make one of their rare approving references to Hegel, attributing to Hegel the view that every phase of every state implies all the moments of state history (575). We can again draw the consequence that both the capitalist departure from state authority and its return to state techniques are immanent in the procedures of every state, no matter where or when. The capture of desire by states, "traverses a long history" (575), but neither state nor flux can emerge as the sole victor. The problem of designing the relation between them defines the "political" issues dealt with in the final section of the Plateau.

Ending the text in this way seems once again to bypass the problem of why capitalism occurred at the particular moment in human history that it did. But the topic of the political implies a sense in which not all moments of conflict are the same moment, and not all moments of flux need be the moment of capitalism. Even if 'why now?' is to be answered with 'anyways, always', we still ask, 'why this particular always?'

The last section of the "Apparatus of Capture" Plateau has the title "Axiomatic and current situation" (*Axiomatique et situation actuelle*). It deals largely with how the flux character of capitalism can be used to generate lines of flight, and how to prevent capitalism from recapturing those fluxes in ever more rigid national or transnational organizations. The issue for me concerns the concept of the *situation actuelle*, the logic of the current event. The praxis that Deleuze and Guattari recommend involves the quasi-temporal categories of decision, prevision, and experimentation with precedents (575). Their "coefficients of incertitude" aim at ensuring that governments be short-lived (576).

Deleuze and Guattari present seven political strategies to generate lines of escape by staggering co-existence over time: adjunction and subtraction, saturation, modelling, power (*puissance*), included middles, minorities, and undecidability (575–91).

Of course, there are straightforward roles for succession within co-existence. For example, there are dates when capitalism admitted unions and women (577–8). Occasional choices have real effects on the distribution of employment, taxation, prisons, and so on, which can shape resistance as well as conformity. Our struggle against capitalism is not a struggle against a state of affairs, but a struggle with the ontology of the virtual and its effectuation. Time is a topic of moral philosophy.[5]

We have seen that capitalist history is quantified by differentials, as when the linear process of capital depreciation and the linear process of wartime production together form a non-linear "rhythm" of profit-taking (582). Whenever capitalism switches axioms, it creates a temporal overflow of *puissance* (582–4). When an economic union adds to the number of capitalist nations, by defining them as such, it creates wars of competition. The insecurity of multinational capitalism might get expressed as a war against terror, or as the perpetual peace of technocracy. "States in their history have never ceased to appropriate the war machine; and at the same time, war, in its preparation and its effectuation, became the exclusive object of the machine" (582). The history of states is the appropriation of war, the capture of becoming, and because of this, history as such is subject to unlimited flux.

This is typical Deleuzian logic. When A is separate from B, it is limited by B; when A is immanent in B, it is extended outside itself throughout B. Flux is set in motion precisely by being captured by a system that multiplies assemblable elements and extends them by technical means. History sets events free precisely by invoking axioms to govern their universalization. Co-existential history is not the mere side-by-side presence of nomadic events and the apparatus of capture; it is the becoming of excess through capture. Co-existence is the overflow of, and into, history.

In sum, we can say that capitalism arose *only* at the time it did, and *also* that it is a *permanent* feature of the relation between state and war machine, only by distinguishing unstable layers of temporality.

DESTABILIZATION AND REVOLUTIONARY CO-EXISTENCE

Under the heading of the "included middle", Deleuze and Guattari say that capitalism spreads out into a tight all-inclusive network; this is "not accidental, but is a (theorematic) consequence of the axioms of capitalism, and primarily of the so-called axiom of *unequal exchange*, indispensable to its functioning" (585). We have seen that contingency subsists on the unstable edges of necessary development. The aspects of capitalism that we might have called contingent – its geographic divisions, its primitive accumulation, even its moment of beginning – are here cast as its necessary aspects, and the aspects that are here called contingent involve nothing other than the inexorability of its expansion into the beyond. If capitalism arose in modern Europe and not in thirteenth-century China, it is only in the sense that in China the forces of stability and instability became stable, and did not clash as often as capitalism requires them to. Indeed, it is rarely obvious which social elements are stable, since the extension of stability to the periphery is precisely destabilizing. If modern events by definition are unstable, then asking 'why is this event happening how?' will only be appropriate at the moment when the historian is not even sure what is happening. And an event that occurs only at the moment when its reality is challenged cannot definitively be said to occur at the moment when it does. There will be a time when the event is assigned a date, but the milieu that the event shapes will not have a determinate geo-temporal location.

There are clear cases where it is precisely stabilization that de-stabilizes a situation, as when controlled energy production and urban growth lead to uncontrollable ecological damage and urban blight.[6] But how do we characterize events without knowing which elements are controlled, necessary, and networked, and which are uncontrolled, contingent, and unstable?

The advent of capitalism in a given state's history has some immediately destabilizing and counter-effectuating after-effects. Leaving room for flexibility, we can analyse events in a series of stages: (a) effectuating assemblage, (b) systematization of consistency, (c) expansion towards the periphery, (d) destabilization at the periphery, (e) counter-effectuation in the form of included middle terms that render the assemblage uncontrollable from the periphery inwards, and therefore (f) material in flux as the content for a new effectuating assemblage.

If we have to count the expansion towards the periphery, plus several chronologically posterior returns to the centre, as one single historical unit, the event becomes uncountable, just as its date becomes a multi-valued coordinate. Deleuze and Guattari refer to the social situation at the periphery of capitalism as the "minority", as "multiplicities of flight" (587) defined neither by the system that expands towards them nor by archaic regimes. They are not speaking of anarchy, or decentralized, pluralistic group identities. Minorities create "innovations" as "problems" that cannot be resolved on any terms whatsoever; they are the human material of instability, a "problem concerning non-enumerable sets" (588). While a person counted in the set of minority members is thereby also a countable citizen, nevertheless qua minority she falls into a mass outside the set as soon as she is counted inside it.

The problem is not whether or not a minority is integrated into an axiomatic; the point is that the minority always creates "*another* co-existing struggle" (*un autre combat coexistant* (588)). The logic of co-existence is that as soon as a regime signs a compromise deal with a minority, the minority splits off into factions that refuse to comply; the ruling system would have to retranslate itself into not one but uncountably many directions at once. The capitalist axiomatic, which after all operates not by imposing one code on all citizens but by changing axioms for each circumstance, minoritizing its citizens, needs a new axiom for dealing with uncountable variations. In short, the challenge of the minority is that "it is the formula of multiplicities. Minority as universal figure, or becoming everyone" (*devenir tout le monde* (588)). If becoming is the ontology of co-existence, "becoming everyone" (like "all the names of history") is the ontology of the co-existence of co-existences.

State historical occurrences and minoritarian becomings are not two kinds of things that happen. Any "innovation" has both history and becoming co-existing within it. Yet neither a state nor a capitalist regime can express that element of the event whose temporality cannot be counted as an occurrence at all. By the same token, minority becomings do not solve recognizable historical problems, and they do not add or subtract countable value in anyone's interests. When they do occur on a nameable date, they do not last for a countable duration, and when they last long enough to be noticeable, they do not allow interpreters to say exactly when they noticed it first. Yet they are no less concrete, real happenings than any historical event; in fact, they are so real that they are not limited to particular nations or economies.

Consequently, judgements about whether a minority can be integrated are "undecidable". They depend on a factor that cannot be found among the facts of the situation, namely on whether the minority will in the future innovate a line of escape by multiplying factions and problems. This is Deleuze and Guattari's analogue to the incompleteness of axiomatic systems; there will always be something true of the system that cannot be deduced from it.[7] Social orders normally try to prove that minorities are either enemies or equals, whereas minorities qua minorities keep it from being clear even whether there is any minority there at all. The last few lines of the Plateau distinguish between "the uncertainty concerning consequences, which pertains necessarily to any system", and "the co-existence or inseparability of that which the system conjoins and that which does not cease to escape from it, following lines of flight that are themselves connectable" (590). Our conclusions regarding post-capitalist history, a history that comes not after but during modernity, depends on this distinction between uncertainty and undecidability; or to be precise, between instability in relation to succession and instability in relation to co-existence; or again, between not knowing 'why now' and knowing why each now co-exists with a now that has escaped it.

What defines contingency is not uncertainty. Contingency pertains to all events, in spite of the fact that capitalism *necessarily* generates and suppresses minor revolutions, and that despots *inevitably* arrive to ruin territorial cultures. What makes it contingent is rather that within the event there are masses whose number cannot be counted, singularities not according to code, problems that are not solved but repeated in disguise, possibilities that the times will not know how to use, successors that interrupt it before it is finished, events that co-exist with, rather than succeed, procedures that exclude them, lines of escape that are all connected, and revolutionaries who abandon hope both of solitary escape and communitarian alternatives. In short, events are contingent not because they do something new, but because they do something undecidable.

Whereas capitalism constitutes "universal history" as stages advancing towards freedom, individuality, and efficiency, minoritarianism constitutes universal history by making its own stages stutter. The last page of the Plateau suggests a somewhat Sartrian account of universal history in singular situations: "the undecidable is par excellence the germ and the place of revolutionary decisions" (590–1). The examples of becoming-germ that Deleuze and Guattari sketch (political radio, and some sort of urban design alternative to psychiatry) hint that instabilities germinate throughout a system quasi-causally. The very necessity whereby a historical process proceeds causally step by step makes each element sensitive to effects in every other element of the system, and hence renders each one subject to every contingency that even a single unstable element or undecidable proposition possesses.

We can summarize three Deleuze and Guattarian formulations of historical conditioning. (i) In *MP*'s theory of dates, it would seem that conditions never engender incorporeal events. This is not quite idealism, since the incorporeal enunciation's other pole is a diagram for the relative dating of events. But dating theory does put the event on the side of the abstract machine and the condition on the side of the machinic assemblage. (ii) In *MP*'s theory of actual events, the event seems defined by thresholds in systems of conditions. This is not quite materialism, since the other pole of system is contingency. But actuality theory does put both the condition and the event on the side of the machinic assemblage and leaves the abstract machine as the sphere of indeterminacy. (iii) The theory of temporal co-existence is the middle ground between abstract machine and machinic assemblage, between dates and events. It is a machinic historiography of dark precursors and interstrate communications. This is the concrete version of the third synthesis of time in *DR*, the future as the co-existence of actual history with a minoritarian search engine.

Co-existence is the fourth, revolutionary, stage of history. It does not post-date the other three, and in fact explains why the other three stages are only quasi-chronological in the first place. While the categories of co-existence, particularly threshold and release, add pieces to the puzzle 'why capitalism then?', it unmasks within it the question of the secret date 'why revolution now?'

To recapitulate: the way that the last exchange overtakes a threshold and turns stock into flux seemed to determine how capitalism emerges from state economics. But this did not explain how the threshold could be met in China and still, for contingent reasons, not force the capitalist elements to be systematically extended throughout the social field. We then looked at flux and contingency within the expansion of capitalism. These seemed to explain when, or at least how, capitalism rebounds off the edges of the social field. But what free wealth and labour produce is never capitalism as an ordered system, but connected heterogeneous escape mechanisms. The best possible explanation of why capitalism emerged when and where it did turns out to be a better explanation of why capitalism is opposed than why it caught on. 'Why revolution now?' means something like: 'what (else) am I supposed to do now?' or simply, 'who: me?'

This is what it means to say that history becomes co-existence, and that all questions of beginnings, and all questions that ask 'why now?' have answers in the form of co-existence relations. Co-existence is ineliminable just because the matters that escape at the periphery have no rules in common. They have no principles of succession among them, their problematic character is univocal and interactive, and they are open to assemblages, whether their modes of escape are territorially archaic, communally signifying, productively indifferent, or revolutionarily singular. The successive stages of history show themselves at the ultimate moment, and only then, to have co-existed all along. In this way, the final explanation of what makes events actual in a historical sense is also the explanation of how temporality is revolutionary co-existence. Time understood historically has roughly the same structure we saw in *DR*: time is three heterogeneous structures co-existing simultaneously as three kinds of becoming, three kinds of origination, three kinds of events, three simultaneous kinds of three successive stages of historical events existing simultaneously. History is the simultaneous co-existence of (a) a succession of territorial empires arising from causal conflicts, (b) a succession of state histories each expressing universal history under a new form of co-existence, (c) a succession of flux-states in a timeless axiomatic of capitalist flows of labour and wealth, and (d) a co-existence of incorporeal date-assemblages in a virtual chronology of minoritarian escape mechanisms. For a historical event to be actualized at a particular moment in time means nothing other than for it to exhibit all four kinds of temporal relations at once, all of which are real, and all of which are diagrammed together concretely.

To wrap up the 'why now?' problem, there are too many passages where

Deleuze and Guattari give reasons why capitalism did not exist in China, and too many where they imply it should have. The only way to solve the problem is to distribute the elements of both accounts throughout the multi-levelled temporality of co-existential history. Different answers to the 'why now?' question will be given simultaneously, according to the multiple senses of temporality that exist simultaneously. To put it (too) simply, pure succession is territorial; succession-in-co-existence is the state; and the co-existence of succession and co-existence is capitalism and its revolutionary potential. All of these co-exist.

'Why capitalism now?' has direct, but co-existing, therefore unstable, answer-particles, as well as unanswerability particles, depending on which temporal micro-level we are at when asking. Insofar as capitalism arose in some places before others, it is because co-existence has a succession-effect; when a regime does not become generalized, it is because stable co-existence co-exists with unstable co-existence; insofar as capitalism emerges everywhere, it is insofar as co-existence is captured by all successive historical periods. The revolution is not something new that the future has in store; it is tucked in between the temporal levels in universal history.

NOTES

1 This has similarities with Sartre's (1960) progressive-regressive method for the study of history.
2 André Leroi-Gourhan's (1964, pp. 130f.) description of the millennia it took for humanoids to move from making one-sided to two-sided arrowheads is a striking and discouraging example.
3 At *MP* 564, the phrase "the impression that" might sound as though it is a false impression. At 574, Deleuze and Guattari clearly use the same phrase to denote a true impression. I think they imply the same in the earlier passage too.
4 Deleuze and Guattari cite Bradbury and discuss TV; the Deleuzian sci-fi writer Maurice Dantec (1999) makes this motif explicit.
5 See Antonio Calcagno (2003).
6 Michael Hardt and Antonio Negri (2000) explicate such phenomena.
7 Alain Badiou's *L'être et l'évènement* (1988) hangs on this ontology.

Bibliography

DELEUZE

The translations of passages from Deleuze's texts in this book are my own. However, I find all the major published translations of Deleuze's works into English to be excellent, and I have made liberal use of them.

A L'Abécédaire. Paris: Vidéo Éditions Montparnasse, 1997.
B Le Bergsonisme. Paris: Presses Universitaires de France, 1966.
C1 Cinéma 1: L'Image-mouvement. Paris: Les Éditions de Minuit, 1983.
C2 Cinéma 2: L'Image-temps. Paris: Les Éditions de Minuit, 1985.
CC Critique et Clinique. Paris: Les Éditions de Minuit, 1993.
D Dialogues (en collaboration avec Claire Parnet). Paris: Éditions Flammarion, 1977.
DR Différence et répétition. Paris: Presses Universitaires de France, 1969.
ES Empirisme et subjectivité. Paris: Presses Universitaires de France, 1953.
F Foucault. Paris: Les Éditions de Minuit, 1986.
FB Francis Bacon: Logique de la sensation (2 vols). Éditions de la Différence, 1981.
LS Logique du sens. Paris: Les Éditions de Minuit, 1969.
NP Nietzsche et la philosophie. Paris: Presses Universitaires de France, 1962.
P Le Pli: Leibniz et la baroque. Paris: Les Éditions de Minuit, 1988.
Pp Pourparlers. Paris: Les Éditions de Minuit, 1990.
PS Proust et les signes. Paris: Presses Universitaires de France, 1964.

DELEUZE AND GUATTARI

AO L'Anti-Oedipe. Paris: Les Éditions de Minuit, 1972.
K Kafka – Pour une littérature mineur. Paris: Les Éditions de Minuit, 1975.
MP Mille plateaux. Paris: Les Éditions de Minuit, 1980.
QP Qu'est-ce que la philosophie? Paris: Les Éditions de Minuit, 1991.

GUATTARI

AH Les années d'hiver. Paris: Éditions Bernard Barrault, 1986.
CS Cartographies schizoanalytiques. Paris: Éditions Galilée, 1989.

WORKS ON AND RELATED TO DELEUZE AND GUATTARI

This bibliography includes only texts to which I refer in this book. There are of course many excellent books and papers written on Deleuze and Guattari that I am not listing here.

Alliez, Éric, *Les Temps capitaux*. Paris: Éditions du Cerf, T. 1 1991, T. 2 1999.
—— and Félix Guattari, "Systèmes, structures, et processus capitalistiques". In Guattari, *AH*, pp. 162–92.
Amin, Samir, *Unequal Development: An Essay on the Social Formations of Peripheral Capitalism* (trans. Brian Pearce). New York: Monthly Review Press, 1976.
Ansell Pearson, Keith, *Germinal Life: The Difference and Repetition of Gilles Deleuze*. London: Routledge, 1998.
Antonioli, Manola, *Géophilosophie de Deleuze et Guattari*. Paris: L'Harmattan, 2003.
Badiou, Alain, *L'être et l'évènement*. Paris: Éditions du Seuil, 1988.
—— *Deleuze: La clameur de l'Être*. Paris: Hachette, 1997.
Balazs, Étienne, *La bureaucratie céleste*. Paris: Gallimard, 1968.
Balibar, Étienne, "Sur les concepts fondamentaux du materialisme historique". In Louis Althusser *et al.*, *Lire le Capital* (1965). Paris: Presses Universitaires de France, 1996, pp. 419–568.
Bergen, Veronique, *L'ontologie de Gilles Deleuze*. Paris: L'Harmattan, 2001.
Bergson, Henri, *Matière et mémoire*. Paris: Presses Universitaires de France, 1959.
Bogue, Ronald, *Deleuze on Music, Painting, and the Arts*. Chapter 2, "Music in Time: History and Becoming". New York: Routledge, 2003.
Braudel, Fernand, *Écrits sur l'histoire*. Paris: Flammarion, 1969, pp. 135–53.
—— *La dynamique du capitalisme* (1976). Paris: Flammarion, 1985.
Butler, Judith, *Precarious Life*. London: Verso, 2004.
Calcagno, Antonio, *Politics and its Time: Derrida, Lazarus and Badiou*. Doctoral Dissertation, University of Guelph, 2003.
Cixous, Hélène, "What is it O'clock? Or the Door (We Never Enter)" (1994) (trans. Catherine A. F. MacGillivray), in *Stigmata: Escaping Texts*. London: Routledge, 1998, pp. 57–83.
Dantec, Maurice, *Babylon Babies*. Paris: Gallimard, 1999.
Debord, Guy, *La societé du spectacle*. Paris: Éditions Buchet-Chastel, 1967.
DeLanda, Manuel, *A Thousand Years of Nonlinear History*. New York: Zone, 1997.
—— *Intensive Science and Virtual Philosophy*. London: Continuum, 2002.
Dennett, Daniel D., *Consciousness Explained*. Boston: Little, Brown, and Co., 1991.
Derrida, Jacques, *Schibboleth, pour Paul Celan* (*S*). Paris: Éditions Galilée, 1986.
Feynman, Richard P., *QED: The Strange Theory of Light and Matter*. Princeton: Princeton University Press, 1985.
Foucault, Michel, *Les mots et les choses*. Paris: Éditions Gallimard, 1966.
—— "Revenir à l'histoire" (1972), in *Dits et écrits, 1954–1988*, T. II, 1970–75. Paris: Gallimard, 1994, pp. 268–81.
François, Alain, "Entre Deleuze et Bergson: À propos de la deuxieme synthèse du temps". In Pierre Verstraeten, and Isabelle Stengers (eds), *Gilles Deleuze*. Paris: Librairie Philosophique J. Vrin, 1998, 63–87.
Haghighi, Mani, "Neo-archaism". In Brian Massumi (ed.), *A Shock to Thought*. London: Routledge, 2002, pp. 131–48.
Hardt, Michael, and Antonio Negri, *Empire*. Cambridge, MA: Harvard University Press, 2000.
Hegel, G. W. F., *The Philosophy of History* [*PH*] (trans. J. Sibree). The Colonial Press, 1900. *Vorlesungen über die Philosophie der Geschichte*. Frankfurt am Main: Suhrkamp Verlag, 1970.

—— *Phenomenology of Spirit* (trans. A. V. Miller). Oxford: Oxford University Press, 1977.
Phänomenologie des Geistes, Frankfurt am Main: Suhrkamp Verlag, 1970.
Heidegger, Martin, *Being and Time* (1927) (trans. John Macquarrie and Edward Robinson). New York: Harper & Row, Publishers, 1962.
Holland, Eugene W., *Deleuze and Guattari's Anti-Oedipus: Introduction to Schizoanalysis*. London: Routledge, 1999.
Husserl, Edmund, *Zur Phänomenologie des Inneren Zeitbewusstseins. Husserliana X*. Haag: Martinus Nijhoff, 1966.
Jameson, Frederic, "Marxism and Dualism in Deleuze", *South Atlantic Quarterly*, 96 (3), 1997: 393–416.
Lampert, Jay, *Synthesis and Backward Reference in Husserl's Logical Investigations*. Dordrecht: Kluwer Academic Publishers, 1995a.
—— "Hegel and Ancient Egypt: History and Becoming", *International Philosophical Quarterly*, XXXV, 5, 1995b: 43–58.
—— "Origen on Time", *Laval théologique et philosophique*, 52, 3, octobre 1996: 649–64.
—— "Dates and Destiny: Deleuze and Hegel". *Journal of the British Society for Phenomenology*, 33, 2, May 2002: 206–20.
—— "Hegel on Contingency, or Fluidity and Multiplicity". Forthcoming in the *Bulletin of the Hegel Society of Great Britain*.
Lawlor, Leonard, *The Challenge of Bergsonism*. London: Continuum, 2003.
Le Lionnais, François, "Le second manifeste", in Oulipo, *La litterature potentielle*. Paris: Editions Gallimard, 1973.
Leroi-Gourhan, André, *Le geste et la parole, 1. Technique et langage*. Paris: Éditions Albin Michel, 1964.
Libet, Benjamin, "The Experimental Evidence for Subjective Referral of a Sensory Experience Backward in Time: Reply to P. S. Churchland". *Philosophy of Science*, 48, 1981: 182–97.
Malabou, Catherine, "Who's Afraid of Hegelian Wolves?" In Paul Patton (ed.), *Deleuze: A Critical Reader*, Oxford: Blackwell Publishers Ltd, 1996, pp. 114–38.
Martin, Jean-Clet, "Des évenèments et des noms". *Rue Descartes*, 20, 1998: 129–36.
Marx, Karl, *Grundrisse* (trans. Martin Nicolaus). London: Penguin Books, 1993.
Mbiti, John, "African Religions and Philosophy", in Albert G. Mosley (ed.), *African Philosophy: Selected Readings*. New Jersey: Prentice Hall, 1995, pp. 88–115.
McTaggart, John McTaggart Ellis, *The Nature of Existence*, Volume II, Cambridge, UK: Cambridge University Press, 1927.
Merleau-Ponty, Maurice, *La structure du comportement*. Paris: Presses Universitaires de France, 1942.
Michelet, Jules, *Histoire de la Révolution française*. Paris: Bibliotèque de la Pleiade, Éditions Gallimard, 1952.
Miller, Christopher L. (1993), "The Postidentitarian Predicament in the Footnotes of *A Thousand Plateaus*: Nomadology, Anthropology, and Authority", *diacritics* 23.3: 6–35.
Needham, Joseph, *The Grand Titration: Science and Society in East and West*. Toronto: University of Toronto Press, 1969.
Negri, Antonio, "The Constitution of Time" (1981), in *Time For Revolution*. London: Continuum Books, 2003.
Nietzsche, Friedrich, *Thus Spoke Zarathustra* (trans. R. J. Hollingdale). Harmondsworth: Penguin Books, 1961.
Patton, Paul, *Deleuze and the Political*. London: Routledge, 2000.
Pernoud, Régine and Marie-Véronique Clin, *Jeanne D'Arc*. Paris: Fayard, 1986.
Proust, Françoise, *L'Histoire à contretemps: Le temps historique chez Walter Benjamin*. Paris: Éditions du Cerf, 1994.
Rancière, Jacques, *Les noms de l'histoire*. Paris: Éditions du Seuil, 1992.
Sanders, Ed, *The Family* (1970). New York: Signet Books, 1990.

—— *Investigative Poetry*. San Francisco: City Lights Books, 1976.
—— *Love and Fame in New York*. Berkeley: Turtle Island Foundation, 1980.
—— *The Z-D Generation*. Barrytown, New York: Station Hill Press, 1981.
—— *1968: A History in Verse*. Santa Rosa: Black Sparrow Press, 1997.
Sartre, Jean-Paul, *L'être et le néant*. Paris: Éditions Gallimard, 1943.
—— *Critique de la raison dialectique*. Paris: Éditions Gallimard, 1960.
Sibertin-Blanc, Guillaume, "Les impensables de l'histoire. Pour une problématisation vitaliste, noétique et politique de l'anti-historicisme chez Gilles Deleuze". *Le Philosophoire*, 19, 2003: 119–154.
Simont, Juliette, *Essai sur la quantité, la qualité la relation chez Kant, Hegel, Deleuze*. Paris: L'Harmattan, 1997.
Spivak, Gayatri Chakravorty, *A Critique of Postcolonial Reason: Toward a History of the Vanishing Present*. Cambridge, MA: Harvard University Press, 1999.
Verstraeten, Pierre and Isabelle Stengers (eds), *Gilles Deleuze*. Paris: Librairie Philosophique J. Vrin, 1998, 63–87.
Žižek, Slavoj, *Organs without Bodies: Deleuze and Consequences*. New York: Routledge, 2004.
Zourabichvili, François, *Deleuze: Une philosophie de l'évènement*. Paris: Presses Universitaires de France, 1994.
—— "Deleuze et le possible (de l'involontairisme en politique)". In Éric Alliez (ed.), *Gilles Deleuze: Une vie philosophique*. Le Plessis-Robinson: Institut Synthélabo, 1998, pp. 335–57.

Index

abstract machine 75–6, 81–4, 95n. 12–13, 169
aion 37–8, 102
Ansell Pearson, Keith 30n. 15–16
anticipation and retention 14–15, 43–4
archaism 42, 127, 137, 159, 162–3, 170

backward causality 157
Badiou, Alain 41, 52n. 4
Balazs, Étienne 114, 127, 134–5, 146
Balibar, Étienne 142n. 18
becoming vs. history 1–2, 7, 10–11, 98, 100, 113n. 7, 145–6, 149–54, 166, 168
beginning (territorial) 121–4, 152
  vs. creation (capitalist) 132
  vs. origin (despotic) 125–31
    original accumulation (capitalist) 136–8, 161–2
Bergson 4, 13, 23, 29n. 2, 34–6, 49, 55, 76, 95n. 9, 100
Bergsonisme 34–6, 55
Bogue, Ronald 70n. 3
Braudel, Fernand 114, 141n. 12, 142n. 16, 142n. 19, 145

capitalist history 122–3, 131–8, 146–7, 159–71
Cartographies schizoanalytiques 75, 84
Cinéma 1 and 2 35, 42, 45–6, 50, 52–3n. 9, 70n. 5
co-existential history 1–6, 33–4, 42, 46–8, 117, 127, 138–40, 154–60, 161–71
  levels of the past 49–51, 58, 92
  staggered co-existence 161–3
communication between events 7–8, 65–8, 93, 99–100, 107
consistency 144, 158–60
contingency 115, 120, 132–3, 135–7, 140, 144–5, 147, 157–9, 163, 167–70
contraction, of present 14–19, 22, 26, 29n. 2, 34, 43
  of past 48–51

Critique et clinique 92–3
current situation 165–6

dark precursor 66–9, 120, 144, 169
DeLanda, Manuel 141n. 10
delay 56–7, 68, 92–3, 118, 137–9, 159–60
Derrida, Jacques 4, 28, 84–7
despotic state history 125–31, 156–69
destination 85, 99, 109
destiny 49, 72, 90–4, 96n. 21
deterritorialization (relative) as history 144–5
diachronics 132, 136–9, 142n. 18
diagram 81–4
distance (temporal) 5, 8, 18, 56–7, 68, 75, 87, 92–3, 107, 111

Empirisme et subjectivité 29n. 4, 29n. 8, 52n. 1
empty form of time 38, 55, 63, 101–3
eternal return 56, 58, 63
ethics 70n. 2, 104–6, 110, 153, 166
evolution (cultural) 116–18, 156–9, 162
expression and content 77–8

falling back into history 118, 145–8, 151–3
flux 18, 21, 38, 75, 99–100, 104, 112, 121, 124, 132–3, 135–7, 162–7, 170
forgetting 110
Foucault 82–3, 109–11, 141n. 12
Foucault, Michel 109–10, 117, 140–1n. 3, 153
free indirect discourse 72–7
future as search through the past 51, 54–5, 58, 64, 69
  as desire 60–4

Hegel, G. W. F. 7, 14–15, 19, 27–8, 34, 71–2, 86–92, 94, 121, 140, 145, 150, 165
Heidegger, Martin 85, 95n. 16, 145, 149
historicism 145
Holland, Eugene 140n. 1

Hume, David 13–17, 29n. 2, 29n. 4, 29n. 8, 42
Husserl, Edmund 4–5, 13–14, 16–17, 20, 23, 86, 95n. 9, 147

incorporeal enunciation 72–7, 100–1
instability 163–9
instant 14–19, 22, 37, 43, 72–3
intra-temporality 22–7, 33, 50, 59–66
   dimensions of time 43–4, 59

Kant, Immanuel 11n. 1, 15, 55, 149

lived present 15
Logique du sens 29n. 6–7, 37–8, 97–113

Marx, Karl 120, 139, 141n. 6
McTaggart, John McTaggart Ellis 34, 52n. 2
measureless time 37
memory, organic 19–22
   pure 5, 35–6, 42–4
   and signs 20–1, 24–7
minority 4, 86, 148–51, 167–70
modernity 88–90, 146–50

names of history 1–11, 77, 91–3, 103, 129, 139–40, 168
   Joan of Arc effect 1–11, 99, 102–4, 110–12
   Lenin abstract machine 81–4, 103
need and fatigue 23–4, 30n. 15–16
negation 27, 121–2
neo-Platonism 14, 86
Nietzsche et la philosophie 9, 70n. 1, 95n. 11, 141n. 5
Nietzsche, Friedrich 2, 9, 58, 70n. 1, 107, 146, 152–3
now 15, 27–8, 148, 152–4

Oedipus 120–1, 124–5
outside 109–11, 125–8

past, four paradoxes 26, 44–50
   reterritorializing on 148–52
Patton, Paul 141n. 4
Pourparlers 74
pre-existence 48–9, 157–9
present, empty 102–3
   former 33, 39–46, 55
   lived 14
   paradox of the passing 26, 28, 32–4, 44–6, 70n. 1
      myth of time passage 52n. 7
   vanishing 27–8

presentiment 121–5
Proust et les signes 52n. 5

quantity 136–7

representability and generalizability 21, 36, 38–42
retrospectivity 15, 42, 81, 115, 119–21, 145–8
revolutionary history 94, 105, 139–40, 148, 153, 166–71
rhythm 22–4

Sanders, Ed 105–6
Sartre, Jean-Paul 95n. 9, 171n. 1
serial history 141n. 3, 141n. 12
Sibertin-Blanc, Guillaume 11n. 5
Simont, Juliette 29n. 9
simultaneity *see* succession vs. simultaneity
speed 23–4, 77, 111–12, 137–8, 146–7, 159, 164
Spivak, Gayatri Chakravorty 142n. 14
Stoics 25, 63, 78, 106
strange stories 68, 92
   strange objects 101
storehouse of the past 41–2, 50, 61–2
structuralism 117, 140–1n. 3
succession vs. simultaneity 4–10, 12, 18–19, 23, 34, 37, 41, 43, 50, 52–3n. 9, 66–8, 71–3, 82–4, 91, 100–3, 106, 131, 138, 158–71
"*Sur quelques régimes de signes*" Plateau 116–18
synthesis, passive 15–20, 50
systematization (in despotic history) 130–1, 163

territorial history 121–5, 159–60
threshold 158–60
time arrow 17–18
today 153–4
   current situation 165–6
   tomorrow 78

universal history 3, 115–16, 119–21, 124–5, 128, 131, 133, 138–40, 144, 164–5, 169, 171

variation 76, 78–84, 104

Žižek, Slavoj 99–100, 113n. 7
Zourabichvili, François 30n. 17, 52n. 5, 113n. 8